RANK-AND-FILE REBELS: THEORIES OF POWER AND CHANGE IN THE 2018 EDUCATION STRIKES

T0283386

Precarity & Contingency

Series Editors: Sue Doe and Seth Kahn

The Precarity & Contingency book series publishes scholarship—broadly construed to include empirical (both quantitative and qualitative), historical, and critical/theoretical projects— that addresses precarious academic labor. While its focus is primarily on academic labor in higher education, it encourages projects that address other labor issues on campuses (including K-12) and/or precarity in labor sectors outside education. The series embraces new visions of and innovations in leadership in the academic environment that might more effectively address current labor crises. It also encourages projects that explore intersections of academic labor activism with other forms of activism, such as LGBTQ+, gender, race equality, ability/disability activism, and environmentalism, among others.

The WAC Clearinghouse, University Press of Colorado, and the Colorado State University Center for the Study of Academic Labor are collaborating so that these books will be widely available through free digital distribution and low-cost print editions. The publishers and the series editors are committed to the principle that knowledge should freely circulate and have embraced the use of technology to support open access to scholarly work.

Other Books in the Series

Robert Samuels, *A Working Model for Contingent Faculty* (2023)

RANK-AND-FILE REBELS: THEORIES OF POWER AND CHANGE IN THE 2018 EDUCATION STRIKES

By Erin Dyke and Brendan Muckian-Bates

The WAC Clearinghouse
wac.colostate.edu
Fort Collins, Colorado

University Press of Colorado
upcolorado.com
Denver, Colorado

The WAC Clearinghouse, Fort Collins, Colorado 80523

University Press of Colorado, Denver, Colorado 80203

ISBN 978-1-64215-190-9 (PDF) | 978-1-64215-191-6 (ePub) | 978-1-64642-500-6 (pbk.)

DOI 10.37514/PRC-B.2023.1909

Produced in the United States of America

Library of Congress Cataloging-in-Publication Data

Names: Dyke, Erin, 1984– author. | Muckian-Bates, Brendan, 1990– author.
Title: Rank-and-file rebels : theories of power and change in the 2018 education strikes / by Erin Dyke and Brendan Muckian-Bates.
Description: Fort Collins, Colorado : The WAC Clearinghouse ; Denver, Colorado : University Press of Colorado, [2023] | Series: Precarity & contingency | Includes bibliographical references.
Identifiers: LCCN 2023037873 (print) | LCCN 2023037874 (ebook) | ISBN 9781646425006 (pbk) | ISBN 9781642151909 (adobe pdf) | ISBN 9781642151916 (epub)
Subjects: LCSH: Wildcat strikes–Teachers–United States. | Collective bargaining–Teachers–United States. | Teachers–Political activity–United States. | Teacher participation in administration–United States. | Teachers' unions–United States. | School boards–United States. | School management and organization–United States.
Classification: LCC LB2844.47.U6 D94 2023 (print) | LCC LB2844.47.U6 (ebook) | DDC 331.88/113711–dc23/eng/20230913
LC record available at https://lccn.loc.gov/2023037873
LC ebook record available at https://lccn.loc.gov/2023037874

Copyeditor: Don Donahue
Designer: Mike Palmquist
Cover Art: "Sangria Chocolat," by Malcolm Childers. Used with permission.
Series Editors: Sue Doe and Seth Kahn

The research reported in the book was made possible (in part) by a grant from the Spencer Foundation (#201900232). The views expressed are those of the authors and do not necessarily reflect the views of the Spencer Foundation.

The WAC Clearinghouse supports teachers of writing across the disciplines. Hosted by Colorado State University, it brings together scholarly journals and book series as well as resources for teachers who use writing in their courses. This book is available in digital formats for free download at wac.colostate.edu.

Founded in 1965, the University Press of Colorado is a nonprofit cooperative publishing enterprise supported, in part, by Adams State University, Colorado State University, Fort Lewis College, Metropolitan State University of Denver, University of Alaska Fairbanks, University of Colorado, University of Denver, University of Northern Colorado, University of Wyoming, Utah State University, and Western Colorado University. For more information, visit upcolorado.com.

Land Acknowledgment. The Colorado State University Land Acknowledgment can be found at https://landacknowledgment.colostate.edu.

Contents

P&C

Acknowledgments

Erin

I would, first and foremost, like to thank all the educator-organizers in West Virginia, Oklahoma, Kentucky, and Arizona who were generous with their time and critical reflections, and whose movement work made this book and so much more possible. My co-research team in Oklahoma who co-created and undertook our oral history project—Autumn Brown, Heather Anderson, Jinan El Sabbagh, Hannah Fernandez, Stacey Goodwin, Mark Hickey, Steph Price, Megan Ruby, Kristy Self, Jennifer Williams, and Angel Worth—were critical partners in documenting educators' experiences in the 2018 strike and worked to highlight narratives missing or marginal from the larger public story of what happened in our state. Much appreciation to the Spencer Foundation for supporting our project. Sarah Milligan and the Oklahoma Oral History Research Program taught me how to do oral history and of its importance, and they are preserving and making accessible our collected narratives.

Lois Weiner's generous mentorship and comradeship challenged and deepened my thinking. From her, I learned much about how to engage in (and the importance of!) scholarship with and for educator and social movements for the long haul. I am indebted to my co-editors Rhiannon Maton and Lauren Ware Stark and all the contributors to our special issue series on contemporary educator movements for *Critical Education*, including Tamara Anderson, Vanessa Arrendondo, Chloe Asselin, Nina Bascia, Paul Bocking, Keysha Goodwin, Jesse Hagopian, Crystal Howell, Noah Karvelis, Sachin Maharaj, Dana Morrison, Tricia Niesz, Leah Z. Owens, Kathleen Riley, Caleb Schmitzer, and Jessica Shiller. Reading and engaging closely with their work throughout writing this book has significantly informed my own thinking.

It's difficult to put to words how formative my experiences have been learning in, with, and from the Twin Cities' Industrial Workers of the World IUB, SJEM, and all those who grew the union to what it is today. In 2018, Brendan and I shared our preliminary thinking with IWW education workers from across the country at a gathering organized by SJEM. This experience, my participation in the SJEM summer reading group in summer 2021, and learning from SJEM members' analyses and organizing during the 2022 MFT strike were critical sites of learning for me. Every time I have the pleasure of listening to and learning from Linda's stories of her family's union history in the 1934 Minneapolis general strike, I am inspired to reflect on the importance of storytelling in the labor movement and on my own family's union history in Chicago. My Grandpa Henry met his union buddies for coffee at the McDonald's on Archer regularly until his death at 85—may we all develop lifelong friendships-in-struggle.

Thank you to series editors and longtime higher ed unionists Seth Kahn and Sue Doe for their commitment to our book and their support, patience, and flexibility while we finished it. We leaned on many people throughout this process: Meg Krausch provided a close reading and review of our first draft and offered important insights that informed our revisions. Our feminist writing group has been a consistent source of support and friendship during the past six years. Gus, Harry, Hazel, Liam, Meryl, and Morgan have helped me to glimpse an educational world we can fight for. My mom wrote me a note inside a gifted copy of *Anne of Green Gables* when I was 9, "Someday, maybe you'll write a book!" I didn't think I ever would for most of my life. My parents' love and support has always made impossible things seem possible.

My partner, Kevin, was endlessly supportive throughout all my (many) emotional anxieties in writing this book. That and his care work—cleaning, cooking, childcare, emotional support—is the main reason this book (and me) exists. August and Lucy, my Haymarket rebels, maybe you'll read this one day! Someday, maybe you'll write a book!

Lastly, and most importantly, I am so grateful to have traveled this journey with Brendan. I left every single conversation we've had since we began this project feeling transformed in my thinking. Your brilliance and principled way of being in the world are an inspiration to me. What a gift it has been to study and co-write with you!

● Brendan

First, I would like to acknowledge my fellow educator friends and comrades who, through their tireless efforts to improve the quality of public education in West Virginia, transformed the country. Standing alongside you all on the picket line or chanting outside of lawmakers' offices during the 55 Strong strike has forever changed me for the better. Your wisdom and insight for a brighter future, your strategies for bringing together all education workers into this fold, and your work connecting everyday people into the labor movement will be forever insightful to those looking to begin organizing.

I am eternally grateful to the education workers and activists who gave deeply of their time to us. As a former teacher myself, I know all too well the struggles of keeping up with the workload educators have. Being so candid about the fight for stronger unions and stronger community responses to attacks on public education cannot have been easy, but we hope to tell your story as truthfully as we can. Your stories and your actions have helped shape the future, and it is our duty to record it accurately.

While there are countless educators I could list here, I want to personally thank a few who have shaped this work, both from their personal activism and their feedback. Jessica Salfia and Elizabeth Catte's book 55 *Strong: Inside the West Virginia Teachers' Strike* cataloged the feelings, emotions, and personal stories of West Virginians so soon after the strike had ended. It is a perfect time capsule of that moment in history, and one which Jessica, in addition to her teaching responsibilities, took up with gusto. Emily Comer's grassroots organizing experience that predates the strike, and her sit-in at Senator Manchin's office during the Kavanaugh hearings in late 2018, have been a personal inspiration to me. To my union mentor, David McQuain, who not only recommended me for my first teaching position, but who signed me up for my union, taught me how to be an effective building representative, shared deeply with me his own personal struggles as an educator-activist, and helped me feel confident when times were toughest as a first-year teacher. Lastly, Jay O'Neal's tireless efforts and journey–from teacher, to activist, to organizer–have been a guiding light for me over the past half decade and I am deeply grateful for his friendship. It was Jay who invited me to attend my first Labor Notes conference in April 2018, giving me a chance to speak about our collective struggle to a packed room of union supporters. Jay likewise invited me to help form the West Virginia United caucus and listened to my plans for how we could operate a cohesive group based on solidarity unionism and social justice. I am indebted to you for your comradery and commitment to the labor movement.

As a new teacher, I wanted to learn much within the realm of social-justice-minded pedagogy. Robert Haworth spoke with me during my first year as a struggling educator, hoping to retain some semblance of autonomy and critical pedagogy in my classroom. His insistence to me that I continue striving for a more democratic future remained at the forefront of my mind as I entered the 2017–2018 school year, not knowing what was yet to come but ready to do my part nevertheless. Becky Tarlau, associate professor at Penn State, provided an informative framework to me for how to interpret the content of this work. Her background on the Brazilian Landless Workers Movement (MST) and critical pedagogy allowed Erin and I to better analyze the relationship between the four surveyed states and their organizational approach to the state. Coming to West Virginia in the spring of 2019, Becky joined us at West Virginia's first Troublemakers School and participated in a joint union picket for National Nurses United in Greenbrier County. I am grateful to have known both of you from more than your research, but from your activism as well.

Understanding the complexities within state NEA affiliates would have been almost impossible without the work of Ellen David Friedman. In January 2019, during a terrible snowstorm, Ellen made the trip to Charleston to meet with WV United caucus members to discuss how we could best structure our new foundational approach to unionism. Having only met Ellen once prior, at Labor Notes in 2018, I found her insight forged through decades in the struggle for social justice unionism. It was evident from the first time Ellen and I met that she lived and breathed militant education unionism, and for her constant support in providing a better analysis throughout this work, I am forever grateful.

None of this could have been possible, however, without the support from my fellow IWW members. Upon hearing of the impending West Virginia strike, union members from across the US and Canada, too many to be named here, reached out to inquire how they could best support us. Your support on the picket lines, at the capitol, and the financial assistance you provided kept up my spirits when times felt darkest. The radical insight you gave me when we collectively decided to wildcat helped me to see that this work can, in fact, be done by the workers themselves. To fellow Wobblies Barry Conway and Humberto Da Silva, who came down to meet with me and film the historic strike, you helped us to preserve an important piece of West Virginia history before others felt the need to do so. I am indebted to you both for documenting our struggle.

I am likewise forever indebted to my co-author, Erin, for her brilliance, her insight, her scholarship, and her friendship. I met Erin virtually soon after the West Virginia strike ended so that I could speak with her students about the strike's impact on us and what her students could expect to see soon in Oklahoma. Upon being presented with the idea of writing the history of these strikes and their aftermath, Erin and I committed the next four years of our lives to ensuring that it came to fruition. Erin graciously brought me to the *Free Minds, Free Peoples* conference in Minneapolis in 2019 where we presented the initial findings in this work. Being in spaces where we could share our insights with similarly radical-minded educators was something I had yet to do at this scale. Our conversations there laid the groundwork for much of this book. Erin shared with me a vision for what this could be, provided innumerable edits, comments, and feedback for my sections, and helped me pursue this joint venture in a way that suited my writing sensibilities. I found my voice in this work because of your support.

Lastly, the work of writing a book of this magnitude could not have been possible without the continued love and support I received from my wife, Hilary. When it became clear in January 2018 that a strike was imminent and we were uncertain where our next paycheck would come from, Hilary and I were just a young family new to our careers in education. But, as she would later do when I told her I wanted to write a book cataloging the strike wave, Hilary offered her immediate support. And while my three children–Sophia, Aidan, and Brody–did not particularly enjoy my being away to work on this, I hope that this book will remind them of the power they have as they mature into young adults.

Prologue: Country Roads Shut Down a State

As the first state to strike in the spring of 2018, the actions of West Virginia rank-and-file educators served to inspire Kentucky, Oklahoma, Arizona, and many other states and districts across the US to collective direct action mere weeks and months following. We foreground our study of the 2018 so-called "red state" education strikes within a narrative constructed by Brendan via his own participation as a high school social studies teacher in West Virginia and interviews he conducted with fellow education workers across the state. The story begins just after rank-and-file educators pressured their local and state unions to undertake what started as a discrete two-day action and eventually culminated in a wildcat strike. Against the wishes of their state union leaders, school boards, and state officials, who called for schools to re-open prior to substantive guarantees for increased wages and a halt to rising health insurance costs, rank-and-file education workers across all fifty-five of West Virginia's counties struck for an additional seven days to secure their gains. This groundswell moment of widespread refusal to accept a handshake agreement between state union leaders and the governor helped to ignite a resurgence in education worker militancy across the southern and southwestern US and beyond.

The Beginning

On Thursday, February 22, 2018, West Virginia's first day out on what was meant to be a two-day strike was as invigorating as it was frightening. An estimated five thousand individuals met at the capitol to protest the mediocre reforms to educators' and public employees' insurance that had been put forth by state legislators and the dangerous pro-school privatization measures that were still being considered. Protesters demanded long-term funding for the state's Public Employees Insurance Agency (PEIA) and a larger raise for all public employees. Kym Randolph, West Virginia Education Association (WVEA) director of communication, recounted the long lines at the capitol, with some waiting for more than two hours to make it inside the capitol building to make their voices heard. "The place was packed," Randolph said. "It was very loud. That is by far the largest crowd inside the Capitol in a long, long time" (Larimer). Rallies became so intense that even the state attorney general, Patrick Morrisey, who had called the strike "illegal" one day prior, barricaded his office with a large taxidermized black bear, supposedly to prevent assembled teachers from breaking down his door. For Jessica Salfia, a high school English teacher from the Eastern Panhandle, the feeling of going on strike was otherworldly. "For me, I had a sense of being part of something historic," Salfia explained to Brendan in 2018. "There was no doubt we were doing the right thing.... I had been organizing my county, being one of the loudest and most powerful voices of dissent. I had been advocating that we needed extreme action. So, I rolled up my sleeves and kept talking to folks and explaining what we could accomplish by following the southern counties."

As Thursday rolled into Friday, a smaller crowd assembled. Disheartened by the lackluster response to what was supposed to be the second and final day of the walkouts, posters on the rank-and-file-created and -moderated West Virginia Public Employees UNITED Facebook group (WVPEU) wondered whether or if any tactical changes would be made to win their strike. Prior to the February 17 announcement by WVEA and American Federation of Teachers-West Virginia (AFT-WV) for a statewide strike, information from a union leader meeting in Flatwoods was leaked on the page that county union leadership would be directed to disseminate the benefits of a rolling walkout to members. Rolling walkouts prevent indictments–legal requirements to return to work on the threat of arrest, fines, or a combination of the two–by only shutting down a particular industry long enough to force the legal process to begin. Once an indictment has been filed, workers return to work just as another group of workers go on strike.

This process slows down management's ability to control their workers if they must rely on the state to enforce their demands. Workers circumvent the legal power of their state government while shielding their members from fines and incarceration. A rolling walkout would have had five counties go on strike all at once. Their teachers and service personnel would be expected to go to the capitol or attend an impromptu picket. If an indictment was filed, teachers would already be back to work. Then, the following day, another five counties would be on strike until another indictment was filed, and so on throughout the legislative session until demands were met.

One WVPEU poster expressed reservation about this leaked proposal. "When we went on strike in 1990, we had our counties go out all at once. You either go out together or not at all." The defined timeline of the initial two-day strike coupled with the leaked proposal led to public education workers' general uncertainty about the duration of and plan for the strike and whether the rolling walkouts would be effective. Some wondered: Would the walkouts simply be a two-day break? On the second day, many education workers did not attend the capitol rally but maintained picket lines and continued food services for low-income children in their local counties. With fewer bodies gathered centrally at the capitol, momentum appeared to wane.

Amidst the uncertainty, Republicans seemed to believe they could test the resolve of teachers and support staff once the weekend had ended. After striking for two days, Thursday and Friday, Governor Justice announced that he would hold a three-school tour of the state that Monday in the hopes of gaining some insight into the grassroots anger that was fueling this struggle. Miscommunication between union officials and members led to confusion about what this meeting would entail. Would it be a town hall open to the public? A private meeting with local union representatives? These questions were not resolved until early Monday morning as Justice, a billionaire who owns more than fifty coal mines and businesses, had already begun to fly, via helicopter, to his first destination of the day. Some wondered if this was intentional, sowing mass confusion in the lead up to the meetings to drive down turnout. Whatever Justice's intentions, teachers showed up in full force.

● The Coal Baron and the "Rednecks"

At his first stop in Wheeling, Justice was greeted by a crowd of teachers who at first remained largely silent and deferential to the governor. Over time, however, the crowd began to push back on Justice's insistence that he was a champion of public education. Justice's proposal was simple–a task force would investigate the concerns for PEIA premiums, and he would call for a special legislative session to address issues of taxing oil and natural gas industries to pay for these changes. The proposed PEIA task force would travel the state and engage with community members to learn which proposals citizens would like to see implemented to pay for halting increases to PEIA. Yet, Justice's olive branch of peace was tinged with a paternalistic overtone. "I love you," Justice told those assembled in the performing arts center at Wheeling Park High School. "But I'm not happy with you. You should be appreciative of where you are." Justice insisted that while teachers were making their voices heard, "You need to be back in the classroom. The kids need to be back in the classroom."

Tensions grew worse after a speaker shouted at him that he should put as much pressure on legislators as he does teachers. Justice's response: "I can be the town redneck, too," was met with angry boos from the crowd. His elitist tone continued throughout the Wheeling town hall. Justice suggested a natural gas severance tax to fund PEIA was simply impractical and may not pass the legislature. At this point, teachers began to walk out of the event in protest. On stage, Justice was visibly frustrated, stating, "I didn't have to come here."

One audience member, Gideon Titus-Glover, a sixth grader from a local middle school, used his time at the microphone to question why Justice, a billionaire who owned one of the largest tourist destinations in the state, would push for a larger tourism budget instead of higher teacher wages or benefits (Novotney). As Justice attempted to get out of the awkward situation, Gideon interrupted and said, "If you're putting money into public schools and making smart people, that's a smart investment" (Novotney). Justice would later quote Gideon's business advice the following day during a press conference officially calling for an end to the walkouts. The hashtag #GideonForGovernor began trending for the rest of the day.

After arriving at his first stop almost an hour late, Justice left Wheeling to travel to his second destination, Martinsburg, again delayed. At Spring Mills High School, in the eastern part of the state, Justice opened by posing the rhetorical question, "Nobody's going to shoot at me or anything, are you?" Many felt this was in poor taste, considering the then-recent Parkland school shooting in Florida which had claimed seventeen lives. Audience members responded with boos and sighs to the governor's poor attempt at humor before Justice added, "Okay, you don't have to promise" (Da Silva). It became clear to many teachers who had viewed Justice's first stop on social media that this was little more than a promotion tour. Indeed, Justice's statement that, "I didn't have to come here," was possibly the most truthful thing he said that day. What had begun as a poor attempt at finding some common ground turned into a hostile back-and-forth between public employees and their governor.

Justice is West Virginia's first billionaire governor. He is the first governor to not hold prior elected office and to have made most of his wealth in coal and large agribusiness. He initially ran for office as a Democrat but switched to the Republican party soon after his election. As the wealthiest person in West Virginia, he positioned himself as a working-class champion. The widespread negative response to these meetings chipped away at his cultivated public image. When he was still a Democrat in April 2017, Justice called a press conference to announce his veto of the state legislature's recently unveiled annual budget. On a white-clothed table in front of him, he lifted the lid of a silver serving tray to reveal a large pile of actual bull manure. "We don't have a nothing burger today," Justice told the crowd, referencing a popular Republican analogy. "And we don't have a mayonnaise sandwich. What we have is nothing more than a bunch of political bull you-know-what" (B. Murphy). At the time, the West Virginia American Association of Retired Persons State Director Gaylene Miller said that Justice's theatrics weren't offensive. "That's just how the governor is. That's what we've come to expect. He's a homespun kind of guy and I think his honesty is refreshing" (Jenkins, "Justice Vetoes Budget").

Now, West Virginia's wealthiest citizen was touring the state in a private helicopter to belittle and deride public employees for having the tenacity to ask for slightly better pay and no increases to their already bloated health insurance. The irony was not lost on teachers.

● Empty Promises

As the governor fled Martinsburg for his final destination, teachers were watching his tour with bated breath. Education workers in Morgantown, where the third town hall was held, had just wrapped up their shift on the picket lines when they flooded into the auditorium of University High School. Unlike the previous two destinations, the auditorium was packed; so much so that not all who wanted to attend could get inside. When Justice shuffled on stage, he was greeted with no applause or adoration. The silent tension of the moment was palpable.

Audience members demanded that Justice increase public employee salaries five percent—which translates to $2,000 annually—for the next fiscal year. In addition, teachers demanded that PEIA be fully funded through a combination of tax increases on oil and natural gas industries and legalizing and taxing marijuana. Justice pushed back on these proposals by suggesting that he had already made the same case to the legislature the previous year. "Did I not last year, at the state of the state, say that the severance tax on gas and coal should be tiered and it should go up and down, with the prices and if we would have done that, we would have been clear sailing like you can't believe," Justice told his audience (Hudock). The governor may have made these proposals to his audience and at his state of the state address, but it seemed clear that these were empty words. A host of oil and natural gas industries donated to key Republican legislators in the past to ensure severance taxes would remain at comically low levels year after year. The third day of the strike ended with Justice wrapping up his publicity tour and little else. Justice informed educators that he admired them for standing up for their students and for exercising their freedom of speech. This appreciation was couched within a threat, however. If teachers did not return to work the following day, punitive actions might be taken to force them to comply.

That Tuesday afternoon, the walkouts continued into their fourth day. Each of the state's fifty-five counties shut down once more. State union leadership from WVEA and AFT-WV announced that they arranged with Governor Justice a tentative deal to increase public employee pay by five percent alongside a sixteen-month freeze on insurance premiums. The PEIA task force that Justice said he was keen on creating would be developed a few weeks later. Flanked by state leadership from the main education unions, Justice stated that this deal was contingent upon teachers returning to work after a "cooling off" day on Wednesday. "The long and the short of it is just this: We need our kids back in school," Justice said. "We need our teachers back in school. They want to be back in school" (Larimer). Attempting to appeal to a sense of community togetherness, Justice presented a kinder side than he had shown publicly only the day prior. "I've said many times we ought to look at education as an economic driver. But maybe I was looking at it as what is the prudent thing to do and not necessarily looking at education as an investment" (Raby and Virtanen). One problem—a bill to increase teacher pay at this point in the year would have to go through committee, dominated by hostile Republican lawmakers, or passed during a special session. The handshake agreement was not binding. Ending the strike before passing the legislature would mean that if a pay raise bill failed to pass, then educators may lose the momentum to strike again. What had been touted in national media as the end of the teachers strike turned out to be its apex.

Teachers had a different opinion of the supposed deal.

● West Virginia Educators Go Wildcat

West Virginia public employees do not have the right to collectively bargain. What little leeway they do have to negotiate contracts is limited, and certainly no legislature would need to honor any deal with teachers simply because the governor said he had struck a bargain with union leaders. It seems that most public employees were aware of this fact. A crowd arrived at the capitol that evening of the fourth day of the strike, furious at the compromise and chanting, "We won't back down," as their unified voice rang out in collective opposition to the handshake agreement.

Weakening the power of unions over the past several years seemed to backfire on unwitting Republican lawmakers. Introducing anti-union right-to-work laws and continuing to block collective bargaining for public employees meant that rank-and-file workers' only recourse was to take the deal into their own hands. State unions held a vote of authorization two weeks prior to the strike. The vote of authorization only said, "I hereby give authority to the state associations to call a statewide action." Mass actions leading up to the wildcat strike had provided education workers a taste of collective power, a power that emerged from their own relationships and labor within their communities and at the capitol. Public education workers came to realize they did not have to agree unilaterally with the terms of the Justice deal; they could refuse it.

Wednesday, February 28 was meant to be a "cooling-off" day yet had become the most anxiety-provoking day of the strike. Emily Tanzey, a middle school English language arts teacher, recounted to Brendan that she was driving back from Charleston to Morgantown that day, pulling over at each rest stop to check her phone and see if she should go home "or return to the Capitol to raise hell." Tanzey chose to return home, only to find that a secret meeting was soon to take place at an old mall that could serve as a central meeting point for her county's educators. At this meeting, "teachers demanded our local union leadership and region reps to wildcat." The informal gathering had been posted on one of the several secret Facebook groups set up by Monongalia County educators, which was replicated throughout other West Virginia counties in various formats. "I honestly felt that the state union leaders had conceded, and I was skeptical of us actually making the progress that had been promised [without a wildcat]," Tanzey said.

A wildcat strike is a strike that is undertaken by workers without explicit authorization from union leadership or a formal vote of authorization. Wildcat strikes tend to happen during periods of union complacency. They are often localized because a large member base is difficult to organize into a single action without the support of union leadership and its infrastructure. In West Virginia, the wildcat strike was not called from a central leader or voice so much as members found the power within one another to stay out to remain united.

On the WVPEU Facebook group, video began circulating of state and regional union officials pleading with members at these informal, rank-and-file organized meetings across the state to accept the deal and return to work. Pleading turned to hostility as members openly defied their unions, yelled back in protest, and walked out of their state and county union meetings. Other counties that held secret meetings, like Monongalia County educators' secret mall meeting, during that supposed "cooling off" day were also likely recorded and sent around on social media, providing access to the tenor of the general mood for those not in attendance. Impromptu organizing efforts spread across the various secret pages and back channels that teachers and service personnel had set up during the walkouts to ensure all workers maintained open lines of communication. Rank-and-file meetings were set up in schools and churches so that teachers and service personnel could determine whether they would accept the deal as it stood or if they would inform their superintendent there would not be enough staffing for the following day.

By late afternoon on the "cooling off" day, three counties–Wayne, Cabell, and Mingo–announced they would not reopen the following day. Posters on the WVPEU page shared the state map of striking counties as it gradually turned red once more, with independent updates on what their own county planned to do in response. Watching the map galvanized those who felt they had been betrayed by their union leadership but were in no position to fight back. "I remember staying up late and watching the map turn red, first a few counties, then all at once," said Joshua Russell in an interview, a social studies teacher from Preston County. "The last counties to go were in the Eastern Panhandle, and we all watched to make sure we were 55 united for one more day." The concept of remaining united created an atmosphere whereby teachers lived out the old labor adage that, "An injury to one is an injury to all."

Many WVEA and AFT-WV state and county leaders were fearful and displeased with members' militancy and the prospect of a wildcat. Earlier in the strike, the Preston County WVEA president, for example, called a meeting at a local auditorium with teachers, service personnel, and the county superintendent in attendance. She began chastising those who argued in favor of continuing the walkouts beyond the initially planned two days in front of the county superintendent and board of education. "It was clear from that meeting that [she] was listening to leadership, but ignoring the masses," Russell said. "We knew at this point the teachers across the state had it together."

County superintendents who had previously sent out automated phone calls to parents informing them that students would be back in school on Thursday, March 1 were forced to rescind those statements soon after. In Monongalia County, Superintendent Frank Devano informed parents that he was "proud to announce that school would be in session for a normal school day" on Thursday. A few hours later, an exasperated Devano called parents and guardians back to say he was "unsure when they [the schools] would reopen." By 6:00 that evening, six counties had announced closures after the "cooling off" day, with an additional two counties on two-hour delays, no doubt an attempt to see if enough workers would report to duty for schools to legally be in session. By 7:30 p.m., sixteen counties had closed and four more were on two-hour delays. As each successive hour passed, it was becoming clearer and clearer that whatever the "cooling off" period was intended to resolve, it failed. It was at 10:30 p.m. that all schools had announced closures indefinitely, and state union leaders were left uncertain of their position. What good was a union if the legislature couldn't rely on union leaders to bargain a deal to end this strike. With whom could they bargain?

Wildcatting turned out to be the right call. On Hoppy Kercheval's popular statewide radio show, Talkline, Wednesday afternoon, state Senate leader Mitch Carmichael declared that he would not bring a vote to the floor on public employee pay. Senate Republicans claimed that a five percent pay raise plan would need to be developed further before they could commit to vote (Jenkins, "Some Education Workers Return"). The Senate had adjourned Wednesday evening without passing a pay raise and reports from educators began coming into the WVPEU page that the Senate's attorneys were allowed to go home early so they could be prepared to read over the bill Thursday morning. When Kercheval asked Carmichael if the pay raise had a chance of passing, Carmichael stated that it was unlikely that there were enough votes to make it happen.

Social media began exploding out of anger. Brendan made a post to the West Virginia Industrial Workers of the World Facebook page explaining that the Senate was unlikely to pass the pay raise. At the time, the page had only around one thousand followers, yet the post reached more than 130,000 viewers and more than one thousand shares. One poster commented, "Then the unions should tell everyone to walk out tomorrow. That was the deal that they made with Justice." Another poster stated he had seen "Mitch Carmichael through the doors at the Capital [sic] today laughing at the crowd at the end of the session. This is no laughing matter. Thousands of workers are fed up. Thousands of families worried about their future and this guy is laughing. . . . These guys are abusing the position and hurting hard working WV people!!! It's time to get involved. Enough is enough!"

● More than Wages and Insurance

It was at this moment that thousands of rank-and-file educators' organizing efforts came to fruition. Wednesday became more than a wildcat; it was an awakening. Education workers online and in-the-field independently organized themselves since the previous summer. On Martin Luther King, Jr. Day, a month prior to the strike, independent rank-and-file educators with WVPEU had organized a lobby day to bring education workers to the capitol and plead with lawmakers to make the necessary changes to state funding. The outpouring of anger directed towards PEIA policy makers was first birthed online, as thousands read the tragic stories of their fellow workers having to go without medical care for fear it would lead them into inescapable debt. It was community members and local volunteers—churches, businesses, sports teams, and activists—who organized food drives to keep students from going hungry. It was the average worker who offered car rides and chartered buses to attend rallies at the capitol, sometimes more than four hours away. If the workers could bring the state legislature to their knees on their own, then why shouldn't it be the workers who chose when to accept any deal?

"I thought the wildcat was absolutely necessary," Russell said to Brendan. "Union leadership was not listening. During the 'cooling off' day I was happy at the prospect of getting back to work, but the legislature began to screw around with the five percent and our local leaders told us we needed to go back to work as a 'good faith' gesture." Staying out to stay united was critical to the continuation of the strike. "We watched as the more militant counties led the way by closing," Russell explained. "At this point, my opinion was that if one county closes, we all close." While some county representatives from WVEA tried to persuade others to return to school, to accept the deal as it was in good faith while waiting to see what the Senate did, militancy ultimately won out. Russel illuminated how rank-and-file pressure ensured the continued strike: "Our school was about 50/50 when it came to continuing the strike, so there was a lot of worry that if we stayed out, school would still be open. One by one, though, teachers in the group chat started taking sick days. Eventually, the WVEA representative got the point, called our superintendent and he had to call off school."

The rising of class-consciousness flourished as a direct result of the strike turning into a wildcat. "One huge change I noticed is that I became closer to my co-workers, especially those who also had ancestors who had been involved with other labor movements," Tanzey said in an interview, reflecting on when the strike turned into a wildcat. "I think for many teachers at my school, there was a sudden awareness that education is also an occupation that needs protections, is also disenfranchised." Many educators who had previously eschewed politics, electorally or otherwise, began to post political statements on their personal social media pages. Those who had previously been afraid to share their views, or were unaware of what they were, now no longer hid their views. Tanzey said, "I think that many teachers realized they are part of a larger labor movement that is happening in the US and globally. Workers hold the power. It's about time we make our bosses see this!"

The wildcat strike positioned state lawmakers as the "bosses," shifting the balance of power away from local boards of education or even administration. Workers wanted investment in education through progressive taxation. "Workers in the capitol were chanting, 'Tax our gas!' and my coworkers at school were suddenly talking about gas companies exploiting us, stealing our resources, and making a profit while our state is left with nothing," said Emily Comer, a Spanish teacher in Kanawha County, in an interview with Brendan. Taxing these natural gas companies would mean the difference between a teacher working a second or third job after school just to make ends meet. It meant the difference between being able to hire and retain experienced educators who otherwise could teach in any surrounding states and make on average around ten thousand dollars more. It was the difference between being able to retire knowing that necessary medication would not increase precipitously, eating away at what little retirement teachers received.

As the walkout progressed, the Senate continued to drag its feet. Meanwhile, the state map continued to turn red day after day. Educators were fighting back.

● Sparking the Fire of Rebellion

By Friday, March 2, it became clear that nothing short of an occupation would suffice. Carmichael had stalled on putting forth a five percent pay raise bill that the House had voted overwhelmingly to approve, sending it to the finance committee where it stayed as members of the committee debated the merits of four or five percent raises. When the Senate was planning to adjourn early Friday afternoon, Jay O'Neal, a social studies teacher in Kanawha County, posed the following on the WVPEU group: "It's going to take added pressure to make sure our demands are met. There has been some talk at the capitol about not leaving the building until they meet our demands. Would you support this?" In 2011, Wisconsin public employees had followed a similar path when they occupied their capitol building in Madison. Protestors refused to leave, creating a fully functioning community inside, with a sleeping area, food station, and information relay center–an event that some suggest served as a precursor to the Occupy Wall Street Movement later that year (Buhle and Buhle). The occupation of Madison's capitol building had lasted more than two weeks, and in that time, protestors had gathered and directed anger towards Republican lawmakers in full force. As tensions escalated, and rifle ammunition was found nearby the capitol building, Dane County Circuit Judge John Albert ordered the removal of union protesters.

Occupying Charleston would mean an increased potential for violence and state repression. Some posters worried that there were few resources for teachers who had traveled hours for what they had assumed was simply another large rally before the weekend. "If this happens, I think it should happen Monday," posted Matt McCormick, a Mercer County teacher. "The Senate will adjourn for the weekend soon and won't feel appropriate pressure if it starts today." Others worried that mass arrest would take place if an occupation did occur. "So far we have acted peacefully," stated one WVPEU member. "This will force the police to physically remove us." Jake Jarvis, a reporter for the Charleston Gazette-Mail, had reported only a week earlier that the House of Delegates had voted to give Capitol police authority to break up "riots and unlawful assemblage" while preventing them from being held liable "for the death of persons in riots and unlawful assemblages." The message was clear–the state would only tolerate so much from their public employees before pressing down hard against them with the full weight of the militarized police force. Only the day before, the legislature passed a bill that increased the pay for law enforcement officers by five percent for the next fiscal year. During the summer health care sit-ins, too, Capitol police arrested protesters, including an Episcopalian priest who many assumed would be immune to state arrest given his position. Educators' fears of potential arrests or violence were not unfounded.

The occupation had been put on hold until a critical mass could mature around the idea. The weekend would determine whether such action would be necessary at all. In what might have been the most widely watched West Virginia Senate Finance Committee meeting in history, committee members met over the weekend to discuss whether to approve the five percent pay raise bill as it stood. Some back-and-forth occurred when Senator Greg Boso began to argue that a five percent raise across the board would be too costly for the state, instead amending the original House bill to four percent so that all state employees would see a raise, a noteworthy stall tactic. The Senate eventually took up the four percent pay raise bill and passed it later that evening, only to realize that they had unintentionally passed the original five percent pay raise bill. Senate Majority Leader Carmichael recalled the bill and passed it with the amended language before it was rejected by the House.

The weekend's standoffs continued until the following Tuesday when West Virginia public employees ultimately won their strike, maintaining momentum despite anger, resentment, and exhaustion. On Tuesday, March 6, after much delay, Senate Republicans finally passed a five percent pay increase for all public employees and members accepted the legislature's conditions. PEIA premiums and deductible increases would be frozen for sixteen months as a statewide task force was set up with the mission to find a dedicated source of long-term, sustainable revenue for the insurance plan. Seniority was kept in place and legislation that would enable charter school creation in the state was taken off the table for the rest of the session.

West Virginia public employees had won tangible, material gains in their strike. Yet, in another sense, the strike had won something bigger than itself. "Outside of West Virginia," teacher Adam Culver shared, "I hope our story continues to inspire other teachers and workers to fight for what should be theirs. As much as this story is about classism, capital accumulation, and social movements, it's also just about keeping promises and taking care of the people who are taking care of your world. . . . It takes everyone to make this world work, and no one who is contributing should be struggling." Indeed, the fire of rebellion that had been sparked by West Virginia educators would not be contained. What had started as a fight over insurance and low wages, as we explore in more depth throughout the book, became something greater than any had anticipated.

P&C

Commonly Used Abbreviations

AEA – Arizona Education Association

AEU – Arizona Educators United

AFL-CIO – American Federation of Labor and Congress of Industrial Organizations

AFT – American Federation of Teachers

AFT-WV – American Federation of Teachers-West Virginia

CORE – Caucus of Rank-and-File Educators

CTU – Chicago Teachers Union

JCTA – Jefferson County Teachers Association

KEA – Kentucky Education Association

KY 120 – KY 120 United Facebook Group and Organization

NEA – National Education Association

NEU – National Educators United

OHB – Ocean Hill-Brownsville School District

OEA – Oklahoma Education Association

OTU – Oklahoma Teachers United

PEIA – West Virginia Public Employee Insurance Agency

TTN – Oklahoma Teacher Walkout: The Time is Now Facebook Group

TU – New York's Teachers Union

UFT – United Federation of Teachers

WVPEU – West Virginia Public Employees UNITED Facebook Group

WVEA – West Virginia Education Association

WV United – West Virginia United Caucus

P&C

RANK-AND-FILE REBELS: THEORIES OF POWER AND CHANGE IN THE 2018 EDUCATION STRIKES

● Introduction

> Past events exist, after all, only in memory, which is a form of imagination. The event is real now, but once it's then, its continuing reality is entirely up to us, dependent on our energy and honesty. If we let it drop from memory, only imagination can restore the least glimmer of it. If we lie about the past, forcing it to tell a story we want it to tell, to mean what we want it to mean, it loses its reality, becomes a fake. To bring the past along with us through time in the hold-alls of myth and history is a heavy undertaking.
>
> – *Ursula K. Le Guin,* Tales from Earthsea

In the spring of 2018, a wave of rank-and-file rebellion swept schools across four Republican-led states in the south and southwest US. One after another, education workers and local union activists in West Virginia, Oklahoma, Kentucky, and Arizona pushed their trade unions, school boards, and school administrations to shut schools down until their demands were met. They called on legislators to increase taxes on the wealthiest extractors of resources and labor in their respective places (namely coal, oil, and gas) to increase pay for all education workers and public employees, provide better health insurance, and restore education funding. After experiencing year after year of budget cuts, often alongside increasingly intense accountability and surveillance measures, educators said, enough.

Mass strike actions are not new to schooling since education unions formed in the early to mid twentieth century. Historian Jon Shelton recounts more than three hundred strikes in the "long 70s" that roiled cities and states across the country from New York to Oklahoma to Montana to California. Yet, for the past thirty or more years, teachers' strikes have been few and far between and never with such widespread public support (Feldman and Swanson). Many have, very rightly, argued that the 2018 education walkouts are a new and exciting shift with deep implications for the future of labor (Friedman).

Through interviews with strike organizers across four states, our own experiences in education labor organizing, and our participation in and proximity to the strikes in West Virginia and Oklahoma respectively, this book undertakes a critically constructive study of the spring 2018 educator uprising, a part of a resurgence of teacher uprisings, including strikes in the Los Angeles Unified School District, Oakland Unified School District, Chicago Public Schools, and Denver Public Schools, among many others in the US and across the globe (Stark and Spreen). Rooting our study in a longer historical view and within a wider education justice movement perspective, we know that a revolutionary shift within the education labor movement requires looking backward just as much as we look to the present and future. It requires that we engage deeply

P&C

embedded hierarchies of power that have always existed, in some form, within the education system.

Our main purpose in writing this book is to reinvigorate the feelings of excitement and raw energy that comprised this shared collective experience among educators and all those–students, caregivers, families, community members, movement workers and scholars–involved in education labor struggles. At the same time, we hope to also encourage healthy, critical reflection to understand several salient tensions that arose and continue to arise within contemporary educator movements. The collective experience of rebellion was/is differentiated, along the lines of rank, race, class, gender, immigrant status, and geography, among other ways. Rank-and-file educators ignited the kindling of agitation among one another into militancy. They pushed hesitant centralized state union leadership to shift from decades of electoral-focused strategies to direct action, if briefly. Differences in power and voice among strike participants and those most directly impacted ensured certain visions for the struggle moved forward while others were constrained or remained marginal. We suggest that grappling with these differentiated, in-tension experiences of the strikes is important for creating and realizing shared visions of just and liberatory education in labor movement spaces. We humbly acknowledge that such critical reflection is only possible in hindsight.

Secondarily, while our study centers on K–12 education struggles, we seek to offer insights that may contribute to post-secondary academic labor organizing. While higher and lower education labor contexts and organization differ in many respects, they are indelibly connected. Issues of public disinvestment and privatization, state or institutional curricular mandates that aim to limit and repress educators who foster study of historical and ongoing social oppression, the precaritization of (all but especially the most feminized) education labor–higher and lower education struggles can and should learn from one another.

We begin by providing a summary of the strikes, then framing the strike wave within its historical context, drawing mainly on the work of teacher strike and labor history scholars. We argue the history (and present state) of teacher labor is a history of racialization and genderization and continues to be so. To understand our present moment, it is important to remember how organized teachers have, in moments, accepted narrowed forms of professionalization that understood (White) teachers as experts and, within education and educator unions, devalued ways of knowing and being incompatible with the status quo. In other moments, educators rejected White professionalization, advocating approaches to militant labor organizing accountable to the communities and social movements they worked in, with, and for. Within such a framing, our analysis of the spring 2018 strikes is driven by a desire to, as Shelton states, "show that teacher organization is at its best when it is a part of a larger social movement and when it can show how intimately related are teacher working conditions, student learning conditions, and social equality" (197).

● Teacher Strike Waves During "the Long '70s": Introducing Unionisms

During the 1960s, 1970s, and early 1980s, strikes and direct action were a common strategy in education labor organizing. With aims toward quelling disruptive teaching labor, the capitalist and bipartisan governing classes appropriated Civil Rights-era language to promote individual choice, school privatization, and the dogma of scientific measurement as antidotes to educational inequality (Baker, "Paradoxes of Desegregation"; Shelton). In West Virginia, Oklahoma, Kentucky, Arizona, and everywhere, these reforms have disproportionately impacted students at the intersections of working class, BIPOC, immigrant, and disabled. Such neoliberal capitalist reforms, co-constitutive with legal and structural attacks on workers' rights and capacity to organize toward more militant aims, have created a now multi-trillion-dollar global education industry (Stark and Spreen). In the past three decades, education trade unions like the American Federation of Teachers (AFT) and the National Education Association (NEA) have largely avoided strikes and direct action in favor of lobbying for pro-public education elected officials. The successes of these neoliberal moves and the decline in education labor militancy are intricately entwined with political, racial, gendered, ethnic, and cultural tensions within the education labor movement (Shelton; Podair; Golin).

During the long 1970s of intense militancy in teacher labor, White educator unions often, yet not always, deferred solidarity with civil rights struggles for integration, community control over the curriculum and school, ethnic studies, and increasing teachers of color. Prior to school desegregation, Black teachers and Black teachers' associations engaged social movement activity entwined with labor organizing for pay and resources equal to White teachers and schools (V. S. Walker; Hale, "On Race"). During integration, White teachers' unions generally did not prioritize fighting against the mass push-out of Black educators, and many AFT and NEA state and local associations remained segregated until as late as the 1970s (M. Murphy; Urban). While there have long been waves of social movement unionism on the margins of the broader education labor movement, Shelton writes that, in tandem with the passage of anti-union labor law, like the Taft-Hartley Act in 1947, "anti-Communist backlash in the postwar years helped to choke off more radical forms of social movement teacher unionism" (31; Blount; M. Murphy). Andrew Feffer's history of this era in New York City demonstrates that anti-communist AFT leaders colluded with state investigations that fired *en masse* K–12 and higher education teachers involved in social movement unions. With the marginalization, push-out, or, in some cases, imprisonment of more radical anti-racist teacher organizers, major unions in many, especially urban, places became more narrowly focused on carving out and protecting the professional status of an emergent White and Whitening middle class teaching force (Urban).

One significant example of the differences and tensions in unionism during this era is Jerard Podair's study of the United Federation of Teachers' (UFT's) series of strikes in 1968 against New York City's (OHB) neighborhood experiment in Black community control. Prior to the creation of the Black community-led OHB, during the 1930s/1940s, a small yet strong, multi-racial women-led faction of the communist Teachers Union (TU) engaged a community-based mode of organizing, developing strong relationships with students, families, and community organizations and a platform grounded in anti-racism and anti-poverty. The TU fought for many years to win leadership in the UFT (M. Murphy 170; Taylor). During the red scares of the 1940s and 1950s, the TU was decimated, with a majority of TU members arrested or fired *en masse* (Podair 170).

In the 1960s, many years of tireless grassroots organizing by a coalition of Black-led community groups, including the remaining TU organizers, won a community-elected district governing board, with hiring and firing power and control over OHB's curriculum (Podair 5). The board sought to redefine school success against narrow individualism and along the lines of community responsibility (Podair 76). The Albert Shanker-led UFT struck in response to the power carried by the local district board and the firing of several racist teachers resistant to Black curricular control. UFT leaders were particularly upset that elected board members comprised a majority of so-called "uneducated" poor Black mothers, whose movement work made the OHB experiment possible in the first place (Podair 87).

Shelton, building from the work of Podair and other teacher strike scholars, offers a more expansive argument to understand these racialized tensions and their relationship to the demise of militancy among teachers' unions during the past thirty years. Resonant with Podair, he suggests that many strikes during this era were rooted in White ethnic teachers' resistance to efforts of Civil Rights and Black Power activists to gain control over school curriculum and personnel.

Shelton further argues that such resistance was nurtured, in part, through the discursive moves of a "producerist" coalition of corporate interests and White working- and middle-class Americans to construct militant teachers' Whiteness as contingent. If one was striking, one was "flout[ing] the law and siphon[ing] off the resources of hardworking Americans" (2). In other words, a striking teacher was a "non-producer," at risk of being tainted by the anti-Black, anti-immigrant racialized tropes used to demean welfare and housing subsidy recipients. Alongside racial politics, teachers' strikes during this era hinged significantly on gender politics. Often, striking teachers were derided by city officials, school boards, and the producerist coalition, generally, as women unwilling to do women's work, like unpaid caregiving duties–grievances at the heart of many union campaigns in this era. More importantly, women teachers balked such gender policing and claimed their right to undertake so-called men's work, participating in decision-making on city, state, and school district budget-making and resource allocations.

Yet, Shelton tends to underemphasize the role and responsibility of the major teachers' unions in the marginalization and repression of social movement unionism, or ways of thinking about and practicing labor organizing toward transforming unions, schools, and society toward radical democracy and social justice aims (see Dyke; Maton and Stark). He frames teacher labor opposition to community control more so as a clash created in the confluence of circumstances in a political moment: "Indeed, the public-sector labor movement in American cities came of age at the exact moment that, first, African American activists organized to rectify the abject inequality that New Deal liberalism helped to institutionalize, and second, cities faced both declining tax revenues and taxpayer resistance" (195). Shelton rightly points to the significance of producerist responses to teacher militancy during the long 1970s in facilitating the rise of neoliberalism. However, historians of teaching, teachers' unions, and the McCarthy era illuminate the longer, active institutional investments of the AFT and NEA in a narrowed White teacher professionalism, and resistance efforts on the part of rank-and-file educators to democratize and practice alternative modes of unionism (Blount; Feffer; M. Murphy; Tait; Taylor).

Despite violent government repression and resistance from trade union leadership, Cindy Rottman et al. argue that marginal yet powerful feminist and antiracist rank-and-file efforts have always existed throughout the history and present of the U.S. education labor movement. Often women- and people of color-led, such efforts understood that labor challenges within the education industry are deeply connected to intersecting issues of systemic racism, sexism, poverty, gentrification, and colonialism. More recently, the 2011 Wisconsin teacher protests against educational austerity began to popularize the tagline that "teachers' working conditions are students' learning conditions' (Buhle and Buhle). The 2012 Chicago Teachers Union strike, led by the more radical Caucus of Rank-and-File Educators (CORE), is one of the most recent and powerful examples of social justice unionism, with its emphasis on community organizing and antiracism (Nuñez et al.). Their demands went well beyond bread-and-butter gains to attend to the everyday living and learning conditions of their students and families (McCartin and Sneiderman). Demands were premised on analyses of the interrelations between school reform and gentrification, regressive tax increment financing policies, the decimation of public housing, and various methods through which land and wealth in the city was and continues to be upwardly redistributed to the already wealthy (Brogan 146). In 2019 and into the years of the pandemic, several major urban strikes continued to push for social justice demands, predominantly led by social justice caucuses within the United Teachers of Los Angeles, the Oakland Education Association, and again, the Chicago Teachers Union (Stark).

Throughout the book, our analysis of the 2018 strikes attends to differences and tensions in ways of thinking about the purposes and practices of union organizing in public education (unionisms, plural), differences that include orientations to militancy, union democracy, social oppression, wider social movements, and to the work of public education system in/for transforming society.

● Timeline of the Spring 2018 Strikes

Strikes are not a new phenomenon in West Virginia, Oklahoma, Kentucky, or Arizona, and educators in these places have long been on the frontlines. West

Virginia educators' 1990 statewide struggle revolved predominantly around educators' poor wages and education funding. In Oklahoma in 1990, educators struck for four days and won increased wages, smaller class sizes, and increased education funding through the passage of HB1017 (Cameron). At the time (and prior to the state's passage of anti-union Right to Work legislation in 2001), the state's major education union, the National Education Association-affiliated Oklahoma Education Association (OEA), was more robust with a much larger membership and union leaders supported and led the action. Previously, OEA called for a statewide strike in 1968, also due to low wages and education funding. In 1988, Kentucky Education Association (KEA) leaders organized a walkout in protest of the Governor's proposal at the time to cut public education funding that shut down ninety-two of the state's 178 districts (R. Walker) and engaged in statewide strikes previously during 1966 and 1970. In 1970, educators across the state struck for six days to win major investments in educators' pay and school funding (Brandt). As recent as 2004, leaders of KEA and its most populous local, the Jefferson County Teachers Association (JCTA), called for a statewide strike in response to cuts to healthcare benefits. The strike was averted after lawmakers met in special session to restore funding. Even as Arizona has had strong anti-union laws on the books since 1947, educators in two of the state's largest districts at the time, Tucson and Scottsdale, struck in 1971 and 1978 respectively, for increased wages and school funding (Eberhart-Phillips; Kennedy).

The 2018 strikes revolved around many of the same issues as the previous actions. All four states continue to be ranked at or near the bottom of average state teacher pay and education funding that disparately impact the states' most economically and racially marginalized communities. In addition to low wages and funding, each state had specific moments of catalyzation. West Virginia's struggle gained momentum due to increases in public employees' insurance premiums and the proposed privatization of their state insurance program. Kentucky public employees and educators became outraged in response to a quickly proposed pension reform bill, tacked on at the last minute to a routine wastewater treatment bill, nicknamed the Sewer Bill. Kentucky's teacher pension fund was siphoned during the 2008 recession to address state budget shortfalls. The reform, pushed by conservative lawmakers, proposed cuts to pensions, especially for new hires, to avoid restoring pre-recession funding levels and would have limited teachers' representation on the pension board. In Oklahoma, while sentiments for a walkout had been brewing for at least a year in many districts, legislators proposed and failed to pass a bill in February 2018 that would have provided educators with a $5,000 pay increase and increased education funding, funded by tax increases. Similarly in Arizona, low wages and steep education funding cuts during the decade prior combined with the energy and momentum from other states' educator uprisings produced a political moment of possibility.

Here, we offer a general timeline of events for the spring 2018 strikes, which may be useful for reference as we narrate in more detail and historicize the actions in subsequent chapters.

Table 1. Timeline of Spring 2018 Strikes

West Virginia	February 22, 2018	Due to pressure from rank-and-file educators, especially those organized loosely with WVPEU Facebook group, WVEA and AFT-WV called for a two-day statewide strike, which eventually turned into five days.
	February 27, 2018	All the state's fifty-five counties continued to strike. On this day, state union leaders announced a handshake agreement to resolve wage raises and the imperiled public employee insurance program.
	February 28, 2018	Initially supposed to be a "cooling off" day before a return to work, educators locally organized and shared information via social media, especially via WVPEU, to continue the strike until the legislation was officially passed and signed into law.
	March 6, 2018	The legislature passed a five percent pay increase for all public employees and a sixteen-month freeze to insurance premium hikes with the promise to identify a long-term source of funding for the program.
Kentucky	March 29, 2018	Republican Governor Bevin and party leaders unveiled and quickly passed an austerity reform to Kentucky teachers' pension fund (drained to address budget shortfalls during the 2008 recession), attached to a hundreds-of-pages-long wastewater treatment legislation (dubbed the Sewer Bill).
	March 30, 2018	Union leaders called for rallies at the capitol while rank-and-file organizers called for a statewide sickout. Educators shut down more than twenty school districts.
	April 2, 2018	Union leaders continued to argue against a widespread job action. All of the state's one hundred twenty counties shut down while educators protested at the capitol. This was facilitated by more than half of districts already out on spring break.
	April 13, 2018	After Bevin vetoed proposed legislation to raise taxes to reform teachers' pension fund, educators shut down more than half of the state's public school population. Legislators eventually overrode Bevin's veto. On this day, state legislators also passed HB 169, also known as the Gang Crime Bill, which many Jefferson County educators argued would fuel the school-to-prison pipeline and fought to center in the educators' strike.

Table 1. Timeline of Spring 2018 Strikes, continued

Oklahoma	March 8, 2018	With pressure from rank-and-file educators, the OEA called for legislators to provide a $10,000 raise for all teachers, a $5,000 raise for all support staff, and a restoration of $200 million in public education funding. OEA gave a deadline of April 1 for legislators to meet demands or face a statewide walkout.
	April 2, 2018	Oklahoma educators shut down near eighty percent of the state's public schools just after Governor Fallin signed a bill that provided $6,000 raises for educators, relative to experience, and a $1,250 raise for support staff, funded by a regressive increase to the tobacco sales tax and no additional public education funding.
	April 12, 2018	After nearly two weeks of striking, citing declining support among superintendents and the refusal of legislators to move on any additional legislation, OEA president, Alecia Priest, called on educators to return to work.
Arizona	April 9, 2018	Organized by members of Arizona Educators United (AEU), educators began meeting up before school, wearing red ("red for ed") to hold weekly "walk-ins" at their school sites across the state, which grew steadily in participation during a few weeks. AEU, a grassroots, rank-and-file led group, worked together with the state union, Arizona Education Association (AEA) to prepare for a statewide strike.
	April 19, 2018	Seventy-eight percent of AEA members voted to strike, demanding a twenty percent salary increase, the restoration of education funding to pre-2008 levels, competitive pay for all support staff, permanent salary including annual raises, and no new tax cuts.
	April 26, 2018	Arizona educators begin their strike.
	May 3, 2018	Arizona educators end their strike after winning a nineteen percent pay increase, partial restoration of nearly $400 million in pre-recession funding cuts, and a promise to restore the rest in the next five years.

● Knowing Your Enemy: The Terrain of Struggle for Public Schools and Universities

While there were specific moments of widespread outrage that created ripe conditions for the spring 2018 rank-and-file rebellion, the seeds of the strikes had been brewing for years, even decades. Public education is one, if not the major, expense for state budgets, and in each of these Republican-majority governed states, tax cuts for wealthy corporations, particularly in oil and gas industries, have long been absorbed through educational disinvestment. While union leaders struggled to develop and maintain relationships with legislators to pass educator-friendly bills, they held little sway in relation to the influence, wealth, and resources of oil and gas, among other corporate interests. State leaders illuminated their gendered and classed disdain for predominantly women educators in these places as the strikes loomed. Oklahoma's Governor Fallin likened educators to teenagers who wanted a new car, Kentucky's Governor Bevin described striking educators as frauds and accused them of leaving children vulnerable to sexual assault and drug abuse (Reilly, "How Republican Governor Matt Bevin Lost Teachers"), West Virginia's Governor Justice called teachers "rednecks," and Arizona's Governor Ducey accused teachers of being political operatives and of playing games (Ruelas and Cano).

Likely, governors (and many other state leaders) made these public epithets because they were in a serious bind. They faced pressure from below and from above. Macks Hopland, a Minneapolis educator and movement scholar, writes on Facebook of the recent 2022 Minneapolis Federation of Teachers' (MFT) strike, "As striking educators . . . knowing who our enemy is, is essential for understanding and winning the fight." In the MFT strike, as with many other unionized urban districts that have struck in recent years, at first glance, the common enemy may appear to be district negotiators or the school board. Yet, as Hopland writes, part-time employed school board members rarely have the professional expertise or day-to-day access to district activities, and much of their information is filtered through the superintendent. It may then seem that the district superintendent is the main power holder, in charge of hiring the negotiating team and who oversees the daily operations and budget of the district. Or, in the context of the statewide strikes, it may appear that state lawmakers are the main power holders, as they control the proposal and passage of legislation to fully fund public schools and universities. In response to these analyses, Hopland argues yes and no.

"Public education is one of the top expenses in all municipal [and state] budgets, and thus is one of the main tax burdens, specifically of property taxes, at the local level. Because taxation and education are by nature redistributive institutions, those with the most wealth in society try to limit their taxes for education as much as possible." Hopland argues that educators must take a wider view in understanding power. Using Minneapolis as an example, Hopland writes that most major Fortune 500 companies target the superintendent or state lawmakers, via corporate foundations or lobbying and campaign donations, to enact reforms that benefit their interests (also see Berkshire and Lafer). Ultimately, Hopland suggests that while public sector unions may sit across the negotiating table from district leaders or in the offices of state legislators, corporate interests' power and influence filters through legislators and district leaders. He argues that understanding how power operates at all levels can better inform educators' strategies.

Public higher education faces similar challenges. With declining state investment, university leaders work to curry favor with wealthy donors, build revenue-generating arms that have little to do with public education for the common good (i.e., athletics programs), encourage faculty and graduate students to subsidize their wages through grants and for-profit product development, reduce their labor costs in whatever ways possible, and continue to raise tuition and fees. These conditions create situations in which public universities, like Erin's, host a local food shelf for the substantial number of students who can barely afford to eat and, at the same time, pay their head football coaches $7.5 million per year in wages (Wilson).

Ralph Wilson and Isaac Kamola write that controversies around so-called leftist indoctrination on K–12 and university campuses have produced ethical, intellectual, and political debates that center the issue of free speech. Yet, they argue, "Often missing from these discussions, however, are questions about power and money" (17). Their research zooms in on one of the most powerful and far-reaching conservative political networks:

> [T]he Koch donor network has an extensive track record of weaponizing free speech arguments more generally. Its members have long used the First Amendment to push back against civil rights, environmental and consumer protections, government regulation, and labor unions. Free speech arguments have been used to justify policies that shield wealthy political donors from campaign finance limits and transparency requirements, thereby maximizing their influence on the political process. (21)

They write that "a handful of plutocratic libertarian donors seek to disproportionately influence political, economic, and social life . . . Political operatives within the Koch network have long viewed higher education as a primary battlefield in the fight to remake the world according to their radical libertarian image" (28).

Like Hopland, Wilson and Kamola suggest that educators must follow the money and understand how and why neoliberal and neoconservative capitalist interests wield their influence in public education policy. Because education, and particularly public education, is a "primary battlefield," educator labor movements operate within a unique industry and comprise a critical front in the struggle for a world that makes life not only possible but just and joyful.

● Thinking Across Lower and Higher Education

The study of the resurgence in militancy may offer important insights for labor struggles in higher education, which has, like lower education, experienced significant decreases in public funding and increases in precarity for all workers, an onslaught of privatization and for-profit schemes (Bousquet), and ever-narrowing spaces for programs and departments that cannot demonstrate their value to capital. Legislation to limit and surveil the study of race, gender, and sexuality in many states affect both K–12 and higher education contexts (Pen America). Similarly, labor movements in higher education have experienced tensions and struggles between professionalization and community-based movements for educational self-determination, e.g., struggles for Native, ethnic, feminist, and queer universities (Meyerhoff). As with lower education, participation in and visions for higher education movements are differentiated by rank, class, gender, race, and indigeneity, among other ways. The early-mid twentieth century state repression of left-teacher organizing in collusion with anti-communist AFT leaders against anti-racist, anti-poverty higher education unions (like New York's College Teachers Union) led to a decline in social movement unionism and a chilling effect on the kinds of research and scholarship undertaken by academics in this era (Feffer).

Like lower education, higher education faculty and non-academic workers undertook efforts to unionize most dramatically in the 1960s and 1970s. Between 1966 and 1994, 172 faculty strikes were undertaken across the nation (Herbert and Apkarian 262). Previously, like the NEA, the early Association of American University Professors (AAUP) was resistant to unionization. In fact, "the AAUP founders went to great lengths to reject the union label" (Reichman, quoted in Herbert and Apkarian 254). With the casualization and feminization of higher education labor, today, only twenty-five percent of all higher education faculty are unionized, concentrated in the Northeast, Upper Midwest, and West Coast (Dobbie and Robinson 130). Yet, like in our 2018 "red" state contexts, majority women contingent faculty have increasingly organized outside formal unions to challenge the low wages and precarity of their working conditions (Berry).

Even as higher education experiences pressures and reforms that are inter-related with those of lower education, their struggles and movements are often articulated at a distance. Within the field of education itself, this distance is rooted in the history of the initial formation of teacher education and its eventual shift from seminaries and normal colleges (a step above secondary education) and into universities (Ogren). As Wayne Urban notes, normal colleges were relatively freer places that "exhibited substantially more signs of gender equality than colleges and universities, even those that were coeducational" (xvi). The consolidation of teacher education within higher education was bound up with the exclusion and devaluation of women's capacity to participate in the formation of the traditions of knowledge that inform curriculum and pedagogy (Grumet). As women and gender minority faculty and faculty of color bear the brunt of casualization in higher education, so are their contributions to research and academic knowledge constrained.

In higher and lower education, teaching labor is underwaged in relation to the prestige and power associated with tenure-track (particularly private) university research labor (Kahn, "We Value Teaching" 596). Like K–12 education, higher education, too, has long grappled with decreased public funding, privatization via increased reliance on donor funding, political censure of justice-oriented academics, and threats to liberal studies in favor of social engineering (Newfield). Today, most teaching labor in higher education (upwards of seventy-five percent) is undertaken by low-wage contingent, non-tenure track faculty who are majority women and faculty of color (Schell ix). Even as many contingent faculty have sought to find ways within and outside of unions to contest, for example, denial of healthcare, low wages, and employment instability, tenure track faculty have not always joined or supported their efforts (Kahn et al.). Examples where tenure-track faculty have done so illuminate its significance. Seth Kahn, William Lalicker, and Amy Lynch-Biniek write of an example: "tenured faculty at LSU advocated for secure positions and improved compensation for their contingent colleagues by forming alliances with an activist group on their campus, even in the face of budget crises and threats of termination" (8).

Many contingent faculty labor unionists and activists have sought to learn from the much more highly unionized public sector of lower education. Kahn suggests that in more precarious, lower-wage higher education fields, like composition and writing studies, "our scholarly forums are becoming less labor averse," with more robust discussion and analysis of contingent faculty issues and organizing ("We Value Teaching" 593–594). While few faculty are unionized in the US, William Herbert and Jacob Apkarian noted an upsurge in higher education strikes in the years between 2012 and 2018 (42). The majority constituted graduate student-led and non-academic employee-led actions while fourteen were undertaken by faculty (28). The signs of solidarity that simultaneously striking University of Illinois-Chicago graduate student workers posted to social media to support striking K–12 educators in 2018 suggests the significance and necessity in thinking these rank-and-file movements across higher and lower education together. Both share the same enemies.

More broadly, and perhaps further suggesting the significance of studying our contemporary strike wave moment, Shelton argues that the American public largely viewed the demise of the labor-liberal coalition and the rise of neoliberal capitalism via the lens of the recurring Civil Rights era teacher strikes (20). He explains, "Neoliberalism relies on the notion that virtually every aspect of life is better off organized by a marketplace because the 'competition' sorts out the winners from the losers" (21–22). Certainly, today neoliberalism remains a strong discourse that continues to significantly shape educational policy from the top down. The widespread favorable media coverage and overwhelming public support for the recent strikes and the centrality of educators and schooling in local and national pandemic policy debates suggests that education labor continues to be an important lens through which many people make sense of predominating political ideologies.

● Public Narratives of the Spring 2018 Strike Wave: Forefronting Intersectionality

Within the mainstream media, coverage of the teacher strikes has largely framed the struggles in terms of professional dignity. In September 2018, *TIME Magazine* dedicated its cover story to the teacher rebellion, telling the personal stories and struggles of thirteen teachers from across the strike wave states. A Kentucky teacher describes her experience:

> Right now, I have a broken tooth that I can't afford to have fixed. I've had to take a sick day before because I didn't have enough gas to make it to school. I donated plasma twice before my first pay day this year just for gas money. I was really embarrassed when I first had to start doing that because I think of myself as a professional. I have a master's degree. (Reilly, "I Work 3 Jobs")

Similar stories were highlighted in the New York Times (Lowe), among other prominent media. The coverage in these influential media marked a stark shift from previous years of reporting that articulated bad teachers and their tenure protections as the root of educational failures. As Haley Sweetland Edwards' November 2014 *TIME* cover story title illustrates—"Rotten apples: It's nearly impossible to fire a bad teacher, Some tech millionaires may have found a way to change that"—discourses of neoliberal education reform were decidedly the norm. In her book, *The Teacher Wars: America's Most Embattled Profession*, journalist Dana Goldstein argues that teachers have, since the invention of compulsory common schooling, existed as scapegoats for the supposed failures of education to achieve the most progressive visions of the institution—social equality and prosperity. Yet, as many critical scholars of education suggest, the institution has and continues to accomplish what its creators intended, namely social control and assimilation into a predetermined social order (Ali and Buenavista). The romanticization of education as a progressive, inherently good project masks the powerful interests invested in weaponizing education, often in the name of progressivism, to maintain and reproduce the existing social order (Bowles and Gintis). Meanwhile, the accordance of professionalism has always been dangled in front of teachers like a carrot on a stick.

On the left, analyses of the strikes have suggested they illuminate the necessity for a renewed faith in the working class. Eric Blanc, for example, writes:

> Many of the big, strategic lessons from the teachers' strikes aren't widely or universally accepted on the Left, or even among socialists. One is that the working class is still the most powerful social agent for progressive, radical change. It's sometimes hard even for Marxists to believe

this because many of us haven't seen it demonstrated in our lifetimes. But now we're seeing it in practice, and it should give us a lot of confidence about our strategy and our political priorities. ("Betting on the Working Class")

Blanc's take represents one important left narrative shaping understandings of the strikes–a renewed faith in the role of workplace organizing and the rising working class to end the worst ravages of capitalism and create a socially democratic future for all. The strike wave seemed to demonstrate to many that, against the media's imaginary of rural and/or Southern White people as ignorant and racist (cf. Vance), the working class can organize and is organizing, their class-based solidarity breaking down barriers of race, gender, and more.

Blanc's reporting on the strikes, based on his interviews with teachers and union leaders during the walkouts, engaged a tone of agitation and celebration for working-class revival. As studies of teacher strike history suggests, militancy is not the only indicator of a radical and just movement. In Chapter One and in the book more broadly, we further elaborate the significance of understanding the underlying theories of change and power (or unionisms) that inform and provoke such militancy.

Fewer media narratives emphasize the racial, generational, and gendered historical specificities of teaching, education labor, and the broader landscape and genealogy of social movements that made the strike wave possible. Editors for *Rethinking Schools*, an outlet for social, racial, and labor justice in education, call on us to understand the ways the strikes were made possible by preceding feminist and intersectional movements: "While it will take broader, sustained efforts to win all the demands raised during the strikes, the walkouts were lessons in social mobilization, led largely by women and drawing inspiration and energy from #BlackLivesMatter, #MeToo, and the March for Our Lives" (Karp and Sanchez).

Ben Jarovsky, for the *Chicago Reader*, contributes to this historicizing work, arguing the "red state revolt" was made possible by the 2012 Chicago Teachers Union strike, led by the community-based organizing of CTU president Karen Lewis and CORE. Jarovsky calls for a more nuanced approach to understanding the differences in public and Democratic Party support for Chicago teachers, fighting for a majority Black and Latinx-serving urban school district and against Democrat-supported moves to take power away from parents, students, and teachers through school privatization and related reforms. In the spring 2018 strike wave in Republican-led states, the Democratic Party was quick to support, aiming to swing the electoral political tide in these more rural states that had, as of yet, not been targeted to the same extent by school privatization proponents.

Alia Wong for *The Atlantic*, argues that media coverage of the continuing strike wave can tend to homogenize interrelated yet quite differently composed struggles. She suggests that the platform of striking Los Angeles Unified School District (LAUSD) educators in January 2019 reflects the fact that educators there are, unlike almost anywhere else in the US, predominantly people of color (thirty-four percent White while the majority, forty-three percent, are Latino according to district data). Many key union organizers have roots in immigrant justice, ethnic studies, and other local movements.

Beyond an increase in education funding, LAUSD teachers, like their Chicago counterparts in 2012, demanded smaller class sizes, the halt of charter schools and school choice/privatization, community-based schools, and increased positions and pay for support staff, like nurses and librarians (Wong). While West Virginia and Kentucky have longer memories and legacies of militant unions in the coal and steel industries, for the most part, many of the tens of thousands of teachers involved in the "red state revolt" were participating in collective action and grassroots movement organizing for the first time and, for many, at a distance from the working class-led movements for Black, queer, Native, migrant, and other liberation movements that have historically composed the webs of organized resistance in these places.

Tithi Bhattacharya ("Why the Teachers' Revolt Must Confront Racism") further illuminates the importance of reading these grassroots justice movements together. She argues that we must not ignore that, in many states, increasing racial and ethnic minority public school students is directly related to justifications for decreased per pupil spending. In many states, tensions existed between strike participants urging the education labor movement to build relations of solidarity with intersecting movements and participants advocating for a "unified" front. For example, in Kentucky, some teachers and activists wanted the movement to act in solidarity with opponents of a proposed bill enabling law enforcement to stop-and-frisk suspected gang members on appearance alone. Touted as the "gang bill," many argued that it directly affected and would criminalize Louisville's young Black student population. Those on the side of "unification" won out, and the "gang bill" passed into law in a state that disproportionately incarcerates its Black residents. As Bhattacharya powerfully writes, "Race is not an add-on to the struggle for wages. It shapes the terrain of struggle".

In other writing, Bhattacharya ("Women Are Leading the Wave") also argues that media narratives overwhelmingly failed to acknowledge the actions were led predominantly by women, limiting our understanding of the broader role of gender and heteropatriarchy in the struggle for public education:

> The politicians in the states where the strikes are taking place, have, over the years, shown their deep commitment to generalized misogyny: Oklahoma has the highest rate of female incarceration. Arizona is ranked first for its anti-abortion laws by the leading anti-abortion group Americans United for Life. Kentucky now only has one abortion clinic left to serve the entire state. In West Virginia, the same legislators whose laws led to the strike, are considering a bill to take out the right to abortion from the state's constitution.

She further argues that the conditions (i.e., de-skilling, poor pay) that sparked the walkouts were a result of patriarchal structures of administration seeking to keep women and care work in their/its place. Bhattacharya's calls to intersectional feminist analyses of the movement are important for reckoning with the education system's historic and ongoing cultural violence against Native people and people of color. Scholars of the feminization of teaching have illuminated the ways White women, in particular, have historically been conscripted into the colonizing work of "civilizing" and assimilating young people into a White supremacist society (Grumet; Meiners, "Disengaging from the Legacy"). As Bhattacharya suggests, the most radical visions for what "care" might mean and look like in education has emerged from community-based intersectional feminist movements. For these movements generally, an ethic of care is deeply interwoven with collective freedom. To understand the possibilities and challenges of the new teacher uprisings, we should seriously engage with differentiated understandings of care and the visions of education implied in these.

Tendencies to celebrate teachers as the new, militant front of the American labor movement may oversimplify or avoid engaging with historical divisions and enactments of solidarity between teachers' unions and movements for feminist/queer, Black, Brown, and Indigenous self-determination. It is within this space of tension that we locate our knowledge project. We aim to engage this tension with care, nuance, and with an understanding that anti-union, reformist discourses often cleverly weaponize the language of racial equity to squash labor uprisings. These discourses are promoted by those who have the most wealth to gain by disinvesting in and privatizing public education.

● Red State Uprising

The small but important body of scholarship on neoliberal attacks on public education and histories of education labor tends to focus on major northern or coastal urban areas like New York, New Jersey, Chicago, and Detroit. As is evident from media coverage of the 2016 presidential election, the social and political context of rural states are popularly, perhaps willfully, misunderstood, often fetishized in the mainstream media as "backward." In, for example, the 2016 election coverage, these places have conveniently been represented as the contained source of the nation's ignorance and racism, a straw man covering a deeper, more complex racial and colonialist history of the violent consolidation of land and power by corporations and the wealthy elite (Dunbar-Ortiz). In recounting community-organizing across higher and K–12 education contexts in rural Indiana, G Patterson writes that "the rural bogeyman" serves to mask the ways in which institutional power is wielded to preserve a White supremacist, heteropatriarchal status quo. "[I]n framing rural areas as backward, we crowd out powerful stories of coalition and resistance taking place in those spaces–and we miss opportunities to reflect on what these stories can teach us" (66).

These states all have rich histories of worker rebellion. For example, the coal regions of West Virginia and Kentucky were simultaneously home to some of the most dangerous working conditions between the late nineteenth and early twentieth centuries and some of the most radical, multi-racial union efforts in the United States (Huber). West Virginia in particular is responsible for one of the largest worker uprisings in the US (Battle of Blair Mountain), due in large part to the exploitative nature of coal barons, the anti-union efforts by local coal mine bosses, and the protections these mine owners received from local and state law enforcement (S. Smith). Nevertheless, the popular imagination of Appalachia is reinforced by such works as J. D. Vance's national best-seller *Hillbilly Elegy*, which suggests that the region's poverty is best explained by cultural pathology, not capitalist labor exploitation, public disinvestment, or extraction-fueled climate disaster.

We are not the only ones who have sought to examine the unique contexts of the statewide strikes of 2018. Many educator organizers who participated in these movements have contributed rich descriptions, theory, and reflections within the previous few years. Public historian Elizabeth Catte, folklorist Emily Hilliard, and teacher, writer, and activist Jessica Salfia edited a collection of essays, 55 *Strong: Inside the West Virginia Teachers' Strike*, in which educators describe and reflect on their motivations, actions, and activism. The collection and Nicole McCormick's writing, "Owning My Labor," powerfully illustrates the "cultures of solidarity" (Fantasia) that emerged among the state's educators, and which contributed to their capacity to mobilize again, a year later, to strike against school privatization legislation.

In Rebecca Kolins Givan and Amy Schrager Lang's edited book, *Strike for the Common Good: Fighting for the Future of Public Education*, several organizers authored chapters that provide deeper insights into the education worker-led efforts in the South and Southwest. For example, AEU organizer, Rebecca Garelli, details the grassroots strategy and commitment to democratization in her state's Red for Ed movement. In a special issue of *Critical Education*, Oklahoma and Arizona educators undertake oral history research and candid reflection, respectively, to constructively examine their experiences and offer insights for the future of their movements (Dyke et al.; Karvelis, "Toward a Theory of Teacher Agency"). Petia Edison and Ivonne Rovira incisively synthesize the antiracist efforts of Jefferson County educators in collaboration with community-based groups toward social justice unionism and the walls they came up against in their unions and among White movement leaders. These written analyses alongside our personal interviews and conversations with many of these organizers and others informs our approach to understanding educator movements in the "red" states.

In the emerging literature aiming to make sense of the 2018 "red" state strikes, many more scholarly and media analyses exist that analyze West Virginia and Arizona, and less attention is offered to Oklahoma and Kentucky. While we do not attend to North Carolina educators' organizing here, the work of educators, particularly those in the state's social justice caucus, Organize 2020, deserve further attention for their part in stoking the flames of militancy in 2018. The perceptions of success in the former states and of failure in the latter states may be one important reason for this imbalance. For example, Blanc's *Red State Revolt: The Teachers' Strikes and Working Class Politics*, discusses the events in West Virginia, Oklahoma, and Arizona while Kentucky remains absent from the narrative. His analysis suggests that Oklahoma educators lacked the necessary experience to push their state union to work for them. As we detail further in Chapter Three and elsewhere, the complex racial and gendered tensions that stultified emergent rank-and-file, often women-led, organizing across the state are critical to explore and understand. Further, as Edison and Rovira illuminate in their reflections on antiracist organizing in Kentucky, complex histories and tensions exist between the state's more racially diverse urban centers and its more conservatively-governed White suburban and rural districts. The root issues that led to the different outcomes in Oklahoma and Kentucky are important sites of learning that we aim to attend to here. Further, we aim to offer analyses that might be useful for addressing the specific challenges educators faced as they necessarily move forward.

● Movement-Embedded Methodology

We as authors are interconnected to the struggles that have occurred in our respective states—Brendan in West Virginia and Erin in Oklahoma—and around the country. Brendan was a member of the WVEA and a public school teacher in the state, as well as a current member of the Industrial Workers of the World (IWW). He was an attendee at the 2017 WVEA Delegate Assembly, and his critical writings of union leadership led him to get involved with Jay O'Neal in organizing the WVPEU Facebook page, which served as a key site of agitation and critical information sharing. Leading up to the walkouts, Brendan worked with fellow educators and school service personnel at his high school to understand the proposed changes to their insurance, the political landscape they were facing, and the legal ramifications of following through with an unlawful walkout. He helped to organize the vote of authorization in his school and, when a walkout was called by union leadership, Brendan helped in organizing a county-wide food-drive for students alongside building representatives with the Monongalia County Education Association (MCEA).

As the strike progressed, Brendan acted as an agitator alongside fellow teachers and school service personnel. He stood on picket lines, traveled to the capitol, wrote reports on the strike, appeared on national podcasts, and maintained lines of communication between the Monongalia County Extended Services and the MCEA. When union leadership brokered an unfaithful deal with Governor Justice to end the walkouts, Brendan wrote a release statement from the West Virginia IWW demanding the strike continue until the initial demands were met, which was shared by parents and on state senators' social media pages. He served on the steering committee for the West Virginia United caucus (WV United), a rank-and-file caucus comprising AFT-WV and WVEA members who were active during the walkouts.

Erin has worked as an early childhood educator, an adult community educator, and a teacher educator during her more than fifteen years of teaching. During her master's program in Chicago, she became involved with community-based efforts to fight against school privatization and community destabilization. She remembers her first day on the job at her university's community engagement center when the director fielded angry calls from then-Chicago Public Schools CEO Arne Duncan's office. Immigrant parents and community activists associated with the center had stormed and occupied a local official's office to protest school defunding.

After a few more years working in early childhood education, she went back to graduate school and became involved with the IWW through efforts to reignite graduate student union organizing at the University of Minnesota in the aftermath of a failed campaign to unionize with the United Auto Workers. As the efforts faltered, she began organizing with education support professionals, teachers, parents, and students with the IWW's Social Justice Education Movement (SJEM). With SJEM, she participated in campaigns against a local district's racist curriculum, for more teachers and staff of color, and to create gathering spaces for social justice educators and education activists. For the past several years, she's worked as a teacher educator at Oklahoma State University, working with and learning from so many critical, skilled, committed, and agitated teachers.

During the strike, she attended rallies at the capitol and shifted her classes, composed mainly of teachers in the Tulsa and Stillwater areas, to more closely reflect on and make sense of the strike. In its aftermath, she collaborated with a team of twelve Oklahoma educators to collect, archive, and study oral history narratives of more than fifty educators from across the state a year to a year and a half after the strike. These oral histories are archived and publicly accessible through the Oklahoma Oral History Research Program at Oklahoma State University's Edmon Low Library.

We initially met through our shared organizing networks with educators and organizers connected to the IWW. Our collaboration on this project grew out of a series of conversations where we realized, first, the significance of a detailed understanding of the relations of labor that composed the strikes. In the media, dominant narratives tended to articulate striking teachers as a united front led by their state education unions. We knew this wasn't exactly the case. Second, we share a desire to create and inspire practically useful conceptual tools for analyzing the ongoing movement that specifically attend to racial, gender, and other tensions related to hierarchical relations of power and authority within the education labor movement and between the education labor movement and wider (often community-initiated) education justice movements.

Driven by these motivations for our collective writing, after the strike wave ended, we realized the need to capture experiences in the immediate aftermath to offer a detailed and holistic perspective of what actually went down. In the

P&C

summer and fall of 2018, we formally interviewed twenty-seven key organizers, rank-and-file educators, state employees, and parent activists from all four states–West Virginia (twelve), Oklahoma (six), Kentucky (eight), and Arizona (two). We also draw significantly from the fifty-four oral history interviews Erin and her research team collected in Oklahoma between September 2019 and March 2020. For interviews we conducted in the summer immediately following the strikes (twenty-five), we re-interviewed most a year later to understand how their thinking and experiences have changed over time. We also draw on social, news, and other media discussions among education workers in these places. Our everyday work with teachers, students, and community activists in West Virginia and Oklahoma, countless more informal conversations, organizing meetings, and classroom and panel event discussions further contribute to rounding out our ground-up analysis of the walkouts.

● Understanding Theories of Power and Change (Unionisms): An Overview of the Book

Studying the internal organizational dynamics that composed the strikes, our analysis illuminates the significance of the emergence of solidarity unionism during the strike wave, or rank-and-file-led unionism where educators and staff challenged their reticent AFT- and NEA-affiliated state unions to take direct action. Further, we consider why this emergence was experienced differently across different states, and why some states and groups of people continued to mobilize in the year following to fight retaliatory legislation while others lost steam. As our chapter overview illuminates, we ground our analyses in the longer histories and legacies of race, class, and gender tensions and issues within and across social and labor movement spaces. Building on this, the book considers how members of rank-and-file-led organizations that emerged parallel to or within their unions studied and made sense of their actual and desired relation to power and the state and what this has meant for their continued organizing.

In the first chapter, we develop our theoretical framework and describe the various theories of power and change that emerged and interacted. We distinguish and historicize four main (sometimes overlapping) unionisms: professionalism, business unionism, solidarity unionism, and social movement unionism. We illuminate the ways in which gender, race, and class have been articulated through these histories and theories/practices of unionism. For example, we draw on histories of the NEA to illuminate the ways in which White professionalist discourses sought to recruit primarily White women teachers to become dues-paying members while the leadership and aims of the organization were rooted primarily in the interests of predominantly White men school administrators. Conservative forms of professionalism that dominated the early NEA articulated teachers' and administrators' interests to be one and the same (improving education for the children). Alternatively, southern Black educator associations formed through Black educators' exclusion from White unions articulated social movement-oriented forms of professionalism that understood teachers as community workers. And women, queer educators, radicals, and educators of color took up solidarity unionist approaches to organize within and exert influence over their trade and professionalist organizations. Historical instances of these solidarity and social movement efforts include the transformation of the NEA from a race-segregated administrator-dominated professional association to an integrated teacher-led trade union. To frame subsequent discussions, we conclude the chapter by introducing the various theories and practices of power and change (unionisms) that became salient during the strikes. Specifically, we discuss the emergence and significance of solidarity unionist approaches.

The middle of the book engages three core tensions that organizers and participants grappled with, rooted in issues of race, gender, and class. In Chapter Two, we address the invisibility or marginality of the colonialist and racial capitalist origins of the previous three decades of state disinvestment in public education. Extensive education scholarship has long illuminated that disinvestment and punitive state, federal, and venture capitalist interventions have disproportionately targeted communities perceived as a threat in need of state containment (cf. Ali and Buenavista). In practice, during the walkouts, signs proliferated that made connections between the decrease in education funding and, for example, the dramatic increases in state funding for youth and adult prisons. In states like Oklahoma, where one out of nine children have an incarcerated or formerly incarcerated parent (United Way OKC), these signs arose from direct experience with such containment mechanisms. In West Virginia, school overcrowding disproportionately affects Black children (Agba), and, in Arizona, the state targeted the dismantling of so-called "racist" ethnic studies programs serving the majority minority public school population (Acosta). Like many social justice caucus efforts across the nation (Asselin), organizers experienced conflicts between cultivating union democracy and directly addressing these intertwined issues, fearing loss of support among White, rural, and conservative educators and the wider public. Our analysis, resonant with Edison and Rovira, suggests that moves toward race-blind articulations of the issues did not lead to educators building collective power in each place.

In Chapter 3, we examine the ways in which gender became salient in Oklahoma. Since the development of common lower education in the US, the feminization and heterosexualization of teaching have been strategically mobilized as both a justification and means for depressing wages and disciplining workers (Blount). Some media and scholarly narratives have linked the strikes to the #MeToo movement, suggesting that newly empowered women are not buying pressures to sacrifice their lives "for the children" or put up with abusive working conditions any longer (Bhattacharya, "Women are Leading the Wave"; Russom). Histories of education labor suggests that women, especially Black, Indigenous, women of Color and queer educators, have often been militant leaders and drivers of movements for education justice (Rousmaniere, "Citizen Teacher";

Todd-Breland; V. S. Walker). We draw on these histories as a lens through which to analyze the dispersed, women- and LGBTQ-led leadership in the emergence of the strike, gendered approaches to organizing, and the challenges and possibilities for continued mobilization after 2018.

In Chapter Four, we explore what Paul Bocking describes as the key question that unions contend with: "how to deal with the state" (390). Class tensions materialized in the formation of dual power union organizations that, to varying extents in each state, resisted becoming subsumed into their trade unions' collaboration with superintendents, elected officials, and the electoral process. Our prologue narrates one of the more powerful examples of this tension, when, on the seventh day of the West Virginia strike, teachers across all fifty-five counties rejected the state union leadership's call to return to work after a tentative agreement had been made with Governor Jim Justice. Undertaking a truly wildcat strike, they shut down schools for another week until the agreement was signed and sealed. We engage transnational educator and social movements (Brazil, Mexico, Canada, and US social justice caucus networks) to contextualize this question within each of our states under study, illuminating the risks in state collaboration and the significance of strong, grassroots, and democratic organizations for advancing demands against austerity and related neoliberal school reform efforts.

In the final chapter, we bring together key discussions in previous chapters to consider the study's implications for moving forward. From our analysis, we suggest that dual power organizations emerging in and through solidarity and social movement unionism were key in igniting the strikes (cf. Voss and Sherman). Organizations that engaged solidarity unionist approaches, including commitments to horizontalism and radical democratic participation of members; that engaged sincerely with conflict that arose between teachers and staff of color and White teachers' understandings of the issues, community-based social movements' and teachers' unions, and hierarchies within the rank-and-file (cf. Weiner, "The Future of Our Schools"); and that maintained an oppositional (even if tentatively collaborative) orientation to business union leadership, administrators, and legislators (e.g., via forming caucuses) continued to build momentum and strength against retaliation. Our analyses and conceptual framework of various unionisms can support readers to consider their own commitments to and understandings of theories and practices of power and change in their work and organizing (cf. Maton and Stark). Further, we support readers in lower and higher education to consider how they might engage in discussions and collective study with co-workers and fellow union members to engage differences to develop and put into practice their collective commitments.

● Conclusion

Rebecca Tarlau argues that the US-based academic literature on critical pedagogy has become distanced from its international roots in social movement organizing, while social movement scholarship has tended to minimize the question of pedagogy in organizing ("From a Language to a Theory of Resistance" 369). While critical pedagogy in the academic literature offers critiques of the education system and its role in social reproduction, studies of social movements tend to emphasize the outcomes rather than the messy, interrelational processes of organizing and political education (also see Asselin; Stark; Maton and Stark). This book aims to cross these boundaries as the theory and practice of union organizing is inherently a pedagogical undertaking. Histories of educator unionism can clarify the necessity of building union movements that are democratic and that are consistently working to understand the racial, settler colonialist, and gendered dimensions and impacts of the US education system.

As we write, many K–12 and higher education workers in our communities are working tirelessly to organize to keep their communities safe from the COVID-19 pandemic and against concerted efforts to whitewash and anesthetize our curricula. Our hope is that this book can support resurgent rank-and-file movements to grapple with their tensions in practice, tensions that have existed as long as compulsory schooling.

Chapter 1. Theories of Power and Change in Educator Unions: Situating the Emergence of Solidarity Unionism

Fear was the first pressing concern that compounded the low morale in the months and years prior to the 2018 statewide strike, according to Brianne Solomon, a fine arts teacher from Mason County, West Virginia: "My school and my county had even lower morale than what I considered the state's average of low morale, so we were lower than low. People were afraid and that showed itself in defensiveness, standoffish behavior, refusal to comment, and tension." In 1990, teachers in West Virginia had staged what was then the largest statewide strike in West Virginia history. Forty-seven of the fifty-five counties had gone on strike demanding better wages, new salary scales to reward years of education, and a fiscal solution to the state's health insurance budget crisis. Led by WVEA's president at the time, Kayetta Meadows, teachers won a resounding victory. They forced the legislature to institute a $5,000 wage increase, spread across three years, bringing up the average state teacher's salary comparable to contiguous states. The legislature committed new revenue to address the $2 billion budget hole in the state's insurance plan and committed to reducing wait time on insurance claims. New salary scales were adopted to enable educators to pursue graduate education (Mochaidean).

The 1990 strike was not without consequences. In the capital county, Kanawha, several teachers were arrested for attempting to stop buses from driving through picket lines. One teacher was run over by an irate parent dropping her children off at school (Mochaidean). Teachers received letters from their superintendents informing them that they would be fired if they continued to walk picket lines. The average loss in salary for those who went on strike in 1990 was $660 (Bradley). Solomon said, "In the beginning, we were not sure if we'd be supported [in 2018] and the people who lived through the 1990 strike were fearful because they knew how bad things could get between coworkers and superiors."

Yet, as Solomon recounted, so far, nothing had worked in the decades since to stem the tide of austerity. "We tried reaching out to lawmakers. We voiced opinions and concerns about the growing number of policies that we saw as attacks on public school teachers and public education. We knew we were getting lip service." At times, both the WVEA and AFT-WV called for limited actions to be taken beyond lobbying lawmakers for better benefits. Blue flus, sick outs, and rolling walkouts were all either considered or acted upon in past years. During Governor Joe Manchin's tenure in the mid-2000s, WVEA even organized a one-day walkout that brought with it a few thousand dollars in wage increases spread over three years (Silver).

A decade later, West Virginia remained ranked forty-eighth in the nation for teacher salaries and school funding continued to decline. "I don't think it's been a secret that teacher morale in West Virginia is at an all-time low," Solomon explained. "It has been for quite some time. I think when you're as deficient in morale as we were, you know it's bad, but you don't know how bad it is."

The strike is the most powerful tool available to educators and all workers. As Solomon recounted, the 2018 strike emerged after decades of continued disinvestment scraping away at the achievements of the 1990 strike. The afterlife of that strike remained tangible for many who lived through it: lost wages, precarious public support, arrests, verbal abuse, and even physical violence in some cases. In 2018, decades of smaller actions and electoral advocacy had not yielded much. Educators did not want to go on strike. It appeared to be the only remaining option.

School funding, wages, and benefits are not the only reasons that teachers and staff were dissatisfied with their work. In the years since the 1990s strikes in West Virginia and elsewhere, educators' curricular autonomy has drastically decreased with high stakes standardized testing and curriculum mandates, while class sizes have tended to increase (Bartell et al.). The sharp decline in overall public education funding has intensified educators' work, forcing them to engage in grant writing and crowd-sourced resource drives for classroom materials (Del Valle); to attempt to address the absence of sufficient systemic resources to provide equitable education to students with disabilities and emergent multilingual students (Litvinov and Flannery); and to become expert learners in ever-new classroom technologies, mandated curricula, and grading systems (Weiner, "Heads Up! Chins Down!"). In Oklahoma, emergency certifications, which require no prior teacher education or teaching experience, have exponentially increased to more than three thousand annually in just a few years as traditionally certified teachers leave to find living wage jobs and administrators scramble to fill empty positions (Eger). As their own, their families', and their students' lives become increasingly challenging under late-stage capitalism, the notion that success in education leads to upward social mobility and economic prosperity seemed more and more a cruel myth.

In higher and lower education, these challenges are experienced with relative intensity across job classes. We use the term "educator" holistically to encompass classroom teachers, paraprofessionals or assistant teachers, food service staff, building caretakers, school health workers, school counselors, and all other support staff. We do so to formally recognize the educative and relational work involved in these positions. As one Oklahoma bus driver said to Erin,

> I started buying dollar boxes of granola bars and just handing it to them because my kids were hungry. And this is me making sixteen thousand a year driving this bus. I'm feeding my kids because they're hungry. Because they're my kids on that bus. You know? . . . If the people are taken care of, then they're taking care of the kids, then the kids are

gonna see that. Then they're gonna mimic that when they grow up. I mean a lot of the folks do it because they love the children–regardless of the pay, regardless of being frozen [on buses without heaters], regardless of whatever else.

Education workers in non-licensed support staff positions are often more diverse than majority White women teachers along the lines of race, language, and class yet often occupy the most precarious positions. Unionized support staff tend to bargain under separate contracts and are often either marginalized by teachers' union chapters or relatively ignored. In many places, paraprofessional positions have expanded to accommodate increased class sizes and reduce overall wage expenditures in practice. The 2022 joint strike by Minneapolis teachers and education support professionals (ESPs) in their respective chapters of the Minneapolis Federation of Teachers, and school food service workers organized with the Service Employees International Union Local 284 illuminates the necessity for organizing across job classes. The nearly three-week strike won significant increases in wages, most substantially for ESPs, who were majority educators of color. Demands were articulated as part of a broader movement for racial justice intimately linked to the police murders of George Floyd and beloved former Minneapolis Public Schools' food service worker, Philando Castile (Jaffe).

Like the Oklahoma bus driver feeding and warming her children each morning, education workers across lower and higher education continue to absorb the brunt of austerity in schools and society, with marginalized, precarious, and low-waged workers experiencing the most dehumanizing conditions. In response to the Minneapolis teachers and support staff strike, Paul Cantrell pointedly writes: "District admin is talking about these negotiations in terms of avoiding debt, cuts, bankruptcy. But the truth is the district is already deeply, deeply in debt. It's just that they've hidden that debt off the balance sheets by making it human debt. . . . Running the schools at the cost of educators' [and students'] health, well-being, and mental stability is a form of debt."

We begin the chapter by offering a framework for understanding the historical development of in-tension educator unionisms–business (sometimes called service), professionalist, solidarity, and social movement unionisms. These unionisms, or theory-practices of union organizing within the education industry, entail specific and situated histories of education labor struggles and modes of relating among and across hierarchies of race, gender, class positions and more. These histories and modes of relating offer important insights for understanding the recent resurgence in educator labor militancy and organizing to transform our unions, schools, and society. In the second half of the chapter, we analyze the lead-up to the strikes, engaging the legacies of these differences in ways of thinking and practicing unionism as a mode of analysis. We narrate how and why solidarity unionism, or rank-and-file organizing within and beyond the limits and exclusions of business union structures and state labor laws, emerged as a key approach that made the mass actions possible.

● Unionisms: Business, Solidarity, Professionalist, and Social Movement Approaches

Often, debates in certain traditions of scholarship (i.e., labor economics, political science), can refer to teachers' unions as one generally homogenous, ahistorical entity. From an economics or labor management perspective, teachers' unions are commonly framed as rent-seekers "looking to gain from their involvement in public education through increases in salaries and enhanced working conditions" (Cowen and Strunk 210). The body of research with and for educators' labor organization is much smaller and marginalized within the academy and often quite inaccessible for those without access to university library resources. Few educator preparation programs provide pre-service or in-service educators with opportunities to learn about unions (what they are, how they operate, how to participate). Often, as with most of our interviews, educators learn in and through struggle, through intergenerational relationships with union family members or mentors, and/or through social movement participation (Maton and Stark). Scholars of social justice or movement unionism argue that political education, or "the teaching and learning processes that compel individuals to reflect on the nature of power and its connections to the range of forces shaping both individuals and institutions" (Maton and Stark 2), is central to growing these movements and formulating more effective union practice (Brown and Stern; Morrison; Riley).

Historically and today, in-tension perspectives on the nature of power have always comprised K–12 and higher education unions and union movements. These iteratively inform structures of union decision-making (whether they are more horizontalist or verticalist), who can be a union member or active participant (e.g., the role of education support professionals, adjuncts, and non-teaching staff in guiding the union's priorities), the political purposes of the union, their aspirations for transforming the education system, and the kinds of action unions might take to realize these aspirations. The recent resurgence in union militancy and democratization (Dyke et al., "Introduction") certainly illuminates increased disaffection with highly centralized unions or those narrowly focused on building power via electoral lobbying. Electoralism, in its extreme, locates power with legislators and government representatives. Educators and educator unions' aim to steer this power through working to elect and build relationships of mutual interest with people who can pass public education-friendly laws. Alternatively, militancy, or direct action, locates power within workers themselves. Their collective action and refusal to continue on with business-as-usual serves as a point of pressure to see the conditions of their work improved and to enact broader legislative and policy transformation. The strength and quality of union militancy and union democratization are intimately intertwined with one another. In the context of the education industry, militancy and union democratization are animated by long-standing, intersecting histories of racism and gender and sexual oppression within union organizations and movements, and likewise, histories of resistance and movement-building for increased worker power and the just and liberatory transformation of schools and society.

To read and understand the in-tension unionisms that emerged in and through the spring 2018 strikes, we first engage a longer, deeper history of educator unionism in the US. By understanding these histories and traditions of theory-practice in educator union organizing, we can better make sense of resurgent militancy in our contemporary moment and its challenges.

● (White) Professionalization

It is a bit of a stretch on our part to consider movements toward (White) professionalization alongside other unionisms, as its traditions of understanding power and change are often opposed to unionization. Marjorie Murphy writes, "The ideology of professionalism in education grew into a powerful antiunion slogan that effectively paralyzed and then slowed the unionization of teachers" (1). It was not until the 1960s that many teachers' unions won the right to collectively bargain. Yet, professionalism is one distinct set of multi-faceted traditions for understanding how educators work together to improve teaching and education.

To be clear, many unionists, including social movement unionists, articulate professional dignity and respect for teachers' pedagogical expertise as a core part of contemporary educator movements. Such calls for dignity, trust, and autonomy can exist within educator movements that acknowledge and attend to the class, race, and/or gender hierarchies within the education system. Historically southern Black educator associations are an important example of this (see D'Amico Pawlewicz and View; Hale, "The Development of Power"; V. S. Walker; and attended to in more depth in Chapter Two). We are after a different sort of call to professionalism. Our use of the term (White) professionalization refers primarily to a movement within education to seek for teachers' inclusion and status within the professional class, and to improve the quality and rigor of education through advocacy and cooperation with the state and capital. Diana D'Amico Pawlewicz and Jenice View write, "[p]rofessional occupations gain stature and authority because they know something that their clients do not: the more abstract and esoteric the knowledge, the more social and economic authority for the professional group" (1280–1281). Whereas other unionisms within education are rooted in the structural divisions between the employing and employee classes, professionalism, as a way of thinking, rejects such a structural understanding. Professionalism imagines teachers, staff, administrators, contingent and tenure track researchers and educators–all who work in education as, to put it simply, on the same team with the same or similar interests (our students) while masking their unequal relations of power and decision-making authority.

One of the main ways we can understand this approach is through the historical evolution of the NEA, the national union of which the major state teachers' associations in West Virginia, Kentucky, Oklahoma, and Arizona are affiliated. We lean heavily on two important and expansive histories, Urban's history of the NEA and Marjorie Murphy's history of the AFT and NEA, which centers the AFT. Founded in 1857 as a professional association by, primarily, administrators and university researchers (mainly men), the association aimed to further the profession of teaching, and to advocate for influence over its increasing centralization in the form of teacher credentialing and accreditation. During its early meetings, White women teachers were disallowed from speaking or participating in the association's proceedings (M. Murphy 4). Women fought for the right to speak and were able to organize within the association to promote their interests in the early twentieth century. At the time, women desired for the association to address their interests more directly, namely, academic freedom, better and equal pay to men, the ability to marry, have a family, and continue teaching (most married and pregnant women were fired), and to have more autonomy over their lives outside of school (often contracts included requirements about when and with whom women teachers could socialize). It is important to note here that the NEA was segregated up until the 1950s, and so women's interests in the organization were decidedly rooted in the interests of White women, specifically.

Women began making some gains within the NEA, even electing a woman president in 1910 (Urban 13). In 1920, male central leadership in the organization pushed a reorganization that would shift the NEA from an assembly-style process to a representative process, with state associations wielding more power. Despite halting the reorganization for a couple of years, women-led interest groups in the NEA saw their participation and influence decline significantly (Urban 14).

In the mid-twentieth century, the NEA turned towards building strong state associations and locals through a top-down, "soft" approach to negotiations. Historically, mostly women teachers had little power within their state or the national association. Although teacher strikes occurred in 1946, 1947, and 1948, the NEA adopted a no-strike clause in all their contracts and refused to endorse them to build cooperation between teachers and administrators (Urban 177). Urban explains:

> As long as the associations had to serve both teachers and school superintendents, and as long as administrators had the ear of the NEA hierarchy, independent teacher initiatives, no matter how successful, were ignored. Just as problematic as the NEA's commitment to teachers and to local teachers' associations in the 1940s was its commitment to the equity concerns of women and minority teachers. (106)

Superintendents continued to have significant control of the leadership and direction of the organization until the teacher uprisings of the 1960s.

At this time, the NEA took a hard stance discouraging its members from the rising communist, socialist, and radical progressivist movements in education research and practice (M. Murphy). Instead, it pushed a professionalist theory of change that suggested teachers, school administration, superintendents, and university faculty must work together to lobby for educational changes in the best interest of all children. Urban recounts that the NEA's (at least nominal) commitment to gender pay equality served to bolster women's support of the organization in relation to the (also) male-dominated AFT, a trade union that rejected the notion that administrators and teachers maintained the same class interests. It is important to note here that during this time, the AFT also swiftly subjugated radical political factions within its organization, even colluding with McCarthy-era government witch hunts (Feffer), contributing to its leadership remaining staunchly White, male, and top-heavy (M. Murphy).

It wasn't until the late 1960s and early 1970s that teachers' union movements had begun to seriously challenge professionalist discourses that the NEA clung to in favor of direct action. Within the NEA, smaller groups of teachers organized within the association to push its transformation to a trade union despite that "the state associations often acted to block, delay, or dilute the various changes proposed by teacher militants for the NEA" at their annual representative assembly (Urban 191). In 1968, the Florida Education Association, an NEA-affiliate, took part in the country's first statewide teacher strike, setting the tone for the association's 1973 re-constitution.

Urban notes that, since the Reagan era and until recently, the NEA has returned to its earlier traditions of professionalist discourses, articulating the purpose of educational change along the lines of what is best "for the children" as a rhetorical device to minimize the relationship between educators' working conditions and students' learning conditions. The non-confrontational lure of (White) professionalism aligned with the dispositions required by neoliberalism, namely, self-sacrifice for the good of the profession.

● Business Unionism

Within education labor studies and activism, Lois Weiner has studied and articulated the mode of unionism that dominates established unions in education and in the wider world of organized labor: business unionism. A strong proponent of members' democratic participation in their unions, she suggests such participation is at odds with the predominating "service model" or "business unionism" approach taken by most teachers' unions (and trade unions, in general). For Weiner, in this model:

> [T]he union is run like a business and exists to provide services including lower rates for auto insurance; benefits from a welfare fund; pension advice; contract negotiations; and perhaps filing a grievance. Officers or staff make decisions on the members' behalf. The union as an organization functions based on the assumption (generally unarticulated, unless it's challenged) that paid officials know best about everything....

> Exclusionary ways of operating that are accepted out of what seems like necessity morph into principles. ("The Future of Our Schools" 33–34)

Despite the predominance of business unionism, education labor scholars have illuminated the ways in which educators have attempted to transform their unions and take up social liberation aims via the formation of social justice caucuses. Rhiannon Maton and Lauren Ware Stark describe caucuses as,

> meso-level organizational forms that exist both within and apart from their broader unions. At times they are formally recognized by their broader union as a "caucus" or group of unionists sharing a specific set of values and agenda, and at other times they operate without formal union recognition while still using this title. Their membership tends to consist of a range of constituents, including progressives seeking radical systemic and structural change, unionists disgruntled with traditional conciliatory union politics, and classroom educators seeking support in the development and advancement of social justice curriculum, pedagogy and politics within and beyond the classroom (Stark, 2019). Caucuses tend to have greater flexibility to work beyond traditional union venues such as district negotiations, and frequently strive to develop deep partnerships with local community groups and constituents. (5)

Via caucuses, rank-and-file members can mobilize their own theories and practices of power and change and organize together to encourage (or pressure) union leadership to distribute resources in ways that support those theories and aims (Stark; Stern et al.).

It is not merely an unfortunate development that the service or business model predominates within established teachers' unions. The infrastructure and organization of business unions arose through battles between workers to exert more control over their own labor power and the state and capital, which sought (continues to seek) to do the same. The genesis of contemporary business unions was a direct result of cataclysmic strikes that had occurred in the US during the pre-World War I era. Typically, in this era, when workers struck, employers would shore up their side with armed guards to force strikers back to work, disrupt pickets, or protect scabs when they crossed the picket line (S. Smith). For example, in the Homestead Strike of 1892, a collection of more than six thousand unionized steel workers clashed with three hundred agents of the Pinkerton Detective Agency, who had been ferried up the Ohio River and begun firing upon the strikers on the shore (S. Smith). In 1894, more than two dozen workers died after the National Guard teamed up with private security forces hired by the Pullman Company to break the nationwide rail workers' strike effort. After the Ludlow Massacre of 1914 and the Battle of Blair Mountain in 1921, where more than twenty-five people (including eleven children) and around one hundred people were killed, respectively, the state began to formally mediate labor-capital relations via the passage of labor laws (Roediger and Esch; S. Smith).

With precursors in the 1926 Railway Act (Wilner), eventually, the passage of the National Labor Relations Act of 1935, also known as the Wagner Act, provided government-protected union activity in the workplace, including the right to collective bargaining and the right to engage in a strike if certain conditions had not been met by the employer. Though the Wagner Act provided a legal framework through which unions could negotiate, it had the effect of shifting unions' focus from militant action to win change and toward building central administrative structures that could negotiate contracts and hold employers to legal account (Brecher). Eventually, as organized labor's relationship with Democrats waned, the Taft-Hartley Act of 1947 amended the Wagner Act and prohibitions on certain labor actions were introduced. No longer could workers legally engage in solidarity strikes, wildcat strikes, or secondary boycotts, to name a few. Since then, labor law has become increasingly hostile to union organizing (Brecher). The latest example, the U.S. Supreme Court's 2018 ruling in *Janus v. AFSCME*, limits unions' ability to recruit members and collect dues.

Restrictive labor law and the power it provides employers has significantly contributed to the centrality of the service or business model of unionism (Tait 6–7). While business unions, in education and other industries, structurally deter rank-and-file membership participation, that has never stopped educators and other unionists from organizing, either within their formal unions and against such business union models (e.g., CORE in CTU) or in organizations that seek to build power beyond the structural limits of trade or business unions altogether. In Vanessa Tait's study of poor workers' movements, efforts on the part of predominantly BIPOC and immigrant worker communities within precarious service, domestic, and childcare labor spheres to address often racist, nativist exploitation were born of necessity after exclusion from and marginalization by predominantly White trade unions.

● Solidarity Unionism

While unions in the general public discourse tend to be synonymous with union organizations officially certified by the National Labor Relations Board (NLRB) to enact their legally mandated collective bargaining rights (e.g., NEA- and AFT-affiliated unions), following scholars of the role of caucuses and autonomous workplace organizing, we take a much broader and simpler definition of union: a group of two or more workers acting together to improve their working conditions. Solidarity unionism as a theory of radically democratic (and often anti-capitalist, anti-racist) unionism arises from the intellectual traditions of industrial union and poor workers' movements in the US and globally (Ness; Tait). Briefly and simply, solidarity unionism suggests workers build collective power by determining their own issues, demands, and actions via democratic processes of decision-making and participation. Attentive to and critical of the limits of business unions and legal impositions on workers' abilities to organize, solidarity approaches rely on creatively withholding labor, whether it's legal or not. As an Inland Steel worker from Chicago in the late 1930s describes, when workers wanted to make a change to their conditions, "the people in the mill . . . had a series of strikes, wildcats, shut-downs, slow-downs, anything working people could think of to secure for themselves what they decided they had to have" (Lynd 20).

While solidarity unionism has many overlaps with social movement unionism, they derive from related yet distinct areas of thinking, organizing, and writing, and so we distinguish it from the latter. Solidarity unionism helps us to understand worker organizing for rank-and-file power in their workplaces and within their unions and derives from the intellectual traditions of industrial unionism, e.g., the IWW. Social movement unionism, in the interdisciplinary and praxis-focused literature broadly within social movement studies, often necessarily employs practices of radical workplace and union democracy to organize with and for broader social movements and toward broader social visions (Stark). Solidarity unionism as a theory and tradition within some of the most aspirationally liberatory movements for industrial unionism may help us to understand the significance of rank-and-file power over their workplace institutions, and social movement unionism pairs such a rank-and-file focus with more pointed considerations of the role and purpose of these institutions within society.

A significant source of trade unions' aversion to radical democracy is their historical exclusion of the meaningful participation of women and Black, Indigenous, and other people of color (M. Murphy; Sakai; Urban). Critical race and Whiteness scholars have argued that up until the mid-to-late nineteenth century, racialized categories were contradictory, changing, and regionally specific to the social and political landscapes of the Northeast, North (now Minnesota), South, Indian Territory (now-Oklahoma), and West Coast. This period in history was one of immense change: Post-Civil War Black, Indigenous, agrarian populist, Chinese worker, and Irish and Eastern European immigrant radical socialist, among other resistance movements threatened the contingent social order of the emerging US (Frost; Roediger).

In the early colonies, the Anglo-European ruling elite had already begun "racially elevating" poor White European indentured servants, the majority of the non-enslaved workforce, by ensuring free White men's "legal, political, emotional, social, and financial status . . . was directly related to the concomitant degradation of Indians and Negroes" (Thandeka 43). Laws and policies emerged that encoded and hierarchized racial and gender difference and responded primarily to White indentured servants' "intraclass collaboration" with enslaved workers, who often conspired to run away together and otherwise caused land and slave owners trouble (Thandeka 44). Legal and social mechanisms of racial and gender hierarchy persisted in the industrializing US, often to tamp down on worker rebellion.

The history of industrial unionism offers an illustrative example of the emergence of solidarity unionism in the US to challenge White supremacy in the US labor movement. Since its inception and heyday in the early years of the twentieth century, the IWW has aspired to be a union of direct, democratic control. While the American Federation of Labor (AFL) during its inception around the same time organized under the premise of "a fair day's wage for a fair day's labor," the IWW organized under the principle, "abolish the wage system." Their principal understanding of the nature of capitalism led the two unions to pursue wildly different organizing roles. IWW membership and local leadership roles were extended to all workers irrespective of race, nationality, ethnicity, gender, trade, or skill level. The IWW's desire to organize the unorganized, the people whom the AFL would never seek to organize, that led to a boom in membership between 1906 and 1917 (Thompson and Bekken).

Theoretically, the IWW seeks to gain power through mass movements within labor unions rather than electoralism. Father Thomas Haggerty, creator of the industrial union structure known as Haggerty's Wheel, desired to organize all workers under the One Big Union which would be democratically operated through a series of industrial committees staffed by rank-and-file delegates within each industry. Once all workers have been organized in this fashion, workers could then shut down the entire economy by engaging in what is known as a general strike (Thompson and Bekken). A massive wave of workers refusing to engage in work would shut down the operating mechanisms of capitalist industry, thereby forcing the bosses to negotiate their terms of surrender. Workers would then have sufficient power built up through this mass strike that would ensure worker control of the means of production alongside the apparatus of managing a non-statist entity of worker-controlled industries.

The IWW's emphasis on worker control through industrial unionism and its eschewance of electoralism put it at odds with more moderate trade unions. In business unions, elaborately written contracts negotiated by paid union staff and directed by union leadership are the main source of employer accountability. In contrast, the IWW seeks for workers to control negotiations in direct systems of governance. Contracts are brief, often seen less as specific obligations of two parties and more of a truce between the working class and the employing class. The main lever of accountability in this approach is the threat of workers' withholding their collective labor (Thomspons and Bekken).

The IWW's efforts toward worker control of production via industrial and concertedly multiracial organizing led to many major uprisings during its heyday in the early twentieth century. Its most successful committee was the Agricultural Workers Organization (AWO), which, at its height, comprised around 100,000 multiracial members across the nation. The AWO pulled off one of the largest agricultural worker uprisings of its era in 1914, creating "'the world's longest picket line' running 800 miles from Kansas up to Rapid City, South Dakota . . . Confronted with a critical labor shortage at the time, the growers had to give in" (Sakai 155). Despite the organization's purported multiracialism, historians of the IWW suggest that its failure, in practice, to create antiracist, anti-sexist leadership and organizing practices, alongside its violent repression by the state, ensured that revolutionary industrial unionism remained (and continues to remain) a marginal theory/practice within the broader labor movement (Sakai).

The IWW offers a window into the lengths toward which employers and the state disciplined and policed multiracial worker organizing. As such, immigrant and poor workers of color have organized themselves, excluded, for the most part, from major business or trade unions. Tait writes, "Many in the traditional labor movement did not believe poor workers could be organized, either because of their fluctuating job status, or because of prejudices against their race, ethnicity, gender, poverty, or immigration status" (7). As such, many poor workers unions challenged unfair working conditions but also, and interrelatedly, took up broader struggles that directly affected them, including for immigrant rights, gender pay equity, and the recognition of domestic, caregiving, and service work as labor worthy of organizing. In her study of poor workers' unions, Tait recounts the economic initiatives of the Civil Rights era movements—tenant and service worker organizing. Tait calls this the "other labor movement . . . composed of independent and community-based labor organizations." She argues, "It is these supposedly marginal workers who are increasingly important in both the US and world economies" (10). Challenging the "image of the working class as blue-collar men," Dorothy Sue Cobble importantly notes that the casualization and precaritization of work is feminized and that "[p]aying more attention to women and to women's jobs, then, is essential if we are to understand the experience of the majority of workers" (2–3).

In higher education, academic workers have long organized via solidarity approaches, as the legal employment status of graduate students and adjunct professors has historically been contested, with universities, often with aid from the NLRB, arguing the contract nature of academic employment. Higher education labor historian Zach Schwartz-Weinstein, in an interview with *Jacobin Magazine*, suggests the significance of thinking the solidarity unionism, by necessity, of graduate employee and adjunct faculty organizing together with the "red state" strikes:

> Organizing in a context in which there is no prospect of legal recognition, as graduate employee unions have had to do in the very recent past . . . is actually really instructive for thinking about how to organize in a Right to Work context. . . . It's important to think about what a union can look like outside of the kind of protections afforded by a Fordist collective bargaining regime and the legality provided by the National Labors Relations Act. (Schapira)

In fact, Rebecca Kolins Givan writes of our current moment, "the line between strikes that are legal and those that are technically illegal is growing thinner and less consequential" (7).

For their part, trade unions have been historically hesitant to support or affiliate with contingent academic labor given the precariousness of recognition, although contingent faculty movements have gained ground in some places (Berry and Worthen). In 2016, the NLRB proposed a rule that determined graduate student workers were not employees eligible for union recognition. In 2021, it withdrew the rule, yet the NLRB's position on graduate student workers' rights is often in flux and dependent on the political party in power (Douglas-Gabriel). Because they were unable to rely on legal recognition, Columbia University graduate employees–key instigators in the 2016 decision–articulated the necessity to forefront solidarity approaches. Union organizer and doctoral student Kate McIntire stated in an interview, "A contract first forces Columbia to share information with us about what those resources actually are, and then allows us to insist on issues rather [than] having to accept what they offer us" (Moattar).

Even in higher education institutions where faculty and employees have been unionized, research on academic casualization suggests that union membership and collective bargaining agreements have not necessarily led to a halt to the restructuring of work in colleges and universities, in the US or in Canada (Dobbie and Robinson; Herbert and Apkarian). SEIU has been one of the major unions to begin to organize adjunct faculty, yet it has been hesitant to engage in strike actions (Herbert and Apkarian). Even so, few faculty in the US belong to a union. Thus, like graduate employees, contingent faculty have had to engage in organizing, often, outside of formal unions. In 2015, for example adjunct labor activists attempted to organize a mass work stoppage of adjuncts nationally. It began when a group of adjunct activists wrote to the Department of Labor "calling for government investigations into wage-theft, teaching load reduction and other unethical/illegal labor practices, garnered nearly 10,000 signatures in summer/fall 2014" (Kahn et al. 5).

This effort led to the organization of the National Adjunct Walkout Day, mainly via social media. While universities were not shut down, large scale protests at universities across the nation took place. In cases where unionized faculty have recently struck, as Seth Kahn writes of the 2016 strike of the Association of Pennsylvania State Colleges and University Faculty (APSCUF), solidarity approaches were key. APSCUF faculty decentralized their work through a strike team that intentionally excluded members of the executive leadership, calling up people with specific skills who may not have previously held leadership positions. Further, the strike team encouraged widespread participation in the organization of the strike up to a year prior to the action ("Solidarity Invoked" 252–54).

In sum, theories of solidarity unionism emerged through early US and international efforts at poor workers', multiracial, sometimes multi-gender, and industrial organizing. With its violent repression and the evolution of the implicit association of the "working class" synonymous with "White men" (Roediger), theories of solidarity unionism emerged through the efforts of workers excluded from trade unions and NLRB recognition. With the ongoing attempts to limit legal recognition and collective bargaining for many workers, e.g., graduate student employees and nonunionized contingent faculty, solidarity unionism beyond the legal strictures of trade unions are emerging as a key approach for building worker power.

● Social Movement Unionism

In the years since the Great Recession, lower and higher education unions (and unionizing attempts) have come under intense attack via legislation that has drastically expanded school and curriculum privatization and cut education funding. Simultaneously, many educator unions have existed on the frontlines of school austerity and the COVID-19 pandemic, demanding, as with the most recent wave of educator militancy, the restoration of resources and robust public health safety measures in schools. Labor studies scholar Saturnin Dandala writes that "while the role of teacher unions in bargaining for the economic interests of their members has somewhat been studied by industrial relations researchers, unions' role in advocating for social justice, such as militating for student welfare, has received little interest among [labor] scholars" (572). However, studies of solidarity and social movement unionism offer significant resources for understanding political differences and tensions from within educator unions.

In higher education, labor studies of contemporary social movement unionism are fewer and farther between. Piya Chatterjee and Sunaina Maira suggest that a significant reason for this is the ways in which higher education resists and marginalizes scholarship that seeks knowledge of its institutions and social functions (12). Much of the existing scholarship of social movement unionism in higher education is rooted in movements within and beyond the university, including feminist, queer, Black, Indigenous, and other liberation movements (Meyerhoff). Louise Birdsell Bauer, in her study of the University of Toronto graduate employee strike, argues that social movement unionism among higher education labor movements is made possible by workers' taking up political identities that reject professionalist discourses that they are "professors-in-training" but rather precarious workers in a system that structurally requires precarity (275). Contemporary precarious worker movements among graduate students and contingent faculty are building social movement coalitions and making important connections between relative precarity in higher education labor and other facets of our current political-economic moment, such as widespread crippling student debt or the ways in which most people's lives have become increasingly precarious via the overall decline in living wage salary and benefits-offering jobs (Bauer).

In the scholarship that emerged from the 2012 Chicago Teachers Union (CTU) strike, several scholar-activists elaborated the significance of the social movement-oriented caucus, CORE, taking control of the union and ousting the stagnant former leadership. Movement and scholarly studies have highlighted CORE's emphasis on community-based organizing and a commitment to building grassroots power (Nuñez et al.; Uetricht). Further, scholars articulated the significance of its analyses of the relationship between Chicago's urban planning policies to gentrify and cosmopolitanize the city and its school closure and privatization policies. CORE's research arm linked various strategies by city leaders to upwardly redistribute public money and power to reshape working class neighborhoods close to the city center into a mass of luxury condominiums. CTU's strike aimed to redistribute that power to the BIPOC working-class communities most directly affected by these oppressive policies (Lipman). In this way, social movement teachers' union activists and scholars have sought to articulate theories of power founded in critiques of capitalism, White supremacy, and heteropatriarchy (Blount; Quinn and Meiners). The small body of education and social sciences scholarship on social movement unionism has most directly attended to theories of power and change in unionisms.

Likewise, within education research, scholars articulate social movement unionism as a form of organizing beyond workers' immediate economic interests and toward transforming social institutions as part of a larger coalitional project to transform and democratize society and governance (Peterson, "Survival and Justice"; Stark). However, Weiner, veteran union activist and scholar, suggests that formal education unions have, since they won collective bargaining rights in the 1970s, pushed aside serious conversations about race, class, and gender through the predominance of business unionism, or representative and centralized leadership distanced from educators' everyday work ("The Future of Our Schools"). This aversion has stultified rank-and-file participation in their unions and their study of for whom, for what, and how they are fighting. In the following chapters, we take up a more sustained discussion of these tensions. In Chapter Four, we discuss the significance of the recent rise of social justice caucuses and transnational networks of social movement unionism and their efforts to challenge often anti-democratic and narrowly professionalist business unionism (Bocking; Stark).

Cindy Rottmann and colleagues write that educator unionists have long organized with and for social movements—from early women's movements to early twentieth century communist and social movements to Civil Rights era and contemporary movements (53–54). Educators organized within their trade and professionalist organizations for broader union responses to the social issues facing their students and families (54). While the CORE takeover of the CTU in 2010 is one of the more widely documented contemporary examples of and catalysts for social movement unionism, analyses and calls to action from teacher unionists suggests the latest wave of social movement unionism has roots in the late 1980s and 1990s as public education began to feel the impacts of the effects of neoliberal policies. In 1999, teacher unionist Bob Peterson describes social justice unionism as a "perspective [that] informs a range of topics—from union democracy to the purpose of schooling, from teachers' relationships with students, parents, and community to the need to radically restructure society" ("Survival and Justice" 11). For him, social justice unionism builds on the best aspects of what he describes as industrial unionism, which "focuses on defending the working conditions and rights of teachers" and professionalism, which emphasizes "teacher accountability and quality of school programs" ("Survival and Justice" 14).

Weiner suggests an important difference between "social justice" and "social movement" unionism, advocating for the latter to describe how educator unions are working and should work toward specific justice-centered political and social visions. She writes that the term social justice unionism has become common place, "I think the idea of a 'social movement' unionism is more useful because it addresses the need for transformation of the unions internally, especially the need for union democracy" ("The Future of Our Schools" 197). However, Stark, in her study of social justice caucus networks uses the terms interchangeably and prefers social justice unionism because it is most commonly used in practice by organizers. For Weiner and Stark, as for us, social movement unionism is predicated on radical democratic participation of its members and its social justice aims. Further, social movement unionism is accountable to the social movements that shape each union's terrain of schooling—whether its anti-gentrification movements, food justice, climate justice, and so on.

As Peterson notes, advocates of social justice or movement unionism also understand the necessity of inter-movement support for winning campaigns and demands ("Survival and Justice"). Just as Bauer suggests the significance of "precarious worker" political identities of higher education workers in building coalitions with related movements, K–12 educator social movement unionists work beyond simply the interests of their communities. They operate with keen analyses of what Lois Weis and Michelle Fine term "critical bifocality," who understand how they and their students' experiences in their classrooms (the micro) is interrelated with global circuits of dispossession and privilege (the macro) (194; Asselin).

In the Global South, social movement educator and student unionism has been closely tied to issues of climate change, dispossession of Indigenous and poor communities' access to land and water, and neoliberal austerity policies. The violently repressed 2011 student strikes in Chile emphasized the US-inspired neoliberal education reforms privatizing and making profits from public schools (Bellei et al.). In Brazil, Mexico, and many other places, educators and social movements have engaged in mass strike actions to protest neoliberal austerity policies (Bocking; Stark and Spreen; Tarlau "Occupying Schools"). At the start of 2019, Zimbabwe educators engaged a national strike to protest rising inflation, which made the purchase of basic necessities for everyone near impossible (Education International). The spiraling inflation is a result of colonialist structural adjustment policies imposed on the nation by the International Monetary Fund and the World Bank.

Across the world, educators have been rising up against privatization, stolen land and poisoned water, and facing outright violence and repression. In Ayotzinapa, Mexico in 2014, forty-three student teachers were murdered for protesting police brutality (Washington). Social movement unionism necessitates participatory and democratic unions yet also seeks to understand, in practice, the relations of repression, dispossession, and containment with which the education system is intertwined. As the movement saying suggests, police brutality of educators in Mexico is tied with colonialist violence in Palestine is tied with my neighborhood and yours, neighborhoods in which schools are always central features and contested terrains.

● The Emergence of Solidarity Unionism in the 2018 Strike Wave

While all four orientations to unionism and more were in play at any moment during the 2018 "red" statewide strikes, we argue that solidarity unionism emerged as a significant means by which rank-and-file educators catalyzed the statewide educator uprisings. Educators organized within and in tension with their trade unions to strike in states where striking is illegal. In all four states, state and local union organizational power had been eroded by anti-union laws and policies (e.g., Right to Work laws) since the 1990s. In Arizona, Oklahoma, and Kentucky, NEA-affiliated state associations articulated themselves not as unions but as professional advocacy associations (Hale "On Race"). Solidarity unionism emerged as a means for workers excluded from the decision-making processes that govern their trade unions and workplaces to pressure their school administrations to shut down. Educators, to varying extents in different places, formed dual power organizations, or organizations that worked in tension and collaboration with their trade unions.

O West Virginia: "Workers Were Not Satisfied with that [Service] Model"

The WVEA stalled organizationally after the November 2016 election. At their annual delegate assembly in April 2017, WVEA President Dale Lee stated, "The WVEA is broken." Few locals had operating budgets, monthly meetings were scattered and never attracted more than a handful of members, and local political action committees could not mobilize enough people to get out strong Democratic votes for endorsed candidates. Building representatives (stewards), who are unpaid, did not always attend monthly meetings nor were they able to share pertinent information with fellow union members in their school on policy or electoral matters. Electorally, the unions could do little to stem the tide of conservative lawmakers sweeping into office on the back of Trump's populism. The state senate swung from a slimmer 16–18 Republican majority to a 12–22 Republican majority. At the 2017 delegate assembly, President Lee announced gleefully that the WVEA's endorsed governor candidate and West Virginia's only billionaire, Jim Justice, had won his race. Governor Justice went on to switch back to the

Republican Party later that year. At the time, his election was hailed as a saving grace to an otherwise poor election turnout.

WVEA members were expected to take on the brunt of these challenges partly because association staff was overworked. An Organizational Development Specialist (ODS) with the WVEA must cover on average 7.85 counties in the state. Commutes from one end of a single staffer's region to the next can range up to two-and-a-half hours. In Monongalia County, for example, there are eighteen K–12 schools in total. This is only one of nine counties that the ODS of the Northeast district must cover. If an ODS only visited schools, one of their multitudinous daily tasks, it would take anywhere from fifteen to seventeen weeks just to visit each school in their region. In a thirty-six-week school year, almost half of the year would have been devoted to making rounds to the counties an ODS represents, ensuring that members' concerns were fully heard and understood.

An emphasis on lobbying lawmakers and pushing for electoral changes did little to galvanize a base of support to fight for strong public education. Emily Comer, a key organizer during the walkouts, said to Brendan in an interview, "I've always belonged to a union and paid my dues, but until the strike I never felt like it held much of a presence in my life in the way much of my other organizing does." Handing out highlighters, calendars, and notepads at the beginning of each year as enticements for new educators may be a good marketing strategy to gain members, but it didn't make members feel they were connected to a union prepared to go headlong into a fight. "Years of asking nicely instead of wielding power helped us get into our current mess, and workers were not satisfied with that model," Comer said. Lobbying is far-removed from teachers' day-to-day work and undertaken by mostly paid professionals who might or might not have experience as a classroom teacher.

In the previous national election, members were mailed endorsement lists while mass emails were sent out months and weeks beforehand. Directives informing members who to vote for, rather than why they should cast their votes in that direction, created a transactional relationship in the minds of many members; vote for the Democrat because the Republican is a worse choice. "It's easy for leadership to say, 'We don't have any power because our members just won't show up to meetings,'" Comer said. "But who wants to show up to a meeting to talk about lobbying? People want to belong to a vibrant, organizing-focused union that puts its money where its mouth is."

The lobbying efforts of WVEA and AFT have produced some results that members have taken note of in recent years. For one, West Virginia—with a population of 1.8 million residents—is one of a handful of states that did not have charter schools at the time of the 2018 strike. Attempts to push pro-charter bills out of the education committee were met with firm opposition from both parties until more than a year after the strike. While the state's educators struck again in 2019 against what they viewed as retaliatory privatization legislation, it passed soon after (Reed). In 2006, teachers across the state staged a one-day walkout to protest a mediocre pay raise proposed by then-Governor Joe Manchin. A few years later, teachers received a $1,000 pay raise across the board, but educators realized this was a drop in the bucket. Rising healthcare costs quickly ate away at the bump in pay, making it evident that the raise was simply an attempt to quell the growing unrest of education workers. Matt McCormick, a WVEA member, said that the tactics of "lobbying a hostile legislature and holding the occasional rally" were typical of this period in the union's history. Even with the one-day walkout, "there was a longstanding trepidation that manifested any time that the word 'strike' was broached."

In 2016, the state senate voted along party lines to approve a bill that would have allowed for the formation of charter schools. Initially, the bill would have allowed for two charter schools to be created each year for the first five years. Senator Greg Boso (R-Nicholas), who represented a predominantly rural district, was in favor of the new educational model, arguing that it would attract businesses and more competitive teacher salaries in rural regions of the state (Ebert).

Lobbying Republicans to vote against the bill did not have the desired effect as it might have had in years past. Party-line voting meant that lobbying allies in the state legislature would only be as effective as long as those (Democratic) allies retained their seats. As Democrats lost control of the state legislature in 2014, union officials turned to lobbying as their main strategy to stymie the rising tide of conservative law-making. The bill was not signed into law, but in an election year, it showed the power of a slim Republican majority. The state unions were generally perceived as lobbying arms, and members who wanted their unions to do more found this perception difficult to challenge.

When members had an idea for making change to union strategy, they were met with little confidence from leadership. Jay O'Neal, co-founder of the WVPEU page, moved to West Virginia in 2015 and quickly realized that it would take more than asking nicely to move leadership in the ways he felt were needed. "When I would go to leadership in the past with some ideas, I got either a non-committal response, it might take forever to get to someone on the board, or I would get a thank you email but no follow up," O'Neal said. "One of the biggest problems is the split between AFT-WV and WVEA, and even though they want most of the same things, it was hard to work between the unions because of their bureaucracy."

West Virginia's initial attempts to halt the floodgates of reactionary legislation came together slowly. Over the summer of 2017, O'Neal and Comer had worked together to create the secret Facebook group that would later be used as a springboard for future direct action, WVPEU. Education workers who had expressed discontent with the lobbying tactics of WVEA and AFT-WV were invited to join and take on an active role within the space. At first, the goal for the secret group was to create a mass collective that workers could join and learn about issues related to their health care, salaries, and education-related efforts at the legislature. Through this group, O'Neal and Comer suggested to WVPEU members that a Lobby Day at the capitol might be the first beneficial use of the group's time and effort.

WVPEU members were tasked with researching issues important to educators, determining which legislator was friendly or hostile, and putting forth presentable material that could then be used by rank-and-file educators on Martin Luther King, Jr. Day, the day that the WVPEU group had set for the Lobby Day. It was around November, however, when O'Neal was summoned to WVEA's main office in Charleston. Apparently, one of the Facebook group members added an executive committee member for WVEA, who informed President Lee that there was an effort to push for lobbying legislators outside of the purview of the union establishment. After meeting with Lee, O'Neal's union leadership gave the greenlight to officially sponsor the Lobby Day–likely because O'Neal, Comer, and others had already organized members and made plans beyond the union via WVPEU.

A few hundred WVEA teachers and their allies attended, bolstered by the belief that 2018 could be a year of a renewed union membership. In the previous year's Delegate Assembly, Lee and David Haney, executive director of WVEA, had called upon locals to make plans of action that would breathe fresh life into the union. With a crowd gathered around the rotunda of the capitol, Lee addressed the crowd thus: "I've heard a lot of people talk about 'It's time for a walkout or time for a strike.' But those are not the first steps in that decision. It's not the first step in what we should do to achieve our goals. If we were to get back to that, there's a lot of groundwork that needs to be laid beforehand." Lee's reference to a strike undoubtedly came from local WVEA presidents and sympathizers, who almost certainly had been witnessing an explosion of reactions across the state demanding the unions take further action.

Earlier that month, Governor Justice spoke at his annual State of the State address and named education as his centerpiece for a new, revitalized West Virginia. His proposal was simple, though; a two percent raise for public school teachers, amounting to around $800 per teacher. This paltry raise would have been eaten up by premium increases to the PEIA. Simultaneously, the WVPEU page began to explode with membership–from a few hundred members in November to several thousand and eventually more than twenty thousand by January. Talks of more militant action permeated the online space, while attempts to lobby hostile legislators continued at the capitol. The result was a perfect storm of impromptu organizing.

Stories began circulating online about legislators accosting teachers for having the gall to push back against premium increases, of representatives outright rejecting attempts to work with teachers to craft policy that could assist in making West Virginia schools better, and of delegates simply misunderstanding basic economic facts and data that the unions presented to them (Howell and Schmitzer). In addition, the state had begun to roll out its GO365 plan at the beginning of the legislative session. This plan would, in one teacher's words, "gamify" an employee's health care. Insurance holders would have been required to log into an online system that would track their health plan. Policy holders would receive points based on the level of exercise that they completed, with an annual point goal that increased each successive year. Failure to meet the set criteria would result in increased deductibles and premiums.

As things were heating up across the state, AFT-WV and WVEA locals began holding cross-union meetings to discuss the impact of the proposed changes to PEIA. A vote of authorization was called in early February that year, which would signal support among the rank-and-file for a walkout. County presidents tallied their votes the following weekend in the town of Flatwoods and found the vote had received overwhelming support–upwards of eighty-five percent of voters stated that they would authorize their union to call a walkout in protest of the proposed changes to PEIA.

On February 17, the following weekend, a collection of United Mine Workers, AFT-WV, WVEA, and service personnel members joined together at the capital to call for unity in action–the walkout that members had wanted to see was announced for February 22 and 23.

O Kentucky: "We Became Activists Accidentally"

Like West Virginia, Kentucky does not allow most public employees to engage in collective bargaining, except for the JCTA, a local affiliate of the state union, KEA. JCTA represents teachers in the most populated county in the state and the county where Louisville is located. Like the WVEA and AFT-WV, the KEA and its local affiliates mostly relied on lobbying efforts to advocate against austerity. In 2017, Governor Bevin had released a series of reports titled "Pension Performance and Best Practices Analysis"–known as the PFM reports after the Philadelphia-based consulting firm that authored the reports–that argued for the systematic dismantling of the state's pension plan and moving it over to a standard 401(k) (Bailey). KEA had lobbied vociferously against the pension reform bill and seemed sure that Governor Bevin's pension overhaul plan would be stopped before it had time to germinate. On a muggy November afternoon, public employees across Kentucky held a "Save Our Pensions" rally at the capitol steps in Frankfort. The rally was called towards the end of a special session initiated by the Republican-controlled legislature and governor's office, where the pension overhaul plan was set to be enacted. The rally, organized by independent activist groups, union sympathizers, and the newly-formed online group, KY United We Stand, had defeated the measure.

Public sentiment had been geared towards defeating the special session and halting changes to public employee pensions in a winter session. Once that session ended, the major state unions believed that it was better to hold off on any collective action until they knew more. Katie Hancock, a social worker and organizer of KY United We Stand, believed that the rally would only be the beginning of the fight. When she helped to organize her fellow social workers under her secret group, the idea was that union and non-union members would be included. KEA had been conspicuously absent from the "Save Our Pensions" rally, even if members had been in attendance. Adding teachers to the online KY United We Stand group shifted a dynamic for Kentucky's state employees in ways that could not have been done solely within the confines of one union or another. "We noticed that we had few teachers on the [KY United We Stand] page, even though they were going to be affected by the same things we were going through," Hancock said about efforts to reach out to and include teachers. "This is why we shifted our dynamic from just focusing on the pension plan to funding public education."

As a non-education state employee, Hancock could be a member of the Kentucky Association of State Employees (KASE), a labor advocacy group similar to the KEA, but one which had less political power as of late. Even still, Kentucky state employees don't officially have a collective bargaining unit. "We have KASE, but as far as I know, they go to our [KY United We Stand] page and share our content to their group, so it's pretty much as if we're doing their work for them." KASE had become de-legitimized in the minds of state workers over the decades of anti-union legislation that Kentucky passed, with KASE's role as advocacy group becoming less prominent and membership declining. Hancock said, "There's no real representation that the average state employee can rely on, so we just decided we had to do it ourselves."

Earlier that year, Bevin's administration had released a series of three PFM reports that highlighted the conservative legislature's agenda for radically transforming Kentucky's state pension system into a traditional 401(k) model, as mentioned above. The reports outlined several critical challenges Kentuckians faced with their pension plan, but it was clear that privatization would be the goal. On the first page of PFM #1, the report states that Kentucky's pension plan for FY 2015 ranks the lowest of all fifty states for funding ratios, setting aside a paltry 37.4 percent of funding levels needed to fully fund the plan. The report states that, "While funding levels are higher for the public safety, local government, teachers, and judicial and legislative programs, all of Kentucky's systems are underfunded and the aggregate challenges remain quite severe" (4).

Initially, PFM #1 introduced the idea that transparency and stricter governance of funds would provide greater control of overhead costs for managing Kentucky's various pension plans (PFM Group, "Interim Report #1"). This was followed by a May 2017 report that signaled a move towards privatization. In PFM #2, the proposal outlined a trajectory of current costs for the state when compared to border states and across the US. The report argued that the solvency of the state's pension plan could not last over the next decade, and for the continued existence of reliable benefits packages, significant alterations would need to be made (PFM Group, "Interim Report #2"). In August 2017, PFM #3, titled "Recommended Options," proposed that public employee retirees would no longer see a cost-of-living adjustment (PFM Group, "Interim Report #3"; Bailey). In a state that does not provide social security benefits to state workers, this would mean living decades on a fixed income. Newer state employees would immediately be funneled into a low-return 401(k) plan in lieu of the state's pension plan, and their retirement age would be raised. Current state employees would be moved to a hybrid model of state and 401(k) plans. Workers would also have to defer retirement even if they had been planning for this ahead of time, and they would no longer being able to accrue sick leave for retirement purposes.

It was in this environment that Kentuckians gathered outside their capitol steps to protest Bevin's push to kick off thousands of Kentuckians from benefits that they had earned through years of service. Matilda Ann Butkas Ertz, a music teacher from Jefferson County who had attended the rally, remembered, "The mood was angry and bitter. Teachers were filled with rage ... At the same time, the governor had made hostile remarks about teachers, included calling us 'thugs,' who were 'not sophisticated enough to understand the fiscal issues,' who were 'greedy ... hoarding sick days ...'" This rhetoric recalled racist ("thugs") and gendered (unable to participate in public budget matters) non-producer tropes mobilized to quell teacher militancy in the long 70s (Shelton), and sought to justify Kentucky educators' absorption of continued state disinvestment.

The November 1 rally had been organized outside of the purview of the KEA, which was still coming to grips with the potential for mass action. Jeni Bolander, a fourteen-year special education teacher from Lexington, recalled feeling that the KEA had given up on members' concerns. "The problems that we faced in 2018 were issues that KEA knew about in 2003," Bolander said, "and yet they let the problems continue to snowball until we were forced to take action." The rally did not necessarily have a large turnout, with anywhere from several hundred to a thousand public employees. But "there were Teamsters, and labor union folks, and everyone just seemed pissed about what was happening to us." KEA had refused to endorse this rally, as they had refused to endorse all actions leading up to the statewide walkouts.

What came of the rally was less clear in the immediate moment. Nema Brewer, organizer of another major social media organizing group that grew out of KY United We Stand, KY 120 United (KY 120), described KY120 organizers' frustrations with the narrow electoral focus of the KEA:

> We became activists accidentally, and KEA is still in the lobbying mindset. There's a big difference between being a lobbyist and an activist. We had gotten to the point that we were done talking, we were tired of sitting down and holding dinner. We wanted to put our boot on someone's throat and flex our muscles. We couldn't hold back anymore.

As the movement grew, so did disagreement around the core issues facing public education, and tensions within the KEA emerged from the longstanding marginalization of Jefferson County educators and BIPOC communities.

O Oklahoma: "I Remember What This Meant to Our Family"

Similar to other states, the lead up to the strikes in Oklahoma had begun at least a year prior within and without the OEA and AFT, even though much of the media attention centered on the strike actions themselves. OEA is, by far, the largest union in the state, though AFT represents many education support professionals and non-teacher school staff. AFT also represents Oklahoma City

educators (AFT-OKC), one of the state's largest school districts and a few surrounding schools. While Oklahoma and Arizona educators may not have imagined that they would be walking out in the spring, the work of NEA locals and
groups of autonomous educators earlier in the academic year facilitated state
educators' response to West Virginia and Kentucky: Oklahoma could walk out
and walking out was the only way to create change.

As we discuss in more depth in Chapter Three, Oklahoma's entryway into
the strike was largely represented in the media and analyses as led by Alberto
Morejon and Larry Cagle–two educators who had headed up each of the two
major Facebook pages: Oklahoma Teacher Walkout: The Time is Now (TTN)
and Oklahoma Teachers United (OTU). However, our oral history and formal
interviews with fifty-four educator-organizers in Oklahoma illuminate that
much of the agitation and initial pressure arose from rank-and-file organization among strong, active union locals and ad hoc groups of educators that
formed a year or more prior, including in Stillwater (see Chapter Four), Moore
(Chapter Four), and Putnam City (see Chapter Five), among many other places.
For many across the state, the failure of State Question 779 in November 2016,
which would have raised the state sales tax by one penny to provide teachers a
$5,000 wage increase, was a major shifting point alongside local experiences of
increased managerial surveillance and loss of teacher autonomy.

A year later, in January 2018, Cagle, a mid-fifties veteran English teacher at
Edison Preparatory High School in Tulsa (at the time), shared with Erin in an
interview that he and a friend and colleague at a different school, Jim (pseud-
onym), formed the early instantiation of what would later become OTU. Cagle's
then-school, located in a wealthier neighborhood in South Tulsa, is highly
regarded in the district and state with an economically, racially, and linguistically
diverse, majority-minority school community. Even as Edison Prep received
praise and high rankings, like many other urban schools in the state, the high
school had become subjected to increasingly narrowed and scripted curricula
and an authoritative administration that created a competitive school culture
among faculty with little support. The school's district administration pushed a
slate of venture philanthropist-backed school reform policies and practices dis-
quietingly like those that, in previous decades, sought (and seek) to capitalize on
the "crises of failure" in post-Katrina New Orleans, Chicago and many other cities. Tulsa Public Schools superintendent, Deborah Gist, was, herself, trained at
the Broad Academy, a two-year fellowship program dedicated to training educational leaders within a paradigm of school efficiency, choice, and market-driven
policies (Casey). Leaders are groomed into advancing the privatization-oriented
schemes backed by the Eli and Edythe Broad Foundation (Saltman). Tulsa's historically Black and Latinx communities in the north and east parts of the city
increasingly experienced school closings, turnarounds, and consolidations to
make space available for new corporate-backed charter school ventures.

At Cagle's Edison Prep, even as one of the wealthier schools in the district,
the high rate of teacher turnover each year provided a telling glimpse of the

conditions public school educators faced in the city. Cagle and Jim recruited a few other educators in two of the city's high schools to organize a sick-out on January 25–three weeks prior to the West Virginia strike. Around fifty teachers between the two schools called in, causing students to spend their day gathered in auditoriums or cafeterias. For their efforts, they received some attention in the news (see Mummolo). Discussing the events two years later, Cagle described himself as "totally a union person" and a union member in his younger days in other cities. However, he had not been a member of Tulsa Classroom Teachers Association (TCTA) or OEA.

The early action caught OEA, TCTA, and district leaders by surprise and they quickly distanced themselves from OTU, calling it a "fringe group." As then-vice president of TCTA, Shawna Mott-Wright stated in a press interview, "I have had no members reach out to me about this" (Mummolo). The early action taken without engaging the union in advance set the antagonistic tone of Cagle and OTU's relationship with OEA leaders from the beginning. Cagle was, per-haps, not wrong to avoid consulting OEA leadership from the beginning as they fought to avoid or limit the strike until rank-and-file pressure from within the unions and on social media made it appear inevitable. An OEA staffer stated: "It's going to happen with or without us, so we need to help" (Blanc, "Red State Revolt" 153). Some members of the TCTA familiar with Cagle felt that his actions were not taken in collectivity but mainly were taken individually and with great risk, for which Cagle, upon reflection in an interview, expressed regret. We explore this further in Chapter Four.

From there, OTU grew initially, as well as lost members quickly after partic-ipants in the first sickout action became fearful of retaliation. By mid-February, students at several schools had organized successful walkouts, including more rural towns like Keifer (Thompson). At Edison Prep, two sisters, including then-junior Faith Shirley, coordinated hundreds of students to walk out on February 14 to protest teachers' working conditions and students' learning conditions. They successfully won their demand to fire their principal at the time, Dixie Speer, who students argued created a "negative climate" at the school (Hardiman).

Cagle described to Erin that organizing the sickouts felt surprisingly easy, in a way that shocked him at the time. With the intensity of the teacher shortage, he knew they only needed a few to participate to shut down normal operations. As OTU grew in notoriety, Cagle reached out to educators in the Oklahoma City area and other regions in the state to begin calling for a statewide teacher walkout, with continued resistance from the OEA. The leader of the most prominent Facebook group, TTN, Morejon, a young teacher in the mid-sized college town of Stillwater, attended an early organizing meeting at a public library in Oklahoma City, accord-ing to Cagle, and shared his plan to create his own page. More social media savvy than Cagle, and, like Cagle, willing to be public-facing, Morejon quickly grew his Facebook group by researching faculty employees across the state's larger districts and direct-inviting them to join TTN, according to Cagle. As a result, the social media group had tens of thousands of educators seemingly overnight.

In the lead up to the strike, the most significant battle between rank-and-file educators and OEA came soon after the two Facebook pages blew up in membership. Initially, OEA leaders turned away from OTU's calls for a statewide walkout. On Tuesday, March 6, OEA president Alecia Priest announced the union's decision to walk out on April 23, after state testing. Immediately, social media sites were filled with furious teachers, who argued that OEA was limiting educators' leverage by holding the walkout so close to the end of the year. The state could have ended the school year with enough state-required instructional time to spare. Thousands of posts along the lines of one educator's comment "Make them fight!" lit up both pages. In the background (described in more detail in Chapter Three), groups of educators with OTU threatened continued sickouts and educators within local unions across the state voiced their dissatisfaction with the state union.

In response to this outpouring of anger and collective pressure, the OEA sent an email to its membership implying cooperation with the state's two hundred superintendents and their support for the April 23 walkout date. Almost as immediately, a Cooperative Council for Oklahoma School Administration (CCOSA) representative sent an email to all school staff that was screenshotted and shared to the OTTN group stating the OEA email was "a misrepresentation of the facts," and that, "CCOSA has not taken any official position on any plans at this time. We know that local districts will make decisions based on their communities." Within the CCOSA, a minority of more enthusiastic superintendents, like Chuck McCauley of Bartlesville, were in support of an earlier date. By Wednesday, March 7, the OEA abruptly announced its decision to push up the walkout to April 2, in time to threaten disruption of state testing and federal funding. OEA's list of demands to be met by April 1 included wage increases for all public employees and school staff and significant increases in school funding. Priest's public image among the state's educators shifted from enemy number one to beloved hero in a matter of just twenty-four hours.

TCTA, the largest local, took on a significant amount of work toward this effort after it became clear it was inevitable, with many teachers new to or inactive in their locals recruited to take on leadership and active organizing roles. This was the case for Hannah Fernandez, a first-year teacher in Tulsa. For many younger teachers participating in and organizing the 2018 strike, the 1990s teacher strikes in Oklahoma and elsewhere were a motivation, even as many did not know much other than the occasional anecdote from a rare veteran colleague who participated in the event. Many had older relatives who had experienced those strikes firsthand as teachers and staff and felt connected to a longer legacy of fighting for public education.

Fernandez remembered her father's experiences, a teacher in Maryland, on strike in 1990. She was well into the second half of her first year as a teacher in Tulsa Public Schools when she learned of the possibility for a statewide strike:

> At first, I was like, "I don't know what I'm doing teaching! I'm not really gonna try to get involved in anything else right now." I just needed

to keep my head above water in terms of surviving. And then as it all approached, there was an article shared [on social media] about my dad's school district [back in 1990]. That was what really drew me in to like, "OK, I remember this. I remember what this meant to our family if this is going to happen." So then I started showing up and doing things.

Fernandez attended a TCTA meeting where leaders invited people to sign up for committee work to prepare for the now certain larger actions that were to take place. She became one of a core group of eight women organizers for the local. This group of women, according to Fernandez, became her community of support in union organizing and in learning to teach as a first-year educator. They also organized several primarily awareness-building actions in the lead up to the strike, including canvassing the county to make people understand the severity of the issues and inviting them to attend legislative events and write their lawmakers of their support for teachers.

Rural educator, Michelle Waters recalled her motivation to support the strike and be involved in her OEA local stemmed from her experiences participating in the 1990 statewide strike as a high school student newspaper reporter:

So, I just remember, you know, the feeling of the spirit of camaraderie and as wanting to support our teachers and recognizing that we needed better education for us, and they need better working conditions. And you know, covering that kind of on an objective level, although it's kind of hard to be objective and, just like, these are my teachers that you're talking about. These are people that I see every day. And just, I remember being excited about that.

Waters' formative memories of the 1990 strike as a student and her family's unionist history in the railroad industry combined with the conditions of her students' rural lives created, for her, a sense of purpose in striking to raise taxes on the state's wealthiest (even as she remained skeptical of the state's effectiveness at redistribution): As Waters described, "educators are on the front lines of that battle," and they "see what's happening."

O   Arizona: "I've been Through that Before"

As a teacher in Chicago, Rebecca Garelli recounted to Erin in an interview that she had participated in the CTU and its historic 2012 education strike, though at the time she did not see herself as an organizer. "I wasn't anybody special, just a regular rank-and-file member. You know, a pretty good foot soldier. I did what I was told, and I did it with a vengeance." As a young person coming of age in the city during 9/11 and the war on Iraq, she had always been politically active, especially at anti-war protests. But she said she was "awakened" by the "racially charged" closings of Black and Brown schools, a main issue for striking CTU teachers.

After moving to Arizona, Garelli shared that she became frustrated by the low pay, horrible working conditions, and, as she described, the pervasive sentiment that teachers had no real power to change anything. "Coming from such a hardcore union town, I was used to being respected. I was used to having rights." She felt that her friends and colleagues did not, at first, share in her frustration, offering up platitudes when she asked questions about why they were forced to attend meetings without pay. "That's just how it is here." After meeting and receiving resources and encouragement from Jay O'Neal and other union activists via social media, Garelli felt supported to create a Facebook page for Arizona teachers. Through the process of managing the explosion of membership and discussion, nine others stepped up to lead the movement of Arizona teachers, forming the organizing core for AEU, which worked in collaboration with but intentionally distinct from the state union, the Arizona Education Association (AEA). Garrelli said, "I was like, 'You know what? I've been through a strike before. I have some ideas of what we could do.'" Indeed, many of the tactics that AEU mobilized were straight from the CTU playbook.

Vanessa Arrendondo, who began teaching in Phoenix, had never joined the union. She said, like many of her colleagues, she had a "negative perception" and felt like she could not afford the five hundred dollars per year in dues. She was already working before and after school to make ends meet. "When I joined Arizona Educators United is when I joined the union." Arrendondo was spurred to action when she joined the newly created Facebook page that kickstarted AEU and took up Garelli and others' offer to start a more formal organizing process. Arizona had the benefit of learning with and from the other three states. Guided by Garelli's experiences and support from other strike organizers, the beginnings of an inter-state network of Red for Ed teacher unionists, the AEU collective learned a few key lessons.

First, they began their work committed to democratic participation. To avoid falling into the same hierarchical forms of out-of-touch decision-making that teachers like Arrendondo's colleagues had been critical of within AEA, they decided to create a more formal system of communication beyond the free-for-all of social media. They began using their social media page more strategically. Arrendondo said in an interview with Erin,

> It started with asking people to volunteer to work as liaisons. We are a grassroots movement. People slowly started volunteering. I created a list, with two lists, one for charter and one for public, which helped people to see which schools were missing liaisons. And then others stepped up and started getting themselves organized.

As AEU developed a liaison network of two thousand teachers across the state, they also began organizing escalating actions. First, wearing "red for ed," along the lines of the CTU strike. Next, they began "walk-ins," where educators, students, and parents showed up before school wearing red to rally and then walk into school together in solidarity.

Learning from the tensions between members, non-members, and business union leadership in the previous struggles, particularly the drastic drop in OEA's membership after they called off Oklahoma's walkout with minimal rank-and-file support, AEA approached AEU with an eye toward collaboration. According to interviews with Garelli and Arrendondo and Garelli's written reflections on the lead-up to the strike in Rebecca Kolins Givan's and Amy Schrager Lang's edited volume on the 2018–2019 strikes in public education, AEU had plenty of leverage to hold their own against AEA, should they need to, given their organization and widespread participation across the state. Their collaboration was mutually supportive. The state union provided resources and organizing expertise and traveled across the state with AEU leadership to host regional trainings for the school liaison network.

● From Fear to Fire

In West Virginia, Kentucky, Oklahoma, and Arizona, the lead up to the strikes emerged in vastly different ways yet with many similar themes, namely, the slow (then quick) collectivizing of anger at legislators and corporate interests who were selling them out and selling out their students and communities. Caught between hostile legislatures, ineffective unions, and neoliberal reformist agendas, education workers found within themselves the foundations for charting a new path forward. Rather than choosing to lobby their delegates for improvements, they staged direct actions at their capitols to demand protections and halt reactionary actions; rather than choosing to rely on paid union staff to help set up channels of communication, they created accessible social media platforms themselves; rather than waiting for an election, they directly confronted their "bosses" in their respective legislative houses; rather than withhold stories of struggle and anger to pacify their rage, they shared their individual messages in collective spaces, generating continual energy for more action.

In each state, the lead up that began with fraught emotions, intense anxiety and fear and shifted toward collective fury, excitement, and possibility as events unfolded and the strikes became a realistic horizon. Mercer County Education Association president, Nicole McCormick's reflections in Givan's and Lang's edited volume speak to the zeitgeist of the moment, "When we fight, we win! When we stand together, we win! Most importantly, when we own our labor and decide that it is ours to give or withhold, we win!" (116).

As the strikes took shape, early feelings of unity and power grew yet also changed and became complicated by differences in understanding the significance of and the in-practice difficulties of building democratic structures amidst struggle, racialized, gendered, and class differences, and tensions and disagreements in understandings over for whom and for what broader purposes educators were withholding their labor. In subsequent chapters, we illuminate the ways in which competing professionalist, social movement, and trade unionisms permeated and interacted within the rising tide of rank-and-file educators.

Chapter 2. Race Shapes the Terrain of Struggle

Like educator struggles in Madison, Wisconsin, and the broader economic focus of Occupy Wall Street in 2011, educator organizers and their supporters in these states demanded accountability from the wealthiest extractors of resources and labor. And like the CTU strike in 2012, the mantra that teachers' working conditions are students' learning conditions emerged as a central frame. At the same time, educator organizers described contending with disagreements or uncertainties about how to maintain popular support while addressing the uneven ways that communities experience education disinvestment, dehumanizing English-centric scripted and standardized test-focused curriculum, and punitive disciplinary policies across racial, class, and geographic divides.

In the following, we aim to better understand the racial politics and complexities of educator organizing in the lead up to, during, and in the aftermath of the 2018 strikes. Our analysis of the 2018 strikes emerges from a deeper study of the entwined longer histories of racial capitalism, settler colonialism, and the construction and development of U.S. public education. This chapter operates, like much of the rest of the book, on the premise that contemporary educator organizing is only strengthened through understanding its complex histories, and that these histories are (always) constitutive of our present moment. Our premise is strongly supported by the experiences of organizers in the "red" state strikes, where efforts to depoliticize the racialized underpinnings of educational disinvestment and neoliberal reforms to make appeals for wider public support appeared to weaken, even fracture, continued organizing momentum following the strikes.

In West Virginia, public discourse and media analyses suggested that race featured relatively insignificantly as an overwhelmingly majority (ninety-six percent) White state. Alternatively, in Kentucky, race featured quite significantly as the educator movement coincided with the state's proposed Gang Crime Bill. The proposed legislation would make gang recruitment a felony, rather than a misdemeanor, and identified a gang as any organization of three people sharing two out of four characteristics: sharing a name, colors, hand signals, and symbols. Individuals convicted under this new legislation would have to serve eighty-five percent of their sentence before the option of parole was available. Outrage over the proposed bill intensified already existing "fault lines" (Asselin) between (mainly Louisville) educator organizers who sought a race-conscious approach and others, who advocated a colorblind economic lens to win wider White support. While Arizona and Oklahoma did not have the same kind of immediate movement crisis that emerged with Kentucky's Gang Crime Bill, we illuminate how public education disinvestment in these states has long been wielded unevenly and via justifications premised implicitly on race and White supremacy.

We begin by drawing from political, economic, labor, and education histories that we feel are key for understanding what, to many, felt like a surprising turn of events in 2018, in right-leaning places. For decades, teacher (and all public employee) militancy had long occupied the position of shameful non-producer and anti-union legislation had been propped by White producerist public sentiments against taxation (Shelton). A longer, deeper history of race, education, and educator labor struggles reveals the very issues that propelled the labor actions—austerity, school privatization, de-professionalization and hierarchization of education labor—are legacies of the last significant wave of teacher militancy in the long 1970s. Then, as now, race, Whiteness, and racism are central.

● Race, Public Education, and Teachers' Unions

The creation of common schooling emerged during a tumultuous time in the mid-to-late nineteenth century when power, land, and wealth did not always appear to be guaranteed to the elite owning class. The shift from an agrarian to an industrializing economy produced pitched, often bloody battles between waged workers (including children) and capitalists (Bartoletti; S. Smith). In industrializing U.S. cities newly booming from rural and transnational migration, the use of state resources to expand and provide working-class immigrant access to compulsory lower education became more desirable as progressive social reformers sought to expand young working class people's access to childhood and "shelter children from the harmful impact of urban-industrial life" (Wolcott 13). David Wolcott and others describe the progressive bourgeois response to drastic urban social transformation as the "child saver movement"—encompassing advocates for compulsory education, juvenile justice, and social work institutions, which included many White, well-to-do women (Lesko; Meiners, "Right to be Hostile"). Ultimately, the child savers sought to expand the parental role of the state in response to what upper class advocates understood as a cultural pathology of the poor and not-quite or not-at-all White.

Many young working class people rebelled against their containment, and, as Madeleine Grumet writes, even preferred waged labor to early urban school conditions—at least if they were forced to work, they would be paid for it. Resources for constructing the infrastructure of public education, including the proliferation of normal colleges (teacher education institutions, which would later expand to become the backbone of the U.S. public higher education system), were won, in large part, on the claims that common education could produce a more compliant, unified society (on the cheap by paying women teachers a pittance (also see Strickland in the context of higher education) at a moment when post–Civil War fears of Native, populist, worker, and freed Black rebellion might unravel the contingent social order.

As K. Tsianina Lomawaima and Teresa McCarty describe in the context of the history of Native education in the US, the state has always pushed a project of assimilation, creating spaces for Indigenous cultural and linguistic practices only when these were understood by the state as safe for maintaining the social order. Schools were a central way the federal government sought to solve the so-called "Indian problem," which is, as the authors write,

> that Native communities have persistently and courageously fought for their continued existence as peoples, defined politically by their government-to-government relationship with the United States and culturally by their diverse governments, languages, land bases, religions, economies, education systems, and family organizations (7).

Lomawaima and McCarty go on to write, "The federal government has not simply vacillated between encouraging or suppressing Native languages and cultures but has in a coherent way ... attempted to distinguish safe from dangerous Indigenous beliefs and practices" (6). During early periods of rapid westward expansion and dispossession of Native lands, the "safety zone" was narrow and Indigenous boarding schools, guided by federal policy, engaged in the most extreme forms of violence, i.e., forcibly stealing children and relocating them to boarding schools great distances from their home communities, severely punishing children for speaking their languages at school (Lomawaima and McCarty). Many Indigenous children perished from staff violence, illness, and neglect as a result of the conditions and practices of these early boarding schools (King). The publication of the 1928 Meriam Report, commissioned by the U.S. Secretary of the Interior, marked a shift from the strict assimilationist logic of the previous era and expanded the "safety zone." The report argued that people have the right "to remain an Indian" only after federal powers had been established within state and tribal relations. As the authors' document, Native communities have, throughout the history of colonization, resisted the prescriptions of the safety zone (as cited in Lomawaima and McCarty).

An excerpt from the Board of Indian Commissioners' 1902 report illuminates the centrality of schooling for the construction and policing of White supremacy and racialization in the pre-Meriam Report era: "Schools alone cannot make over a race, but no one instrument is so powerful in producing desirable changes in a race as are schools for the young" (Annual Report of the Commissioner of Indian Affairs [ARCIA] 781; cited in Lomawaima and McCarty 7). Ongoing efforts continue to construct an education system that seeks to efficiently manage racial, cultural, linguistic, gender/sexual, class, and other differences for the benefit of a racial, heteropatriarchal capitalist social order. In response to such efforts, many students, teachers, and communities have always engaged everyday and formal organized resistance in classrooms, schools, communities, and beyond. From students' subversion of the curriculum through disruptive acts in the classroom (coded as "bad behavior") or teachers' engaging in critical pedagogy behind closed doors to boycotts of mandated testing, parent-led hunger strikes, and student and educator walkouts, education is a continuous site of contestation and struggle.

How such resistance to the management of racial hierarchy has borne out in the context of teachers' unions, historically, has been fraught.

● Race and Teachers' Unions

Scholarship recounting the formation of contemporary teachers' unions in the US tends to focus on narrating the origins and evolution of the NEA and the AFT, and specifically key constitutive struggles on the part of local organizations in Chicago, Detroit, New York, and Philadelphia, among other Northern urban places (Gaffney; Hansot; Karpinski; Lichtenstein; Lyons; McCartin; Mirel; Tyack et al. as cited in Hale, "Development of Power").

However, as Hale notes, "an emphasis on the AFT, the NEA, and their local affiliates privileges a northern and urban perspective that overlooks the racialized dynamics of professional teacher associations in the American South" (Hale, "Development of Power" 445). He further argues that the 2018 strikes and militant organizing across Southern states and the Sunbelt "is built upon" the histories of Black teacher organizing in the South, and further, that "[t]his history reveals that the professional organization of educators' labor constitutes a unique, though overlooked, aspect of labor and civil rights history as it provides a framework to situate a movement that has at times been framed outside the grasp of American history" (Hale, "On Race" 2).

Prior to the *Brown v. Board of Education* decision in 1954, which ended de jure segregation in educational institutions, White teachers' unions excluded Black teachers from membership. The NEA, for example, was segregated until the 1970s, when it consolidated the African American Teachers Association, while some state affiliates integrated sooner (Urban). Under segregation and excluded from White unions, Black educators organized professional associations to advocate and take action to improve access to educational resources, professional training, and equitable pay (V. S. Walker). Unlike the NEA's form of professionalism, which sought to constitute a body of professional knowledge within and managed by White institutions (e.g., colleges of education) that could bolster the prestige and aims of the profession, D'Amico Pawlewicz and View suggest Black teachers' associations advocated a form of professionalism that saw, instead, teachers as "community workers" (1287). Professionalism, within many Black teachers' associations in the South, took the form of pedagogical training that sought to premise education on the cultures, histories, and aspirations of Black students and communities. Across the US in the pre-*Brown* era, educators of color "navigated the gray area of profession as institutional bolster and profession as social justice activism," for example, Mexican American and Japanese American educators created language programs in response to English-only policies (D'Amico Pawlewicz and View 1287).

V. S. Walker writes that African American teachers in the segregated South have been narrowly framed in the literature and popular discourse as either victims of racial oppression or caring maternal or paternal figures. Alternatively, she paints a more complex view:

> [T]eachers were caring individuals, but their behaviors were more than caring. Likewise, although they worked in constrained educational cir-

cumstances, they were not debilitated by these circumstances. Rather the teachers were increasingly well-trained educators who worked in concert with their leaders to implement a collective vision of how to educate African American children in a Jim Crow society. (753)

Within Black teachers' associations, a collective vision centered on fighting for equitable pay and resources for Black schools and an end to segregation. Black teachers' associations and Black educators developed critical coalitions with other civil rights organizations.

For example, the Oklahoma Association of Negro Teachers (OANT) formed in 1893 and existed through the 1960s. It disbanded not long after the NEA opened its rolls to Black Oklahoma teachers in 1955, and its political resources and membership steadily declined with the pushout of Black teachers during integration (Billington). Donnie Nero, founder of the Oklahoma African American Educators Hall of Fame, writes that few of its organizational records exist, beyond brief mention of a few well-known OANT leaders in periodicals documenting the history of the formation and later desegregation of public education in the state. According to Nero, the organization was a stalwart driver for "professional development, training, coordination and structure for African American educators during a time when segregation was the law of the land." In the 1940s, OANT existed at its height of organization and influence, pushing for and achieving significant increases in funding and resources for Black schools, then funded via a dual and completely separate mechanism than White schools in the state (Clayton). While many Black Oklahoma educators, like elsewhere in the nation, lost their positions, the OANT among other Black community and political organizations since Black settlement in the territory proliferated legacies of knowledge, relational infrastructure, and inspiration to contemporary organizing (A. Brown).

Like the OANT, beginning in the 1930s, Black teachers' associations in many key Southern states had built significant momentum for challenging dismal material conditions in their schools, low pay, and racism. Black teacher organizing played key roles in advancing the Civil Rights Movement yet are underappreciated for doing so (Baker, "Pedagogies of Protest"; Hale, "On Race"; V. S. Walker). In Mississippi, Alabama, Virginia, and South Carolina, among other states, Black teacher organizers were able to make such advances because they were able to advance social and racial justice visions and analyses in ways that White-dominated educator unions were unwilling:

> Race functioned to divide the organization of all teachers but at the same time it permitted Black teachers to organize autonomously to address civil rights issues in the larger movement for equal education. This agenda, which spanned over half a century, shaped the Civil Rights Movement's broad democratic social vision in ways that White and northern teacher associations did not. (Hale, "Development of Power" 445)

The work of Southern Black educator associations in this era, as Hale argues, offers an important example of social movement educator unionism that employed a visceral understanding of the role of racialization in the construction of the conditions of educators' work. Black educator associations simultaneously fought for such common good and Civil Rights Movement-relevant demands as curricular self-determination, pay equalization among White and Black teachers, higher professional standards, and, during desegregation, for the right for Black educators to work.

Continuing to use Oklahoma as an illustrative example, Black educators in the state were a critical source of leadership in the Civil Rights Movement locally and nationally. Clara Luper, Nancy Randolph Davis, and Ada Lois Sipuel Fisher are three prominent examples of skilled local educators and community organizers who worked within networks of Black civil rights organizations and mobilized analyses of the relationship between the racist education system and broader social issues to enact significant change efforts for anti-racist policies and civil rights. For example, Luper and other Black educators organized with striking Black sanitation workers in 1969 and faced retaliation in their schools (A. Brown). It is unclear to what extent, for example, Luper, an Oklahoma City educator, infamous leader of the OKC NAACP Youth Council lunch counter sit-in movement that inspired similar efforts nationally, and OEA member, had a relationship with the waning OANT in the late 1950s. The OANT had tended to take a more conciliatory approach of "friendly persuasion" to advocate for equitable integration policies after *Brown v. Board* (A. Brown).

President at the height of public education policy transformations to facilitate the Supreme Court mandate, Fredrick M. Moon is oft cited as a minor opinion in studies of Southern Black teacher perspectives on integration: "I know our teachers feel that if it is a question of losing our jobs or having segregated schools, we will take the job loss" (Haney 90). Many Black teachers did not feel similarly yet lacked the meaningful support of the OEA to challenge Black teacher pushout and post-Brown re-segregation, especially in that state's two major urban areas of Tulsa and Oklahoma City (Billington).

While these struggles played out differently in different places in the North and South, Baker suggests that it was, in fact, in the Southern White institutional response to such struggle from which emerged the foundation and logics of contemporary neoliberal school reform. In this way, nearly every educator's agitation over de-professionalization, high stakes testing, and loss of curricular autonomy has roots in the White retaliation and racial animosity against Black educators' efforts toward racial justice. In response to the successes of such organizing for equal pay, educational quality, and an end to de jure segregation, standardized testing emerged as a tactic to "restrict black access to White institutions and the professions" (Baker, "Paradoxes of Desegregation" xvii). In a striking example, University of South Carolina president, Daniel W. Robinson "helped officials expand testing and tracking in primary and secondary schools, arguing that 'this difference in achievement between the races may be our last line of defense'" (Baker, "Paradoxes of Desegregation" xxii). At the same time, Black educators understood the challenges and risks of both school and union integration:

> African American educators were wary about the suitability of relinquishing their allegiance to their own associations that had their well-being as a primary goal in favor of the NEA whose commitment was questionable. Moreover, school desegregation threatened the professional status and job security of African American educators (Karpinski 14).

Similarly, in Oklahoma, Black educators slowly trickled into the newly desegregated OEA (with the support of the OANT) yet remained supportive of the OANT. In 1958, the Black educator association counted 1,500 of the state's 1,622 Black teachers as members (Clayton). In the 1950s, OANT shifted its efforts to fight against the pushout of Black teachers in the state. While Black membership grew in the newly integrated state NEA-affiliate, the OEA did not elevate or prioritize the issues facing its newer members (Billington), and until it officially disbanded in 1958, the remaining OANT infrastructure and leadership steadily fought for equal pay and the recruitment of Black educators in re-segregated and integrated schools through the 1960s.

The manipulation of desegregation policy to perpetuate a racist education system that could continue to reproduce oppressive and hierarchical gender and class relations is at the root of educators' 2018 grievances. As Baker writes, "officials used their control of education [during the years of desegregation] to construct a more rational educational order that has proven to be more durable than the educational caste system it replaced" ("Paradoxes of Desegregation" xvii).

● Race, Teacher Power, and the Rise of Neoliberal School Reform

The 2012 (and later 2019) Chicago teachers strike is oft cited as the most recent predecessor and influencer of the 2018 resurgence in teacher militancy (Weiner and Asselin). Karen Lewis, then-president of the CTU and member of the CORE, is an example of the ways in which Black political organizing for education justice in our contemporary moment is borne on the backs of Black (women's) teacher organizing. Lewis' inroads to education organizing began during her time as a student activist. As a high school student, she, along with many other students across the city, organized a school boycott, demanding the hiring of more Black faculty and staff and community control of schools. Todd-Breland notes her ideological motivations were rooted, at the time, firmly within the Black Power Movement (219–220). Later, as CTU president, Lewis encapsulated the racial and class project of neoliberal school reform with the following remarks in 2013:

> Children of the elite are given a full, rich curriculum that allows them to explore, create and imagine, while the children of the poor and those

> who chose publicly funded public education are given the drudgery
> of test prep. Children of the elite are given a curriculum that prepares
> them to rule, while our children are given a curriculum that prepares
> them to be greeters at Wal-Mart. (Todd-Breland 227)

Citing Pauline Lipman's work on the neoliberal reshaping of urban education, Todd-Breland writes that austerity policies (at the center of the 2018 red state strikes) are directly linked to the labor-economic needs in late stage racial capitalism: while the children of the elite few have access to well-resourced schools that employ creative curricula and pedagogies, "a larger number of under-resourced neighborhood schools and 'no excuses' charter schools focus on the 'basic skills,' 'ability to follow direction,' and 'accommodating disposition work' required for employment in the expanding pool of low-wage and temporary service sector jobs" (227; Anyon; Bowles and Gintis).

Standardized testing in K–12, for teacher credentialing, and for college admittance continued to proliferate in the decades that followed desegregation from South Carolina throughout the South and nation as "more defensible forms of separation based on class as well as race" (Baker, "Paradoxes of Desegregation" xxii). The implementation and proliferation of high stakes standardized testing in K–12 and for college entrance aimed to limit BIPOC access to White education institutions in the wake of desegregation and had the effect of Whitening the teacher pool (Baker, "Paradoxes of Desegregation").

More recent merit pay and tenure elimination policies, among other achievement logic-based policies, have pushed out a significant percentage of African American teaching faculty (Buras; Jankov and Caref). As scholars of neoliberal urban education policy have illuminated in the context of urban education, such measures have been strategically utilized to support state and local governments to read educational failure in working-class, often working-class BIPOC communities, and most often in neighborhoods that appear ripe for real estate development (Buras; Lipman; Picower and Mayorga). Scholars of the 2001 No Child Left Behind Act argue, the ability to point to supposedly objective data proving failure provided justification to enact drastic punitive measures that had the intended effect of privatizing and de-unionizing public education (Klein; Saltman).

While the demands of the 2018 red state strikes were primarily for equitable wage increases, education historians have documented the ways in which the racialized conflicts of the 1970s were central to shaping White public support for the rampantly individualist regime of neoliberalism in education and other social policy. White teachers' unions were often pitted against Black political organizing for community control and self-determination, and White teachers' notions of (conservative) professionalism existed in stark tension with Black community organizing efforts toward community-based, culturally sustaining notions of professionalism. Shelton articulates these various tensions as they played out at the height of 1970s teacher militancy:

> For some [white] teachers, this new power meant avoiding teaching students whom they viewed as dangerous and difficult to teach. For some white teachers committed to improving education in black schools, many assumed that only through teaching middle-class, individualist values could blacks overcome the "culture of poverty" that entrapped them. For other teachers, however, increased teacher power clashed with the demands by Black Power activists that teachers should shoulder more caretaker responsibilities in the schools. (Shelton 57–58)

It is important to note that educator unionists were far from homogenous in their political perspectives during this era. Yet, more radical educator organizers had been systematically pushed out from their unions and teaching positions during the "red scare" era of anti-communist political repression (M. Murphy; Taylor). In combination with the decimation of major social movement union organizations, like New York's TU, the complex ways that administrators and municipal and state leaders pitted White teachers' and Black communities' class interests against one another, sowed long-lasting divides that, alongside retaliatory anti-union right-to-work legislation, made it increasingly difficult to respond to the proliferation of austerity policies in response to the economic crises many urban and rural municipalities faced during deindustrialization and White flight in that era (Golin; Podair; Taylor).

The histories and legacies of Southern Black teachers' associations, among other educator movements for educational self-determination and equity, help us to understand the breadth and depth of education organizing and the significance of Black educators in advancing the Civil Rights Movement and shaping the terrain and aims of social movement unionism, historically and today. The rise of teacher union militancy across the nation and its conflicts and tension with Black Power, among other anti-racist working-class revolutionary movements of the 1970s, provides necessary context for understanding the dangerous implications for centering color-blind narratives in contemporary educator movements. As education union historians and scholars of anti-racist and social movement educator unionism have unequivocally illustrated, efforts to repress community-based anti-poverty, multiracial, and anti-racist union movements offer a measure of how threatening such approaches are for the social order–repression on the part of national union political leaders (M. Murphy; Urban; Weiner), the state and ruling class (Goldstein; Taylor); and White society (Shelton; Todd-Breland).

These tensions and conflicts have been documented and studied, to some extent, with the emergence of social justice caucuses and social movement unionism in urban contexts (Asselin; Maton; Morrison; Riley; Stark). However, they have been relatively absent in recent analyses of the 2018 "red" state strikes (Hale, "On Race"). As our analysis illuminates, West Virginia, Kentucky, Oklahoma, and Arizona each have their own situated histories and geographies of racialized oppression and resistance in education (and beyond).

● A Race-Conscious Context of the Appalachian Educator Strikes

Race and Appalachian history, alongside the intertwined histories of the western territories that are now Oklahoma and Arizona, have often intermixed through a combination of White violence, genocide, slavery, and forced migration. As White settlers began pushing westward in the eighteenth and early nineteenth centuries, Indigenous groups were forced out of the region almost entirely (Pollard). At the turn of the twenty-first century, two-fifths of Appalachia's Indigenous population lived in twenty-one of the four hundred ten counties, with the greatest concentrations in western North Carolina. No region in central Appalachia between West Virginia, Kentucky, and western Virginia had a single county with more than five-hundred self-identified American Indian residents. Colonialism in Appalachia pushed out whole communities, beginning long before the Trail of Tears and which later became exacerbated by it. As such, much of the previous history of Indigenous Appalachians is marginalized in narratives of the region (Pollard).

Although central Appalachia's Black population is the smallest of all three regions, the historical roots for this modern demographic shift are important. The enslaved population in Kanawha County (formerly Virginia) grew from three hundred fifty-two in 1810 to 3,140 by 1850 in large part because of the precious salt industry along the ten-mile stretch of the Ohio River, the Great Kanawha, which lie three miles north of Charleston (Stealey III). Western markets had an insatiable demand for salt–both for processing and preservation– and the Kanawha Valley's salt mines provided a ready supply for markets out west. Because of the easy access to the Ohio River, which could load barges of the Kanawha brine to markets across six states, central Appalachia's enslaved population boomed in the antebellum period (Stealey III). The region was well-known for its role in the interstate slave trade. Appalachian households ranging from the poorest Whites to the wealthiest elites played a role, directly or indirectly, in trafficking enslaved people. Merchants and non-slaveholding farms benefitted greatly from the slave trade, with each county courthouse having its own slave auction block (Dunaway).

During the Jim Crow Era, Black Appalachians experienced chronic poverty similarly, in some ways, yet also disparately to their White counterparts. In Clay County, Kentucky, for example, Blee and Billings note that "a more complex relationship between regional poverty and migration" exists (367). For example, economic security in the nineteenth century (i.e., land ownership) was possible for Whites but not Black residents. White persisters, those who remained in the county, tended to accumulate more property over time whereas Black persisters, who tended to have little or no base of property, became even more impoverished. In addition to land ownership, resource accumulation and the shift from subsistence farming to commerce and industry made life easier for White persisters than Black persisters. During times of economic depression, White persisters could more easily live with kin than could Black persisters, with the latter living with White nonkin as domestic or agricultural workers more frequently (Blee and Billings).

The second generation of Black families that had grown up in Kentucky and West Virginia knew a similarly racist region. Despite the ground-breaking Supreme Court case *Brown v. Board of Education,* many of the old racist habits that this generation's parents faced were suffered by them as well. As Karida L. Brown states,

> As long as the terms of the old racial contract were maintained, there was no reason for exerting overt, repressive measures to maintain order. Instead, the ideology of White supremacy and the structure of separate and unequal were internalized into the habitus of everyone living in the Jim Crow South. As long as they had internalized these overt structures, there was no longer a need for signs and lynchings; all people knew their place. (98)

After the 1950s, Black Americans were forcibly relocated into central Appalachia in service to the extractive industry—mining and salt manufacturing. After mechanization, fewer Black miners had jobs and competed with White miners for the better benefits of remaining in the mines (Clark). Within a few generations, those families had moved farther North as the economy shifted from agriculture and extraction to service and commerce. Therefore, despite a growth in non-White residents in Appalachia, only three counties in West Virginia and none in Kentucky had at least ten percent minority residents in the 2000 census (Pollard).

The racialized poverty and lower education status for non-White residents account for much of the stereotypes about Appalachia's "backwardness." In 2000, 13.6 percent of the region's total population lived below the poverty line, one percent higher than the national average (Pollard). The gap between White and non-White residents, however, is higher. Twelve percent of White Appalachians lived in poverty in 2000, compared to twenty-five percent of non-White Appalachians, higher than the national average. In eastern Kentucky, the numbers are worse: twenty-four percent for Whites, thirty-one percent for Black residents, and thirty-seven percent for Latinx residents (Pollard).

The predominance of an almost entirely White homogeneity in Appalachia is not simply a benign fact. Instead, it is the result of active and persistent actions designed around a White supremacist framework for the creation of this region. Barbara Ellen Smith explains that this Whitening approach to Appalachia by academics is dangerously reductive. Smith argues instead for a race-conscious perspective on Appalachia which "understands the region as a repository for America's evasions and conflations of race and class but refuses to participate in the obfuscation" (53).

In 2019, 3.6 percent of West Virginians identified as African American, 1.7 percent identified as Hispanic, and 1.8 percent identified as two or more races (U.S. Census). Likewise, in Kentucky, 8.4 percent of state residents identified as Black,

3.8 percent identified as Hispanic, and 2 percent identified as two or more races, significantly higher racial diversity than in the Mountain State (U.S. Census). However, Black and Latinx enrollment in teacher preparation programs in both states are relatively low when compared to states with larger non-White populations. Both West Virginia and Kentucky scored in the lowest categories for Black and Latinx teacher preparation program enrollments for 2018–2019 (Partelow). Thus, although diversity in demographics exists in both states, relative to their student population, both states have low numbers of non-White educators.

O Kentucky's Not Quite 120 United

This imbalance between BIPOC students and a mostly White education workforce presented challenges in both West Virginia's and Kentucky's statewide strikes. As stated in Chapter One, Kentucky's legislature was about to end their 60-day legislative session in late March, only to pass SB 151–the pension overhaul package or Sewer Bill–at the last minute. The JCTA Facebook page proclaimed after the passage of SB 151, "JCTA has called for job actions in the past and the situation may come to that again, but the Association certainly is NOT calling for such an action at this time." This, despite having made a previous post that day that stated, "If you are an education employees (sic) or a supporter of public education and can possibly get to Frankfort IMMEDIATELY, please come NOW!!!" Kentucky's largest local affiliate appeared to ask education workers and their supporters to demonstrate at the capitol, but only if they were capable of doing so without disrupting the school day.

On Friday, March 30, 2018, more than five hundred protesters arrived at the capitol steps shouting in anger that the legislature had passed what should have been a defeated bill at the last hour. A sick-out had shut down schools in more than twenty counties. Even Jefferson County had been forced to close after one thousand teacher absences were called in and several hundred more anticipated. These numbers represented a sizable portion of Jefferson County's education workforce. Jefferson County employs more than six thousand teachers and has more than one hundred schools in its district. According to district spokesman Daniel Kemp, the wave of mass absences meant that all schools would have unfilled classrooms, and around twenty schools would have double-digit absences. A large red banner was unfurled from the capitol's balcony that stated in bold red letters: "Kentucky deserves better." The strike was officially on.

Brent McKim, president of the JCTA, informed media outlets that JCTA would bring a legal challenge against SB 151. First, they would challenge a provision that did not allow teachers to use unused sick days when calculating pension benefits. Then, they would use this challenge to declare that the entire passage of the bill was unconstitutional. Working alongside then-Attorney General, Andy Beshear, whose father had been the Democratic governor of Kentucky until Bevin had taken office, JCTA employed a calculated lobbying tactic more comfortable for both JCTA and KEA leadership.

Kentucky's walkout continued that following Monday. It was on this day that the fruition of KY 120 went from online organizing, under a name of solidarity as an homage to their neighbors in West Virginia, to an actualized struggle of solidarity unionism. All one hundred twenty counties' schools were closed for the first day of statewide action. Many counties' schools were on spring break at the time, and there was some confusion as to whether educators in those counties would be expected to "strike" alongside their fellow educators or continue with their pre-arranged plans.

It appeared that, although the walkouts were able to amass large swaths of energy from rank-and-file educators from across the state, KEA was unfavorable to future actions. The following Tuesday, KEA voted not to support any future strike actions—sickouts or walkouts. Without on-the-ground support from the unions, there was little ability for the KY 120 page or zone leaders to call future actions.

Nema Brewer, KY120 leader, stated to Brendan in an interview that one of the primary concerns for the page was that if continued actions occurred, it might jeopardize JCTA's contract negotiations. Jefferson County is the only county in the state that has collective bargaining rights. It is also the largest school district in the state with disproportionately higher numbers of students of color compared to the rest of the state. Future labor actions could, in theory, force the JCTA to go on the defensive against both their members and a hostile state legislature. Governor Bevin had wanted to put the school district under state control since he came into office. Given that Jefferson County voted overwhelmingly for his opponent in the last election, Jack Conway, Bevin recognized the collective power of organized labor in this part of the state. "There are people in our state who wouldn't care if Jefferson County seceded tomorrow," Brewer stated. "The goal was to keep everyone united. We're not the 119 united or the 1 united, we're the 120 united and what affects one of us affects all of us."

Organizing for continued action, the group had difficulty maintaining cohesion. First, KY 120 had only been in existence for less than a month when the first non-union-sanctioned walkouts began on March 30. Zones and representatives across the state had been established through an impromptu call for members. For a sustained action to occur, longer-term planning would likely have been necessary. KY 120 had many unvetted members who joined out of anticipation of being part of something bigger than themselves, something that could direct their anger towards political action when the unions had been stagnant or too appealing to traditional lobbying tactics. Personal politics oftentimes made organizing a challenge. "We probably have more Republicans on the page than anyone else," Brewer said, "and so we have to be very careful about how we approach certain topics." This process meant that there would be no possibility for members to vote on work stoppages, sickouts, walk-ins, or the like.

Uncertainty around the page's relationship to KEA complicated this issue further. Matilda Burtkas Ertz, a music teacher from Jefferson County, stated, "The local union [JCTA] was not publicly or privately promoting a work stoppage, though they happily supported us in wildcat 'sickouts' after they were initiated organically." While the unions had believed that these actions had defeated a bad budget, Burtkas Ertz said, "From our perspective, it failed. Many in the groups thought this was weak. Yet, we were not at the bargaining table." Some counties faced disorganized sickouts in "a poorly organized game of chicken," and without a plan, these fell through.

Second, the timing of SB151, coincided with spring break and the end of the legislative session. Whatever organization that had been built had to be prepared to mobilize on a moment's notice. Legislative moves to push SB151 coincided with the budget to keep a check on the potential of a work stoppage. Republican lawmakers witnessed the previous rallies that had occurred and knew that passing the pension bill before the end of the session would force them to confront a mass of angry educators. Something similar had already happened in West Virginia. Educators there had gone on strike with sufficient time left in the legislative session to push for a pay raise. Burtkas Ertz realized that "we could have been organized and made our demands" after the session, "but we would be rallying an empty state house with the only prospect of winning being if the governor called a special session." It was unclear whether Governor Bevin would be willing to do so. When teachers went on strike again on April 13, 2018, Bevin was quoted saying, "I guarantee you somewhere in Kentucky today, a child was sexually assaulted that was left at home because there was nobody there to watch them" (CNN Wire). Public employees feared that community support would no longer exist if a strike action continued, so the safer route for some was to vote out the bad representatives in November and hope for the best.

⭘ The Gang Crime Bill

Perhaps the biggest division within the Kentucky strike in 2018, however, was not so much how to continue the strike in opposition of SB151, but how to relate to another piece of reactionary legislation–HB169, also known as the Gang Crime Bill. The bill was designed to increase penalties for offenders if they were known to be affiliated with a gang, or if a gang-related activity could be considered a factor in their crime. Gang recruitment would also be classified as a felony, rather than a misdemeanor charge, with gang members convicted of a crime also required to serve at least eighty-five percent of their sentences. The term "gang" was also redefined. For someone to be considered committing a "gang-related offense," they had to meet two of the following characteristics: three or more individuals, sharing a common name, symbols, colors, hand signals, and geographic region. Governor Bevin welcomed the legislation at the time, saying, "We can no longer have the welcome mat out for gangs.... They are not welcome to prey upon our children" (Bailey).

The overt racism of this bill exposed the fissure within Kentucky's education strike. It is worth quoting Bhattacharya once more: "Race is not an add-on to the struggle for wages. It shapes the terrain of struggle" ("Why the Teachers' Revolt

Must Confront Racism"). When the Gang Crime Bill began circulating in state news, many Black educators reacted with alarm. The rise of KY120 appeared to be a chance to bring together disparate teachers from across the state to oppose the pension overhaul and a bill that would effectively expand and strengthen the school-to-prison nexus. Tyra Walker stated in an interview with Brendan, however, that "when we began discussing the Gang Bill that would impact our students of color, and particularly the Black students in JCPS [Jefferson County Public Schools], the conversation [on the Facebook page] changed. I was in the group one minute then out the next. Not just out of the group but blocked."

In describing her relationship with KY120, Walker explained that its leadership and many other activists who would play a pivotal role in the 2018 walkouts had known each other well prior to the strike. However, during discussions about how to best relate the struggle for racial liberation in the context of the education walkouts, that conversation was muted. "Some of us, like me, were deleted and blocked from the KY 120 page. There was nothing united about those actions." Walker believed that one of the problems that shifted leaders' focus from a militant, take-no-prisoners stance at the beginning of the strike to a more acquiescing stance occurred through a series of conversations with KEA leadership who advocated a more gradual, legalistic approach to challenging Bevin's legislative agenda.

Petia Edison, also a Black educator organizer from Louisville, concurred with Walker's assessments in her interview with Brendan. Like Walker, Edison also knew many future KY 120 organizers years prior when working on state-level issues. KY120 leaders had become well-versed in the art of lobbying and communicating what legislation was on the table during each legislative session, including "reporting back to the groups all the side deals and legislative moves that were happening (in 2016–2017). So once the legislature in 2018 started, we were already solid and grounded in understanding which legislators were friendly to education and which were not." Through a series of messenger groups, Edison, Walker, and several others formed what would later become the formal structure of KY 120. However, like Walker, once Edison brought up the Gang Crime Bill, she was also removed from the organizing structures she helped build. "I encouraged my fellow teachers to push our legislators to say 'no' to the Gang Crime Bill. I was blocked from the KY 120 page because I was called divisive and a gang bill is not an issue that teachers should address. I am appalled at any educator or non-educator that works in the school system who would not be looking out for the best interests of the students."

This falling out process took years to develop. Brewer, a KY 120 leader, and Edison met in 2017 during that year's legislative session. They were in daily communication on Facebook messenger about upcoming bills, discussing strategies for lobbying techniques and identifying potential allies from both parties. They worked to compile and disseminate this information widely and form mass communications with like-minded public employees. Both Brewer and Edison shared a passion for defending public education, as did the JCTA president, Brent McKim.

Both White individuals helped Edison as allies in the struggle for public education, but it was the Gang Crime Bill that separated those bonds. "My relationship with [Brewer] came to an abrupt end when I brought up the gang bill.... [McKim] did not help push for the resistance to the Gang Crime Bill.... The commonality in all of these relationships is the lack of support towards the resistance of the Gang Bill, and they all have White privilege," she recounted to Brendan.

Edison's personal identification with this bill comes from a place of loss and realization. She had to bury a former student in 2015, her school's neighborhood is ranked nationally as one of the most dangerous places to live. Yet, this bill would only further antagonize the relationship between its mostly White teaching force and its majority students of color. "The gang law is a law that legalizes stop and frisk, and the students that attend my school would most likely be stopped and labeled as gang members, and that follows you for the rest of your life. This law isn't just a civil rights violation, it accelerates the school-to-prison pipeline at a speed we will not be able to contain." When teachers walked out again later in April of that year, as we discuss in more depth in Chapter Five, teachers in Louisville were already on high alert not to trust KY120 because of their lack of support during the Gang Crime Bill's passage.

While both Kentucky and West Virginia share a similar history with respect to the development of race, class, and education in central Appalachia, issues of social justice were more prominently articulated along the lines of economic justice—as working-class educators against a small political elite. Red bandanas that educators began wearing during the walkouts were an homage to the Battle of Blair Mountain, the largest insurrection in the United States since the Civil War. To many West Virginians, this battle signifies the state's longstanding history of everyday people of all races, working together, to fight back against the elite. The difference between the Battle of Blair Mountain and the #55Strong strike, however, is that race and White supremacy were more critical leverage points that served as a wedge between workers in 1921 than they were in 2018. Indeed, the racial makeup of the southern coal counties of West Virginia during the Mine Wars (1912–1921) were far more diverse between non-White and White miners than a century later (Musgrave). Out-migration of the state's Black population in addition to West Virginia's low urban density (no city has more than 50,000 residents) created a vastly different terrain of organizing.

● Conflicts in Understanding Racial Justice Demands as Common Good Demands in Oklahoma and Arizona

A race-conscious approach to understanding educator movements in Appalachia with a longer historical lens illuminates that racism and White supremacy have long served as tools to weaken labor movements historically (e.g., during the Mine Wars) and today (e.g., the Gang Crime Bill and White KY120 leaders' lack of solidarity with Louisville teachers and students). Like Appalachia, Arizona and Oklahoma have been significantly shaped by histories and ongoing realities of settler colonialism and White supremacy that shape the educational policies at the heart of educators' grievances.

O The Race Politics of Austerity in Arizona

In Arizona, disinvestment in public education that precipitated the 2018 strike cannot be read outside the race politics that came to a tipping point a decade prior. In 2004, racial minority students officially became the demographic majority in P12 public education, a ratio that has only steadily grown since then. As of 2014, only forty percent of students were White while forty-five percent were Hispanic, according to the 2016 Arizona Minority Student Report by the University of Arizona (Millam et al.). Despite these shifts, Jeanne M. Powers' research illuminates that Arizona's school segregation during the previous twenty-five years has only intensified. Anti-immigrant sentiments among White residents had been building steadily, urged on by prominent state leaders who stoked racist fears of undocumented immigrants as criminals, job-stealers, and the source of the state's poor economic situation.

In 2010, these sentiments came to a head when two nearly simultaneous legislative efforts sought to make it illegal for educators to teach ethnic studies in the state's public schools (a precursor to more widespread educational gag orders today) and the infamous SB 1070 that legally allowed police to routinely asking for citizenship documentation at their discretion. The ethnic studies ban legislation specifically targeted Tucson Unified School District's successful Mexican American Studies program. Then-State Superintendent John Huppenthal, who led the attack, was an ardent supporter of school choice, vouchers, and privatization and helped to oversee the expansion of charter schools in the state. His argument for banning ethnic studies illuminates the centrality of White fear of loss of power as well as the ongoing centrality of the curriculum in maintaining the racial order:

> We are not in the entertainment business. We are in the winning values business . . . This is the eternal battle of all time. The forces of collectivism against the forces of individual liberty and we're a beautiful country because we have balanced those things. Now, right now in our country we're way out of balance. The forces of collectivism are suffocating us—it's a tidal wave that is threatening our individual liberties. And so, we, at the national level need to rebalance this and we need to make sure that what is going on in our schools rebalance this. (as quoted in the Western Free Press and cited in Acosta 3)

While state leaders engaged in colorblind language to articulate both the ethnic studies ban and SB 1070 legislation as having nothing to do with race but with individual liberties, Powers argues that "'common sense' indicators for reasonable suspicion will not make interpretive sense without the common sense of race and the historical and contextual cues it conveys" (200–201).

In the wake of statewide strikes in West Virginia, Kentucky, and Oklahoma, AEU emerged as a rank-and-file-led organization committed to democratic practices and dispersed leadership (as described in the previous chapter). AEU spurred its state and local mainly NEA-affiliated associations to action. The core group of less than a dozen educator-organizers leveraged the resources of the AEA to build a broad infrastructure of training and communication to more than two thousand AEU school site liaisons across the state. In an interview with Erin, AEU organizer, Vanessa Arrendondo, an elementary school educator in rural Yuma, outside of Phoenix, recounted becoming involved after witnessing year after year of increased class sizes, decreasing resources for everyone, and, in particular, for Yuma's emergent bilingual students and families. Like AEU organizer Rebecca Garelli's experience in Chicago, the ongoing, largely bipartisan, efforts to defund public education, implement punitive accountability policies, and expand school choice (for a choice few) is experienced most intensely by Arizona's urban and rural working class Chicanx, Latinx, Native, and communities of color. Student, community, and educator organizers involved in fighting against a statewide ban on teaching ethnic and Mexican American studies in Arizona's public schools for more than a decade certainly have a keen analysis of the entwinement of austerity, racism, and xenophobia (Acosta).

Unlike some areas of Arizona, rural Yuma also has many more Latinx educators, many of whom Arrendondo felt were largely disconnected from the early organizing of AEU and what many understood as a largely White teacher-led Red for Ed movement (Karvelis "Rural Organizing"). Through Arrendondo's organizing efforts and engagement with local community leaders, Yuma became active during the strike and educators rose up to become liaisons and coordinate actions and decision-making across the state. Some of AEU's liaisons were also building representatives for the AEA who found new purpose and responsibility in their dual roles. As AEU organizer, Rebecca Garelli writes, "The AEA understood that our grassroots group, AEU, included the 'drivers of the bus,' and union leadership understood that the educators' voices needed to be out in the forefront" (108).

In an interview with fellow AEU organizer Noah Karvelis for *Critical Education*, Arrendondo said, "So for me, it was very important to ask, 'How do I connect with the leaders?'" ("Rural Organizing" 97). Then again, Yuma educators became disconnected as the movement shifted focus toward electing education-friendly political candidates and legislation. In 2018, AEU had around two thousand liaisons across the state. The next year, the number dropped to five hundred. As Karvelis described in discussion with Arrendondo, "these rallies for candidates and the efforts to pass the #InvestInEd ballot initiative to increase public education funding after the walkout. They just didn't have the same energy." ("Rural Organizing" 100). For Arrendondo, part of the reason the momentum was lost was because they shifted away from the focus on AEU's and the state association's five demands: a twenty percent salary increase, the restoration of education funding to 2008 levels, competitive pay for all support staff, permanent salary including annual raises, and no new tax cuts (The Republic Staff).

Invest in Ed emerged in the aftermath of the walkouts as an initiative of the AEA. It sought to employ lobbying strategies and rallies to push for the passage of Proposition 208. The proposition, which eventually passed in November 2020, restored hundreds of millions of funding for K–12 public education. However, with this shift away from the original demands and toward legislative advocacy, Karvelis and Arrendondo felt that the movement lost much of the original power. Arrendondo attributed this loss and departure as a shift away from directly engaging rank-and-file members in articulating "what they want" and that a return of this energy would require "going back to the members":

> It didn't matter what political party you were. We all believe in the same thing and look at what we were able to do as a grassroots movement with people that had never, including myself, had never been involved in politics. It didn't matter that I didn't have any experience in anything or even how to freaking work an Excel sheet. When we focused on education, it was so powerful. I just have such a hard time letting go of that. It was so powerful. Oh, how do we get back to that?! Because listen—we were able to do something special. ("Rural Organizing" 101)

Here, Arrendondo describes a value that has become core to the emerging efforts toward social movement or social justice unionism across the nation and transnationally: union democratization.

Scholars of social justice caucuses and social movement unionism have articulated the ways in which union democratization in education exists in tension with social movement unionists' efforts to articulate common good and social justice demands for economic, immigrant, and racial justice, among other issues. Unlike West Virginia and similarly to Kentucky, Arizona educator organizers' efforts to push racial justice demands as common good demands were fraught. In a reflective piece theorizing teacher agency in the 2018 strike, Karvelis writes of this tension:

> As one teacher organizer put it during a discussion on centering race, gender, and common good in our demands: "We just can't do that here. Arizona isn't ready for that." This tacit logic dominated the decisions made in Arizona despite many of the organizers, myself included, stated goal of social justice-oriented movement work. This demonstrates that, despite its initial existence outside of the political logics of Arizona, the movement still embraced the tactics of past movements and the inherently understood political limits that exist in the state. There seemed to be an almost unspoken, self-disciplined understanding among activists that some topics and actions were simply off limits. ("Towards a Theory of Teacher Agency" 3)

In her study of the internal organizing practices of New York's Movement of Rank-and-File Educators (MORE) and Philadelphia's Caucus of Working Educa-

R&C

tors (WE), Chloe Asselin describes this as "the extension dilemma," (24). In their efforts to put forward social justice demands, social movement unionists navigate tensions that arise through fears that both fellow (predominantly White) educators and the wider public may be turned off by racial justice frames, while color-blind economic justice frames seemed more appealing.

In Arizona, and other states, the speed with which educators mobilized did not offer much time for the kinds of political education and community-based organizing undertaken by many groups of educators in union caucuses that resulted in social justice-oriented demands (Maton; Maton and Stark; Nuñez et al.; Stark), as Karvelis and others sought to consider. However, studies of social movement unionism illuminate its critical importance. Evidenced by both the prominent battles for ethnic studies and against the criminalization of undocumented immigrants, the state's disinvestment in Latinx-majority public education students is inextricably entwined with the stoking of unfounded White fears of minoritization and loss of power. Such fears have been mobilized to justify austerity policies, efforts to criminalize ethnic studies, and increased policing and surveillance of Latinx communities.

O Oklahoma: Indigenous-led, Latinx-led, and Black-led Movements for Education Justice

In Oklahoma, like in Arizona, instances of more formal rank-and-file organization, like that of OTU, emerged relatively quickly in the months leading up to the statewide strike. Unlike many WE members' years of engagement in community relationship-building and book studies and inquiry groups, which contributed to many members' racial justice problem framing and, thus, the caucus' organizational commitment to racial justice, the predominant problem frame (Maton) that emerged was one that centered on raising taxes on the state's extractive industries and increasing education funding and resources. Formal efforts on the part of rank-and-file educators and the state's unions were largely disconnected from both community-based education justice organizations and from the far more racially diverse and working-class support staff.

Without such relationships, the OEA, its locals, and the tenuous rank-and-file organizations continued a history of avoiding/marginalizing the problem frames of BIPOC educators and community organizations. Such problem frames have long existed through the legacies of Black teacher organizing in the OANT and OEA, Native community-based and educator-led efforts for indigenizing education and in undocumented youth-led efforts for racial and immigrant justice in education. Citizens United for a Better Education System (CUBES) offers an important example in the context of Tulsa, one of the state's two largest school districts. Due in large part to the diligent record-keeping of CUBES leader, Darryl Bright, and the combined cumulative historical and movement knowledge of the predominantly Black elders who make up its leadership, the organization published an extensive report in 2015 documenting Tulsa Public

Schools' "improvement initiatives" for predominantly Black (and increasingly Latinx) North Tulsa schools since desegregation, 1954 to 2013 (Commission on Educational Reinvention). Drawing on oral history interviews, district reports and communications, meeting notes, and other records, CUBES recounts decades of concerted community exclusion from articulating the educational needs and strategies for a just education of the city's African American students.

CUBES formed in 1987 after then-TPS Superintendent Larry Zenke sought to close and consolidate several North Tulsa schools. CUBES, together with the local chapter of the NAACP, ministers, parents, and students boycotted (a sort of community strike) on April 4, 1988. Ministers organized their churches as "schools for the day" during the boycott (Commission on Educational Reinvention ii). Since its initial formation, CUBES and its webs of community organizations have continued to fight against school closures and consolidations, most recently the 2019 closure of Gilcrease Elementary School and consolidation of Monroe Demonstration Academy (BWST Staff). Such closures, consolidations, and charter takeovers of Tulsa Public Schools have been intensified under the leadership of the current superintendent, Deborah Gist, a graduate of the neoliberalist Eli and Edythe Broad Foundation's Broad Academy (Casey).

Accompanying this chronology, the CUBES' Commission on Educational Reinvention report offers a call to reinvent (rather than reform) the education of African American young people. The TCTA has maintained a close working relationship with Superintendent Gist, who has systematically ignored CUBES leaders' calls for a stop to the closure and charterization of North Tulsa schools. Even so, CUBES articulates a vision for public education that understands the necessity of the pedagogical expertise and (accountable) professional autonomy of educators: "The purpose of education must be defined by a collective process that includes a deliberative discourse by educators, with authentic engagement and input from all levels of the District and from grassroots community groups and individuals" (Commission on Educational Reinvention vi). The report articulates an educational vision that centers "interdisciplinary knowledge," authentic and student-centered learning, and understands students as capable of "contribut[ing] something of value to their schools and communities now; and realize that they don't have to wait until they have a college degree, become 'wealthy' or become a 'grown-up'" (ix). CUBES envisions a curriculum that is culturally and linguistically relevant and addresses the "root causes" of racist and systemic inequality (x). Since 1987, CUBES has fought to be heard in the district's decision-making process and to enact their vision for North Tulsan education.

While problem frames resonant with CUBES were present in many individual Oklahoma educators' analyses of the intertwinement of race, school funding, and de-professionalization issues, these frames were absent in the unions' or emerging rank-and-file groups' official problem framing. For example, Oklahoma has one of the highest rates of incarceration in the nation and globe at 1,097 people incarcerated for every 100,000 people, with Black Oklahomans imprisoned at a rate nearly four times that of White residents (Prison Policy Initiative). On

P&C

signs at the rallies and all over the movement's Facebook pages, educators called on the state to "fund schools, not prisons" (Blanc, "Rank-and-File Organizing"). The sentiment makes important connections between the rise of prisons and policing and the decline of public education funding. However, the phrase can also mask the ways in which educational policy and practice is enmeshed with the policies and practices of policing and prisons (Meiners, "Right to be Hostile"). As CUBES demonstrates, community-based movements in North Tulsa do not want just any public education, they want to realize a specific vision that values and centers North Tulsa communities' visions and desires rather than systematically exclude them in favor of profitable education management organizations and private curriculum companies. Unions' and educators' lack of engagement with community-based organizations like CUBES or others in the formulation of demands have alienated many of Oklahoma's educators of color from their unions.

Stephanie Price's story offers an illustrative example of how anti-racist organizing is necessary to strengthen educator labor movements. Prior to the walkouts, Price, a speech-language pathologist in Moore Public Schools (at the time), had little involvement with her union local, The Education Association of Moore (TEAM). She recounted experiencing racism often in her work:

> Personally, I felt that people made comments that were very insensitive, that were racist. Dealing with micro aggressions, things like, "I saw the movie,"–not me, but a co-worker telling me they had seen the movie, *Selma*, and knowing that some of that had happened, but not realizing the entirety of it. And then proceeding to tell me that they weren't sure why Black people needed African American History Month because it was a long time ago, and we should just get over it. Things like when people were protesting in the streets of Ferguson over police brutality, being told Black people are always overreacting. So comments like those over the span of several years that I just kind of took on and never said anything about, and when I did ask for help, I didn't feel that I got the response that I needed or wanted.

These experiences encouraged Price to join TEAM's Committee for Racial and Ethnic Minorities (CREM). In CREM, Price found mentorship and community with other Black women educators who had similar experiences.

CREM was formed initially as a joint minority issues committee within the union to bring issues of racial and cultural diversity to light in the district. Price said, "Essentially a group of people recognizing that there were inequities, and that things could be better, and coming together to figure out how to make that happen. At some point before I became a member of the group, CREM started to do work that was focused on primarily racial justice."

For Price, CREM was an initial steppingstone, the walkouts were another. Price's experience illuminates that rank-and-file-led unionist efforts toward anti-racism can be a way in for many BIPOC and otherwise marginalized educators to become active participants in their unions. "It was because of the walkout and the steps leading up to the walkout that I became involved in the union," Price said. She was energized by the uprising and found meaningful community in left-leaning educators she met, locally and beyond. After the walkouts, Price became the vice president of TEAM during the 2019/2020 school year, continuing to work with CREM to push for racial justice issues in Moore Public Schools, including culturally relevant and anti-racist trainings for district administrators and educators. Through her connections and relationships with educator organizers across the nation, Price became an organizer with National Educators United (NEU), which seeks to cohere and support statewide rank-and-file educator organizations that emerged out of the spring 2018 walkouts.

Price was one of several urban metro area educators galvanized by the strike who attempted to build something like an urban educator caucus across the Oklahoma City and Tulsa areas via the NEA's National Council of Urban Education Associations. However, internal dynamics and territorialism from existing unions stalled the effort. One of the reasons Price was drawn to organize for NEU was because the group centered issues of racial and justice in their work—in fact, it is the first set of three broad demands they list in their literature and website (NEU Website). Finding little support, for more justice-oriented approaches to organizing, and continuing to experience racism on top of many other workplace issues compounded by the pandemic, Price eventually left the state of Oklahoma altogether.

● Conclusion

West Virginia, Kentucky, Oklahoma, and Arizona have vastly different political geographies and histories that inform responses to social and scientific efficiency movements in education. Even as the contemporary rank-and-file movements have won widespread attention through their militant actions, it is important to understand these as one part of a broader terrain of movements that seek to address historical and complex injustices wrought on communities by and through the education system. Conservative legislators' efforts in each of these places to implement educational gag orders that censor and whitewash classroom texts and curricula (PEN America) have created a culture of fear and surveillance for all educators in recent years. The fervor to implement these laws should be read as, in part, a response to and an effort to dampen the resurgence in educator militancy in recent years.

Price's story, the exclusion of Louisville educators and anti-racist issues from KY 120, and the resistance Arizona's educators experienced in trying to center social justice issues illuminates that colorblind approaches to organizing serve to weaken contemporary educator movements, in practice and analysis. White supremacist and settler colonial logics are at the heart of the states' most oppressive efforts to disinvest in its public education system. While colorblind approaches may (at least temporarily) draw in the support of White educators, it alienates many BIPOC and justice-oriented educators. Educator movements lose out on the rich knowledge, passionate commitments, and relational resources of community-based movement organizations, like CUBES, Yuma's community leaders, or Kentucky's BLM-related organizations. Further, color-blind approaches to unionism obfuscate how White supremacy and settler colonialism operate in, through, and against the public education system in ways that disproportionately effect BIPOC teachers, students, and communities *and* depress all, including White educators', wages and working conditions.

Chapter 3. Ungrateful Teenagers and Misbehaving Women

On the second day of the 2018 Oklahoma educators' strike, then-governor Mary Fallin made a now-infamous public comment at a press conference: "Teachers want more, but it's kind of like a teenage kid who wants a better car" (News on 6). Some educators' responses employed a common refrain used to justify the shutdown. As Liz Hogget, Norman Public Schools educator said when asked for a response by the Washington Post, "We're doing this for our kids" (Villafranca). For many Oklahoma educators and beyond, the emphasis on striking "for the kids" was both true and a discursive strategy to ensure public support and avoid (gendered) non-producerist tropes (i.e., "teachers are lazy," "teachers want more money for less work"). Many educators sought (and felt pressure) to appear as though their demands for livable wages were second and inconsequential to their demands for increased education funding. Many educators felt they walked a thin line for such public support, as teaching, like domestic and socially reproductive work generally, is often under-waged or unwaged (women's) work (Brown and Stern). In practice, however, the day after Fallin made the comment, masses of protesting educators packed inside the Capitol building and erupted in a much more confrontational response. Jingling their keys and following Fallin as she walked up the stairs to her office, they chanted in collective anger, "Where's my car? Where's my car?" (Gstalter). One teacher participant posted a video of the event on Twitter and conveyed her strong emotional response to the spontaneous collective rebuke to the governor. "I'm crying," she wrote.

Fallin wasn't the only politician to excoriate the boldness of predominantly women militant educators. State representative Kevin McDugle experienced an uncomfortable moment of fame after a visit to a high school class just before the walkouts. Students pegged him with questions and shared what became a viral social media video in which he proclaimed that he would not vote "for another stinking measure when [teachers] are acting the way they are acting," despite his previous self-stated support of educator-friendly legislation in the year prior (Williams and Hosseini). While neither state leader mentions gender, directly, educators have experienced a long and ongoing history of paternalistic infantilization and rigid gendered expectations of appropriate feminine behavior that have aimed to discipline women's labor dispositions and militancy.

Today, women comprise 98.7 percent of all pre-kindergarten and kindergarten educators, 80.5 percent of all elementary and middle school educators, 56.5 percent of all secondary educators, and 86.7 percent of all special education educators (BLS). At the same time, "nearly half of all principals, including two-thirds of high school principals and three-fourths of superintendents, are men" (Russom). In higher education, while the majority of all tenure track faculty are men, women comprise the majority of part-time (53.8 percent) and full-time (53.9

percent) contingent faculty positions, and women faculty overall earn ten to twenty percent less than men (Colby and Fowler 2). Despite this, in the literatures on educator unionism, few examine in-depth the gendered relations of education labor organizing. Urban's historical account of gender, race, and the history of the NEA, Kate Rousmaniere's writing on the life and work of Margaret Haley, whose leadership and organizing initiative created one of the first educator unions in Chicago at the start of the twentieth century, and Jackie Blount's work on gender/ sexuality and school workers are a few notable exceptions. Many other writings on educator unions and union struggles may mention gender or the contributions of people like Haley or, more recently, Karen Lewis in stoking militant social movement unionism. Yet, less commonly is gender engaged as a central lens of analysis in the history and present of an historically feminized employment sector and a majority women union composition (Brown and Stern).

Since the more widespread resurgence of militant and social justice unionism after the 2011 Wisconsin educator sickouts and the 2012 CTU strike (Buhle and Buhle; Hagopian and Green), an emerging body of scholarship and writing has sought to describe and make sense of this new era of rank-and-file militancy. As we highlighted in previous chapters, anti-collaborationist solidarity- and social movement-focused approaches are not new. Yet the early twenty-first century has certainly marked a turning point after the previous four decades of the combined repression of educator militancy, educational austerity, and the delimiting of educators' pedagogical agency in the forms of mandated corporate curricula, high stakes testing, and school privatization.

Studies of the histories of Southern Black educator organizing illuminate the key significance of gender and women's work in professionalist approaches to educator organizing (V. S. Walker). For Black educator organizing in the North and South, BIPOC women excluded from and marginalized by White teachers' unions sought community-based forms of educator professionalism. The history of the NEA illuminates that, while its origins were rooted strongly in the leadership of predominantly men administrators and academics, it relied on a resounding majority women membership base and was significantly shaped over time by rank-and-file women- and queer-led organizing from within the organization who sought union democratization and the prioritization of women's and queer people's grievances in the workplace (Blount; M. Murphy; Urban). And rank-and-file women educators across the nation, like Margaret Haley and the Chicago Federation of Teachers (CFT), organized caucuses and unions driven by communalistic, feminist, and class struggle orientations to educator labor and socio-political responsibility (Blount; M. Murphy). Conservative professionalist or singularly class-centric analyses of the histories and ongoing present of educator unionism can diminish the ways in which both race and gender animate the structuring and experience of class and class exploitation.

In the context of higher education, college and university faculty have been predominantly men, historically. As women have entered the ranks of the faculty since the 1970s, so has the casualization of faculty employment increased. While contingent, non-tenure track faculty employment was utilized as a stop-gap measure by college and university administrations during the economic crises of the 1970s, shifts toward part-time and low wage academic employment have, in the past few decades, constituted a drastic restructuring of higher education labor. Women and contingent faculty of color represent the majority of casualized labor (Schell). In many places within higher education, contingent faculty are overrepresented in disciplines and departments that more often undertake "care" labor, e.g., undergraduate general education areas like composition courses in English and public speaking in communication studies, and, of course, departments of teacher education, in particular early childhood and elementary education). In the context of writing studies, a site within higher education that has been both the source of intense casualization and adjunct faculty organizing, Eileen Schell writes:

> [W]omen are thought to be particularly good at delivering the kind of care work associated with teaching writing or providing language instruction: painstakingly poring over drafts and making comments, tutoring and administering writing centers and writing programs, holding one-on-one conferences, offering informal advising and support for students struggling with writing and with adjusting to the higher education environment, especially first-generation college students, students of color, international students, and women students. (xv)

Within these sites, women have often been on the forefront of organizing to address the disparities experienced by feminized contingent faculty, advocating for feminist and social justice approaches. For example, contingent faculty labor activists, Sue Doe and colleagues forefront the affective dimensions of organizing. They caution against "[m]easuring success by a limited set of predetermined outcomes [which] can cause activists to overlook important work that is not readily measurable." Doing so can have the effect of delimiting organizing work within "the pervasive, market-driven language of productivity" (214). For the authors, such an approach is hegemonically patriarchal. Rather, they suggest that "social change is spurred by and maintained through emotion," and it gains legitimacy among workers via centering the stories of educators' lived realities and attachments (217).

Histories of educator unions illuminate the struggles of women, in particular BIPOC women, to fight for power within their unions, and in so doing, as Doe and colleagues advocate, they have engaged in particular forms of organizing. More often, women-led and feminist-oriented movements within union organizing sought coalitional approaches, engaged families and community, developed practices of mutual aid and care, and more often avoided more public positions of celebritized movement leader (which, historically, were positions predominantly held by men) in favor of less hierarchical and more horizontalist approaches.

Through an in-depth examination of Oklahoma, we illuminate that educator organizing within and on the periphery of established unions in the 2018 strikes is both a continuation of and historically specific gendered dynamics of power.

● Women and Gender/Sexual Minorities Negotiating Power in Hostile Territory

During the educator uprisings in 2018, Bhattacharya wrote that women educators were building a new labor movement: "These are women fighting for dignity and security in the most commodious sense of those terms. Their gender is not incidental to this strike, their narratives of fear about their families and health, are not backstories to what is merely a wage struggle" ("Women Are Leading the Wave"). Bhattacharya aimed to bring much needed attention to the gender politics of the education strikes, noting that women disproportionately undertake the caregiving labor in their families, schools, and communities. More commonly, the 2018 educator strikes were narrated as popular uprisings, class struggle, and/or a struggle of college-educated professionals for dignified wages and respect. Similarly, gender and sexual politics (through which socially reproductive labor is contested and disciplined) is not incidental to educator organizing but fundamentally shapes its theory and practice (Russom).

Crys Brunner writes that battle metaphors are pervasive as descriptors of teacher activists and leaders: teachers on the frontlines, as warriors, in the trenches, fighting for educational reform and the common good. For Brunner, they "are warriors because they fight for children; they are also warriors because they have entered a domain from which they and their beliefs have been historically excluded" (as cited in Abowitz and Rousmaniere 239). For Abowitz and Rousnamiere, Brunner's conceptualization of women teacher activists and leaders as warriors is important in two key ways. First, it acknowledges how "women leaders negotiate power in a hostile territory that is not of their own making," within the conditions and decision-making of education and within established educator unions that seek to exert influence upon it (239). Secondly, Brunner's conceptualization of the "warrior" challenges pervasive sentimentalization of women teachers as self-sacrificing caregivers and, instead, draws on longer traditions of feminist organizing within unions and education. Abowitz's and Rousmaniere's description of such a model, in which they draw on feminist political theorist Lauren Berlant's notion of the diva citizen, is worth quoting at length:

> The history of women's political participation and activism is typically narrated as cooperative, relational work that is characterized by solidarity and the communal networks which embed the single activist in a larger associational web (see Eisler, 1987; Welch, 1990). As progressive educators, we go against the grain to hold up a model of political activism and leadership that is characterized in part by its acknowledgment of the benefits of individual strength and the singular ambition to influence others. While we understand the limits of the diva citizen–progressive politics cannot survive without cooperative, communal models of political work–there are many moments in schools and in public life at large that call for the diva's assertive, near domineering power. Diva citizens

work for the good of others. Originating outside of power, their motivation is to make power available to others from the margins. They have a
strong understanding and respect for the everyday struggle of everyday
people, and their leadership is informed by resistance strategies and a
"logic of survival" intended to obtain dignity for ordinary people amongst
the institutions and policies they did not build (Bettina Aptheker quoted
in Jones 114–116). (Abowitz and Rousmaniere 243)

With Abowitz and Rousmaniere, we suggest (the marginalized) histories of
traditions of women, feminist, and queer organizing that have shaped educator unions and movements helps us to understand such "cooperative, commu-
nal modes of political work" as distinct and in-tension with (heteropatriarchal)
modes of organizing that rely on centralization of authority and hierarchy. Further, these histories offer important examples of diva citizen leaders who work
to "make power available to others."

In highlighting feminist traditions of organizing within historically feminized education labor, we continue to foreground that traditions and instances
of feminist organizing are not homogenous, but are situated with relation to race,
class, and geography, among other intersections. In noting gendered differences
in modes of organizing, we do not seek to suggest that all women and queer educators organize to "make power available to others," or that historical instances
of feminist organizing are uncomplicated by White supremacy, compulsory
heterosexuality, or patriarchy. Catherine Beecher, as one prominent example,
advocated strongly for the mass hiring of women as teachers during the late
nineteenth century. A class-privileged White woman, she argued for the proliferation of common schooling in the service of nation-building and successfully
made the case that women could be paid much less than men (Grumet). And,
within early feminist-oriented educator union movements, White women leaders foregrounded ethnic and class solidarities yet perpetuated anti-Black racism.
Rousmaniere's racial biography of Margaret Haley details the Chicago Federation of Teachers (CFT) class-struggle-oriented founder's White silence and
exclusion of the city's growing number of Black educators from the CFT. Rousmaniere articulates a context in which Haley's class struggle unionism for White
elementary school teachers, even in the face of her own experiences of ethnic
discrimination as an Irish Catholic, refused to understand the racial capitalist
exploitation of Black workers by industrialists and politicians (11). Her own racist ideologies created long-standing legacies within Chicago's educator unions
that created tension (rather than solidarity) with Black social movements in the
city's schools and communities, "limiting efforts [for anti-racist work]" (Lowe,
cited in Rousmaniere, "White Silence" 13).

Along the lines of Blount, we seek to illuminate that the experiences of rank-
and-file women, gender minorities, and queer educators in their unions and
workplaces have been shaped by particular gendered/sexualized experiences
of exploitation. From the disciplining power of binaristic gender and normative

heterosexual kinship relations, women and queer educators have, often of necessity, birthed alternative forms of power to survive and fight for a more just world (Blount; Quinn and Meiners).

● Gender and Educators' Work

The history and ongoing dynamic legacies of the genderization and feminization of educators' work coupled with historically shifting social conceptions and policing of sexuality and sexual identity, have always impacted and shaped practices of educator organizing. Blount, historian of gender, sexuality, and school workers, writes that schools have always been and are "gender-polarized places," and places where educators were/are tasked by social and political authorities to police and nurture "proper" gender roles and sexual behaviors/identities among school workers (1). As common schooling proliferated in the late nineteenth century, gendering educators' work became a strategy mobilized on multiple fronts to exploit and control women's labor for low wages (Albisetti; Grumet; Strober and Tyack). Women's early pedagogical traditions (starkly different from the militaristic style of many men teachers) and organizing (for equal pay, for community responsibility, to be able to work after marriage and/or pregnancy) were often met with gendered/sexualized retaliation (Bailey and Graves; Blount).

In the early twentieth century, as teaching became "women's work," educator organizing was often fraught with gendered notions of labor value. Often, men (high school) teachers would not support women (elementary school) teachers in efforts to equalize pay across grade levels. At the time, as teaching became staunchly feminized, school administration became decidedly masculinized. In part, the development of the hierarchical administrative structure of schooling was firmly rooted in policing women in public space. According to Blount, as early women educators became teachers of co-educational spaces, opponents circulated fears of their supposed inability to successfully discipline boys, especially adolescents. Blount writes,

> Typically they used persuasion and other nonviolent means of maintaining discipline. Experts eventually conceded that women generally seemed to have as good, if not better, results with their disciplinary practices than many men who resorted to corporal punishment and intimidation. Word quickly spread that women teachers governed their classrooms effectively. (23)

With an increasing number of women living independently and "exerting authority in a public place," fears arose that women were becoming too independent, and perhaps, "that they may not need men." From these fears arose the position of the superintendency, a means for men to serve as a "gender-regulating presence" (23). Many early superintendents were not experienced educators yet supervised women's work and were paid significantly more to do so.

In 1920, women teachers comprised eighty-six percent of all teachers, and ninety-one percent of all women teachers were single women (or seventy-eight percent of the total teacher workforce) (Blount 59). In unprecedented ways, teaching and nursing offered working- and middle-class women a means toward self-subsistence without reliance on a husband's or family's income. Blount recounts the ways in which women school workers were able, in ways previously limited, to live differently: in shared housing and kinship that pushed social boundaries of mentorship, knowledge-sharing, and socialization beyond the watchful eyes of patriarchs. The rise of the eugenicist movement and the spread of White supremacist fears surrounding the decline of White college-educated women's rates of marriage and reproduction created policies and practices that sought to staunch women's ability to live independently of heteronormative family structures. In 1929, a writer in a popular periodical of the time shared an increasingly common sentiment:

> In two ways, at least, these women [spinsters] are all alike, both marked with one stamp. They do not have a normal social life, no matter how good a time they may be having, and they do not have a normal release for the deepest emotions in them, which may therefore, either atrophy or nurture them or find an unnatural and illicit outlet. (Banning cited in Blount 67)

From the 1920s to the 1940s, the rise of the science of sexology and eugenics created social associations between spinsterhood and lesbianism. Coupled with educator organizing, locally and on the part of the NEA, to challenge districts to change policies that banned married women from teaching (among other post-WWII labor shifts) and the genderization/sexualization of single women teachers as diminutively "queer" and abnormal, the demographics of women teaching shifted from majority single to majority married by the 1960s (Blount).

During this era, as women gained access and influence within public space, (predominantly men-authored) research on teaching and teachers' work tended to emphasize uncertainty as to how the increasing numbers of women teachers would impact the socialization of boys and normative masculinity (Bailey and Graves). During the war years, women took up superintendency positions (usually as long as there were no possible men candidates) in greater numbers. After the war, women were pushed out from administration in large numbers as men returned from overseas and sought out civilian jobs (Blount). At the same time, qualities desirable in administrators increasingly drew on certain ways of understanding "masculine": athletic, military experience, and family patriarch. In 1946, one district gushed over its new "ideal" administrator: "The man selected could not be labeled as an effeminate being. He was a former collegiate athletic hero. His physique was comparable to any of the mythical Greek gods. He was truly the ultimate in manliness. The last, but not least in importance of his personal characteristics, was the fact that he was married" (Blount 84). Rank-and-file (majority single) women educators' organizing in the early twentieth century through the 1930s, alongside broader rising labor, anti-racist, and socialist movements, often marked by bloody struggles in the streets and picket lines (S. Smith), among other threats to the status quo of power, produced a retaliatory moral panic on multiple fronts. The post-war years saw a structural repression and push-out of single women, queer, and socialist and communist educators and intensified pressures to police the roles of gender and sexual identity and behavior in schools (Blount).

Scholarly and popular writing on gender, sex, and teachers' work in the first half of the twentieth century tended to focus singularly and only implicitly on White middle class women, "render[ing] Whiteness invisible and foreground[ing] gender as a unidimensional concept rather than a site of intersectional and multidimensional meanings imbued with racialized, classed, and religious standpoints (among others)" (Bailey and Graves 692). As historians of the formation of the common schooling system and interrelated social institutions, i.e., the juvenile justice system, White wealthy women socially organized to wield influence over the development of such institutions driven by (still persistent) motivations to correct the "culture of poverty" (Wolcott). In such a frame, the problem of education is rooted in the "poor" behavior of working class and racialized students, families, and communities. Alternatively, many rank-and-file women and queer educators who organized to exert influence via unions and professional associations recognized the material conditions and challenges facing urban and rural communities during the peak of industrialization and its decline (Blount; M. Murphy).

Gender inequity in teaching and teachers' work is historically complex, intersectional, and cannot be mapped neatly along a progressive timeline. Rather, as Blount writes, "current conditions have developed in specific historical contexts" and struggles (11). As Blount and other historians of educator organizing illuminate, the collective organization and influence of women and gender/sexual minorities in education-related struggles have emerged and waned within specific conditions and were challenged within and beyond historically heteropatriarchal educator unions. By understanding the longer, deeper story of gender/sexuality and educator organizing, we can see gendered differences in theories of power and change put forth by educator organizers, whether within frames of professionalist, trade, solidarity, or social movement approaches to unionism.

● Rank-and-File Women and Queer Educators' Community-Based Approach

Scholars of teachers' unions and teachers work illuminate that the NEA has existed as a historically patriarchal organization with efforts in key points of its history on the part of predominantly women teachers to democratize and wield influence in the interest of rank-and-file educators (rather than men administrators). Early on, the NEA operated mainly as a teacher institute, where predominantly women schoolteachers would convene to listen to lectures provided by men academic educational experts. Growing increasingly agitated by the

NEA's centralization and bolstered by local organizing of, especially, elementary school urban educators, rank-and-file predominantly women teachers organized a teachers' rebellion within the organization in various eras of its existence, the earliest at the turn of the twentieth century.

During this time of industrialization, urban educators and students experienced difficult teaching and learning conditions that mirror, in many ways, today's struggles: overly-prescriptive curriculum; few resources; untenably large class sizes; and corporate evasion of tax contributions that would appropriately fund education. Marjorie Murphy writes of the gendered significance in women educators' organizing approaches:

> The women proposed their own vision of education that was based on experience in the classroom as opposed to university credit; they thought that knowing the community was more important than satisfying the top administrative personnel. In the beginning the women did not regard their battle as being particularly feminist; instead they modeled their cry for human dignity on the example set by the trade unions. Eventually, however, as the educational stage became more contested, they responded more self-consciously as working women and identified the inherent sexism in the educational establishment (53).

Through militancy and collective bargaining women educators (especially elementary level educators who bore the brunt of under- and unpaid care work in schools) sought to challenge the ways in which women teachers were tasked with solving the issues of systemic failure via the extraction of their supposed infinite reserves of emotional, intellectual, and physical labor (Shelton).

For Urban, the NEA's origins in promoting a professionalist approach existed at odds with, and predominated because of, the more men-dominated militancy of trade unionism. Urban suggests that the NEA catered to women teachers' needs and issues in strategically rhetorical yet insubstantial ways for much of its pre-union (pre-1960s) existence. Yet as both Urban and M. Murphy demonstrate in their respective historical studies of the NEA and AFT, the early twentieth century saw a women-led teachers' rebellion within the NEA to decentralize leadership and decision-making, and to push the organization toward trade unionism rather than (White) professionalist respectability.

While Margaret Haley is one of the more well-known figures in initiating and leading women teachers to organize labor unions in the early twentieth century, M. Murphy notes that women-led efforts among primarily elementary school teachers took place in cities across the country. Three thousand teachers organized in local federations and delegations from Milwaukee, St. Paul, St. Louis, New York, Washington, and Philadelphia, among other places. They joined Haley and the Chicago Federation of Teachers at a 1904 Boston NEA meeting to express their frustrations with its administrator-led conservatively professionalist orientations. M. Murphy writes of one speaker, an elementary school teacher, from one of these delegations, who spoke to "enthusiastic applause":

> "[H]igh salaried officials who direct the destinies of the National Educa-
> tion Association ... point out the way to educational perfection for the
> benefit of teachers who receive extremely low salaries." Yet this latter
> class, which [the speaker] termed "the silent partners," had to "pay the
> bills for the support of the association in the main." (57)

At the same meeting, Haley spoke of the need to push for more labor-oriented
forms of organization and "insisted that industrial workers and teachers had a
common cause 'in their struggle to secure the rights of humanity through a more
just and equitable distribution of the products of their labor'" (M. Murphy 58).
Likely, these early efforts of women educator's union militancy and organization
existed in relation to the increasingly eugenicist derogation of White spinsters as
gender/sexual deviants.

Despite the efforts, women educators did not succeed in decentralizing decision-making within the NEA nor shifting its organizational focus toward the
issues that motivated rank-and-file women educators to organize (M. Murphy;
Urban). It was not until decades later, 1960–1973, the NEA experienced a dramatic shift from professional organization to union. In the 1950s and 1960s, the
NEA's national leadership was predominantly White men "often with minimal
experience in the schools," with an organizational structure that diminished the
practical power of the elected representative assembly and centralized decision-making among staff (Urban 171). Around this time, state-level affiliates similarly were dominated by men administrators "who agreed with the NEA staff in
their suspicions about teacher power. The two groups [state affiliate leaders and
NEA staff] together managed to exercise an effective veto over NEA policies and
actions they considered undesirable, especially the establishment of any independent teacher voice" (172).

While Urban wrote his history of the NEA in 2000, his analysis of the NEA's
role in the burgeoning teacher militancy of the 1960s seems prescient in relation to the 2018 strikes. He writes, "While these [1960s New York City teachers'
strikes], like most strikes, originated in local conditions and were affected primarily by local circumstances and concerns, the failure of the NEA to respond
effectively to those conditions and circumstances for its own national organizational advancement" significantly shaped its history in the 1960s (172).

Urban suggests that there is consensus among analysts of this era that the
increasing influence of militant urban secondary educator organizers, more
often men, catalyzed the NEA's shift from professional organization to union.
Yet, M. Murphy disagrees with prioritizing gender over other factors of militancy,
namely generational differences. The post-war years saw an influx of younger men
into high school teaching, dramatically shifting the gender and age demographics
in secondary education: "36.2 percent of secondary teachers but only 25.5 percent
of elementary school teachers were under thirty years of age" (220). Further, M.
Murphy found that few, if any, of the analysts of the rise of teacher militancy in the
1960s knew of or engaged the history of the early years of teachers' union organiz-

ing. "[T]heir oversight of the contribution of the women to the revival of militancy in the union reinforced the stereotypes about women [as anti-militancy]" (221).

The literature (mainly from the area of labor-management relations) aiming to understand the demographic characteristics of attitudinal militancy in the 1960s–1980s supports M. Murphy's assertion that gendering militancy as masculine or the domain of men in this era is problematic. Conducting a study of five hundred twenty-four elementary and eight hundred sixteen secondary teachers in 1990 and an extensive review of decades of research, Samuel Bacharach and colleagues argue that "militancy of this type is best understood as an outcome of the teachers' poor integration into the school organizations in which they work, rather than as an outcome of the demographic characteristics of teachers or the geographic location of their school" (584). In 1989, Williams and Leonard analyzed a survey of four hundred fifty elementary and secondary teachers in Mississippi and found that women were more likely to support collective action than men. In other words, workplace conditions were likely the most pressing factor for militancy in this era.

Like M. Murphy, Blount argues that histories of queer educator unionist leaders have been largely erased from studies of school workers and worker organizing. Prior to the national eruption of social movements for gay liberation, notably inspired by the Stonewall Rebellion in 1969, the firing of gay and lesbian (and suspected gay and lesbian) educators were often isolated, quiet incidents (Blount). Spurred by the momentum of the gay liberation movement in the 1960s and 1970s, queer educators across the nation had been increasingly organizing against their unjust termination. For example, in 1972, John Gish, a New Jersey high school English teacher formed the NEA's first Gay Caucus. In his words:

> Most gay teachers are known to be gay, or are assumed to be gay, by their students and Boards of Education. Just as long as nothing is said, the system tolerates them. I'm fed up with lying to them. I'm tired of using women to accompany me to proms so that a "proper" image is preserved. I'm tired of listening to anti-gay jokes in the faculty room and being forced to laugh with the straights (Blount 115).

Gish, along with several other teachers organizing within their unions and communities were fired for organizing for the rights of gay and lesbian teachers to work. Yet, their actions inspired a wave of organizing within state and local unions across the country, most notably in California. "Morgan Pinney and students at San Francisco State University successfully encouraged the California Federation of Teachers to pass an ambitious resolution supporting the rights of homosexual teachers" (Blount 120). In 1974, Gish's Gay Teacher's Caucus passed a similar resolution in the NEA, providing much needed legal resources and support for so many unjustly fired LGBTQ+ educators. In the AFT and New York's UFT, educators had a more difficult time. Longtime leader of the UFT, Albert Shankar, "did not want the UFT to take a public position on the rights of gay teachers, believing the matter to be too divisive" (Blount 124).

The risks for gay and lesbian teacher activists were high, and many, like Gish and others, were pushed out from teaching altogether. Nevertheless, their successes, Blount argues, were due in large part to the broad coalitions and social movement infrastructure that had been developing and building since the 1960s, which made their efforts possible in the first place (Hagopian and Green). In New York's TU, Clarence Taylor documents the differences in women's, and particularly Black women educators', organizing roles and interests among radical socialist and communist educators. He writes, "By means of committees, women focused on community work, creating an alternative path to leadership" (Taylor 516).

For example, Rose Russell, leader of the TU's Legislative and Political Action Committee, "forg[ed] relationships with political figures and labor and civic leaders and by helping to make the union an important player in the fight for civil rights, adequate funding for public schools, and decent pay and improved working conditions for teachers" (Taylor 532). Russell fought tirelessly for academic freedom and against the repression and firing of radical teachers during the red scare era in the 1940s. Lucille Spence created the TU's Harlem Committee, and focused efforts on community-based organizing for intercultural and anti-racist professional development for teachers. Alice Citron, another organizer for the Harlem Committee, fought for African American history and culture programs in the public schools. Mildred Flacks engaged the Harlem Committees modes of "teacher-community relationship" model in Bedford-Stuyvesant, the city's largest Black neighborhood at the time (550). "Women also led the child welfare, library, social, and parents' committees, groups that were important in helping to define the TU's social movement unionism" (556).

Taylor argues that internal political divisions within the TU intensified with McCarthyist repression of its members and contributed to its demise. Its hierarchical and patriarchal leadership's alignment with Soviet Russia existed in contrast with forms of community-based and coalitional social movement work undertaken and led by some of its most effective women leaders and organizers. From the 1930s to the 1940s, women's positions in executive leadership declined, yet women comprised most of the TU's membership. Despite the decline in executive representation, Taylor argues that women sought influence, instead, via organizing committees:

> They helped create alliances with parents, labor, and civil rights groups with the goal of assuring that all children receive the best education possible. Women took the lead in the fight for sufficient funding of schools, the construction of new school buildings, the reduction of class size, the elimination of racially biased textbooks, and academic freedom. Women, like their male colleagues, worked to improve the working conditions of teachers, but they also became vociferous advocates of social movement unionism" (535).

Belinda Robnett argues that TU's women leaders were not notable celebrities in the union (these were mainly men), but rather served as "bridge leaders" who "kept their pulse on the community. The goal of bridge leaders was to gain trust, to bridge the masses to the movement and to act in accord with their constituents' desires." Bridge leaders worked in the "movement's or organization's free spaces, thus, making connections that cannot be made by formal leaders" (Robnett 26–28).

Like Flacks, Citron, and Russell, the most powerful instances of feminist organizing in education arose from analyses that foregrounded the intersections of gender, race, and class. In Oklahoma, Autumn Brown's educational biography of civil rights activist, educator, OEA member, and catalyst for the national sit-in movement, Clara Luper, illuminates the commitments to building Black power, class struggle, and feminist politics that animated her classroom pedagogy and renowned activist work. For Luper, holding down picket lines for striking sanitation workers, gathering members of the NAACP Youth Council in her home to plan direct actions, and cultivating her students' voice and agency were all deeply intertwined. Brown writes that Luper, among other Black women educator activist contemporaries, has had long-lasting legacies that persist and continue to shape local movements. Most often they are remembered for their civil rights activism yet, Brown contends, their contributions to the state's histories of labor and educator movements as educator organizers are marginalized and not well understood.

These histories of gender and education labor provide a foundation from which to analyze the salience of gender in Oklahoma's strike and for cultivating a more robust intersectional analysis and organizing practice.

● Gender as a Salient Lens to Understand the 2018 Oklahoma Strike

Historical understandings of the feminization and heterosexual disciplining of educators' work and the corresponding organizational approaches and efforts on the part of rank-and-file women and queer educators provides an important analytical lens to understand the 2018 strikes. These gendered dynamics existed everywhere in their own situated, specific ways. As Gillian Russom notes in their writing on the resurgence of educator militancy, many rank-and-file women educator organizers understood the strikes as "a gendered rebellion." Russom cites Petia Edison in Kentucky, "I believe women are sick and tired of being sick and tired" (176). Emily Comer of West Virginia stated, "I know it's not just about my paycheck or my healthcare–the worse the economy gets, the harder my job jets, it's more stressful with more emotional burden on the teachers in my building who are mostly women" (178). Los Angeles teacher organizer, Rosa Jimenez: "[The fact that] teachers, mostly women (in LA many women of color), are expected to be teachers, counselors, nurses, nourishment providers, all while taking care of our own children, reflects capitalism's tendency to extract as much labor as possible from someone with the minimum compensation" (178). As

Russom contends, the 2018–2019 educator militancy must be understood within the context of a broader political climate of women-led organizing, including the Black Lives Matter movement, the Women's March, and the emergence of the #MeToo movement.

Eric Blanc's 2019 book-length journalistic narrative of the 2018 strikes in West Virginia, Oklahoma, and Arizona, *Red State Revolt: The Teachers' Strikes and Working Class Politics*, has become an influential and popular text in understanding this particular moment in educator militancy. Blanc's writing has become a lens through which many educators and labor folks have come to understand what took place in Oklahoma. He makes the case that the strikes emerged via (and their success hinged on) a militant minority of socialist educators with political organizing experience. In his narrative of Oklahoma, he predominantly emphasizes the leadership of Alberto Morejon and Larry Cagle as the respective creators and moderators for the state's two largest agitational Facebook pages, TTN and OTU. In twenty-two pages describing the build up to and unfolding of the strike, Morejon and Cagle are described as rank-and-file leaders up against OEA leaders. He writes that the state's educators were "insufficiently organized to overcome the hesitancy of their union leaders [in the OEA]" (163). He goes on to write:

> Nor would it be fair to pin the blame on Morejon and Cagle. As individuals lacking the benefit of any previous organizing experience, they did the best they could to push things forward, and they stuck their necks out, often at great personal cost. Morejon's efforts, in particular, played a critical role in raising educators' desire to fight and in forcing Republican lawmakers to grant teachers a historic pay raise. What was missing in Oklahoma was a team of like-minded grassroots militants, armed with activist know-how, class struggle politics, and an orientation toward working within the unions to push them forward. (163)

In our oral history interviews with more than fifty educators across Oklahoma's rural, suburban, and urban contexts illuminates the complexities of the origins, motivations, and leadership activities that sustained the lead-up to the strike and the action itself. It was, perhaps, true that insufficient organization existed among educators within, on the periphery, or beyond the OEA that could have challenged the union's dissipation of the strike before any real gains could be made, as was the case with West Virginia's wildcat strike. However, the overemphasis on a few, mainly men, leaders can diminish the widespread distributed leadership and labor of the state's predominantly women educators.

Unlike every other state, Oklahoma educators did not gain any progress on their demands during the two-week strike. Immediately prior to the strike, in an effort to avert it, legislators conceded an average of $6,100 wage increase for the state's educators. While this concession was a major victory, they still fell far short of what educators felt would be necessary to adequately address the extreme disparities facing Oklahoma's public schools after so many years of disinvestment. In August 2017, more than five hundred teaching vacancies existed and nearly five hundred teaching positions were eliminated. In the 2017–2018 academic year, the state issued 1,975 emergency certifications, and in 2018–2019, the state issued 3,038–an increase of fifty-four percent in just one year (Eger).

In Oklahoma (and elsewhere) important networks of community relationships were mobilized for mutual aid efforts–relationships rooted in extended kinship networks, local church communities, and social movement networks. The origins of the strike are not easily rooted in the creation of either of the popular Facebook pages (Krutka et al.). Rather, agitational and organizing efforts took place within, on the periphery of (or, at least temporarily, reactivated) local unions that, since the passage of right-to-work legislation, had decreased in activity, operating mainly to negotiate contracts every few years. In smaller towns or less active locals, negotiations often only take place between the president of the local and district administration. The networks of relationships that emerged in the lead-up to and during the strike are, by and large, sustained by the care work of women, mothers, and the organizing efforts of those on the margins of Oklahoma's evangelistic conservative governing ideology that has predominated its electoral offices in recent decades. This ideology has marked Oklahoma as one of the worst states in the US for women's quality of life, taking into consideration women's access to healthcare, employment and pay, violence against women, incarceration rates, among other indicators (Trotter).

A deeper examination illuminates gendered forms of organizing (and retaliation) that contributed to the tenuous organization of Oklahoma's rank-and-file educators. As we emphasize throughout the book, our analysis (and many of our narrators' reflections) exists with the benefit of hindsight that tens of thousands of striking Oklahoma educators did not have in the moment.

● A More Nuanced Retelling of Gendered Leadership in Oklahoma's Strike

As the most prominently featured rank-and-file leaders, Larry Cagle and Alberto Morejon are often written together as similar actors in their social media agitational capacities with key differences in their respective demeanors: where Morejon was more often cast as polite or diplomatic, Cagle and his OTU Facebook group were considered brash and antagonistic. In practice, their approaches and activities were rooted in quite different theories of power and change–Cagle as self-described politically progressive and critical of the OEA's conservatively professionalist approach and Morejon as a more conservative figure invested in electoral politics and ambivalent about unions altogether.

While OTU's mode of organizing relied heavily on persuasion and lighting up the media, Morejon engaged a more conciliatory relationship with OEA (at first), and approached his work as agitator and facts provider, collaborating with OEA leaders to use TTN to communicate updates and information. While OTU had a considerable social media membership (around fourteen thousand), TTN catapulted to nearly one hundred thousand in the lead up to and during the walkouts. Morejon's approach to organizing engaged gathering and distributing information via TTN (in ways that Arizona educators later found helpful and replicated (Garelli)), closed-door discussions with union leaders, and constructing alliances with school administrations, superintendents, and legislators. After the walkouts, Morejon created and distributed informational "grades" for lawmakers to entice TTN followers to vote for the most education-friendly lawmakers, whether Republican or Democrat, met with and endorsed political candidates, and held well-publicized meetings with the State Superintendent, Joy Hofmeister. He was sought after by such figures because of his status as a leader of the educator movement. In May 2020, Morejon lost this status after he was arrested and charged for "making lewd proposals" to a former junior high school student (Savage). With the arrest, Morejon passed the moderator duties for TTN to another educator and the page changed its name to Oklahoma Edvocates. It continues to exist as an information hub.

According to Cagle, in an interview with Erin, after the strike began, OTU continued to engage in more on-the-ground organizing. While OTU was certainly an emerging organization, it was also quite new, and events unfolded rather quickly. In the absence of a more formal organization or democratic processes for decision-making in OTU (which Arizona organizers learned from by developing a site-based liaison network and practices of democratic decision-making among all members), Cagle quickly became spokesperson and influential leader, traveling to districts across the state, especially rural Republican strongholds, to make presentations on the need for more widespread action. Cagle said he drew his organizing experience and approach primarily from his previous career as a business manager in Florida. For Cagle, results and impact were a priority over organizational structure or process. During the strike, Cagle continued to travel to places around the state to support educator organizing. In one Oklahoma City area district, one school's principal refused to shut down. Cagle and local educators used their cars to block the streets surrounding the school so cars and buses could not arrive on campus. Cagle was fiery about winning, and not just increased wages. As a person who worked an additional one or two jobs, depending on the season, Cagle and many other educators certainly needed the raise. Cagle and OTU, like many educators across the state, sought smaller class sizes, increased wages for support staff, more student supports, among other common good issues. Cagle even attempted to collaborate with the statewide employee union to join the strike (to no effect), and successfully coordinated a solidarity strike with construction workers at the state house organized with the American Federation of Labor and Congress of Industrial Organizations (AFL-CIO).

In part, he said he took up this role because he was unafraid and confident to talk to the media, and in part, because others in OTU were fearful or unwilling to speak to the media. Without the backing of the union or experience and the time to put in place organizing practices of risk mitigation, OTU members felt they were too out in the open, as individuals, and Cagle discovered this was true the hard way. In retrospect, Cagle said he felt he blustered to the media too often, "What can they do except fire me?" he remembered thinking early on. He cringed while recalling a moment when he stated to a reporter that he "double dog dared" the state's education leaders to fire him. Cagle suggested he did not quite understand the stakes at the time, for himself or for others. He certainly came to, later, after being transferred and demoted, "lambasted in the media," and even faced physical attacks, like a brick smashed through his car window in Guymon, a rural town near the panhandle known for its meat packing plant. At one point, he found himself trying to find a way to explain to his students his arrest years prior for drunken driving, which had been pasted across social media and circulated widely. He described losing friends, witnessing co-organizers face retaliation in ways that severely impacted their lives and livelihoods, and, to keep his most recent position, he said he was required by his new district leadership to "promise to never do that again."

Like Cagle, Chuck McCauley is a respected educational leader in his community of Bartlesville, Oklahoma, a town an hour or so north of Tulsa. In an oral history interview, he shared he was a teacher for nine years in rural schools outside the Bartlesville area before he became an administrator at Bartlesville High School in 2001, and later, in 2016, the superintendent of the district. In 2017, a parent advocacy group in town had come to McCauley to ask him to join them in their efforts to advocate for raising teachers' wages in the district. McCauley had heard "rumblings" two or three years prior from educators in his community. As a former classroom teacher from a working-class background and married to a passionate educator, McCauley was supportive and recalled the important gains the state's educators won in 1990 as he was finishing his teaching degree at Northeastern State University in Tahlequah, Oklahoma. He stated the time for action felt more important in 2018 than ever as he felt they were in a more dire position than thirty years ago, with a severe teacher shortage that was impacting the quality of educators in his district. Where he used to have dozens upon dozens of educators applying for an open position in his district, at the time of his interview in 2019, he had two or three, maybe. In September 2017, McCauley addressed the monthly meeting of Tulsa County Area Superintendents to press them to support a walkout for increased funding: "I gave a pretty impassioned plea to them, at which nobody supported. There was not one person in the room that was interested in that at that time."

Over time and as rank-and-file educators became more agitated, witnessed the early actions of OTU and heard and contributed to the rumblings in the hallways and teachers' lounges, McCauley had cultivated allies among administrators in various state and local professional organizations. While McCauley certainly was not a rank-and-file organizer, he played a role in ensuring superintendents supported (at least tentatively) suspending classes during the walkout. As he describes, after the April 1 passage of now legislation that conceded funding and wage increases, he imagined the first day of the walkout would be a "one and done" endeavor: "We felt like we needed to–we already made all these plans. Our community had made plans to suspend classes where we could still make sure kids were fed and the community was taken care of that we should go ahead and do–have a walk out for a day–kind of a victory lap kind of thing."

While the collegial relationship between Morejon and the OEA festered, especially in the aftermath of the "date debate" described in Chapter One (McCauley, Morejon, and an overwhelming number of rank-and-file educators pushed for an earlier date that threatened state testing while OEA pushed for a less confrontational post-testing date), the OEA maintained its relationships with administrators through regular meetings and debriefings. McCauley recounted,

> We canceled school on Monday–suspended classes on Monday, and then sent people to the capitol, and then things went–I think there was all kinds of hope that more would be done, and there was so much distrust and misinformation that was going out for a variety of reasons.... I drove to Oklahoma City every day. The administrator organization, which is called CCOSA, Cooperative Council of Oklahoma School Administrators, they have an office close to where the Oklahoma Education Association office is, and they had a daily meeting at one o'clock for all superintendents that wanted to come, or they had Zoom meetings, and I didn't know it at the time, but I went to that first one, and I ended up leading. I led every meeting. "So, Mr. McCauley, you're the kind of the one that got this started, so, line up," and we had people that were there from across the state just kind of talking about daily updates.

Whereas the OEA only reluctantly collaborated with Morejon and Cagle, the state union collaborated regularly and closely with the state's superintendents throughout. In the end, predominantly men superintendents became, to use Blount's language, gender- and militancy-regulating presences upon predominantly women educators.

In summary, the months-old OTU and subsequent high school student organizing played an important (but not singular) role in catalyzing the statewide strikes through effective yet quickly organized sickout and walkout actions in the state's most populous districts. While Morejon welcomed the celebrated role of movement leader via his large social media audience and used it to make alliances with legislative allies, administrators and, tenuously, with union leaders, Cagle and OTU placed their focus and energies on engaging the rank-and-file (students, fellow education workers) to achieve their demands by any means necessary. Cagle's risky approach was unevenly matched to other OTU members' level of preparedness and comfort. As McCauley's activities underscore, many superintendents were at a tipping point as well, facing severe budget shortfalls and a paltry and ever-shrinking pool of qualified educators. In spite of this, superintendents' support for a teacher walkout was precarious as many feared a more widespread rebellion and sought to manage the walkouts on their terms and in collaboration with the OEA.

● Oklahoma's Rank-and-File Educators Building Relational, Communalistic Organization

While Morejon, Cagle, and McCauley were represented as catalysts or leaders in the media, they were far from the only or even the most significant leaders of the walkouts. In the absence of union leaders' initial interest or capacity in fomenting the action, many educators across the state played important roles in agitating, organizing actions and mutual aid, and strategizing (often on the fly) collectively.

Amy Brown and Mark Stern, in their study of the work of Philadelphia's social justice caucus, Caucus of Working Educators (WE) and the closely intertwined educator activist organization Teacher Activist Group (TAG), found that even as "the bulk of the community surrounding WE and TAG identify as women . . . they were clearly utilizing many political and historical devices that emerged as responses to sexist oppression, misogyny, and patriarchy." Even so, they "weren't quite as vocal about how and why neoliberal policies (education and otherwise) are made possible by and through gender" (178). Similarly, through examining the efforts of so many educators across the state (including many stories untold here), we seek to foreground the ways in which predominantly women's organizing utilized organizing strategies that responded to sexism, misogyny, and heteropatriarchy.

Our interviews suggest that Oklahoma educators' working conditions were the most pressing factor to inspire militancy, and that a mass action had been under informal discussion ("murmurs," "rumblings") in school buildings among rank-and-file educators for a year or more prior in at least Putnam City, Stillwater, and many other districts in and surrounding Tulsa, and Oklahoma City. As TCTA member (at the time) Kate Baker described:

> It almost felt like there had just been kind of something in the air like almost that entire year. . . . I feel like the year before [November 2016 (Wendler)] when we, when the penny sales tax didn't pass like I feel like things started, at least for me, it started to kind of rumble and become like this very like disquieting experience where people went from being like, "Okay, well we're just going to keep puttering along and working this way," to this feeling of like, "We're not getting anything. We're not like, we've tried to get raises this way. It's not happening. We're trying to get more funding this way. It's not happening. Like now is the time to act."

For Baker and many others, witnessing West Virginia educators go out on strike was an important catalyst:

> I think seeing West Virginia go out, everybody was like, "Oh my God, like this, we can do this. Like this is actually a thing that we can do." And I know that it had already been kind of in the works, and like the

P&C

talking and the rumbling was there, but I think watching them do it really empowered our teachers to be like, and maybe some of the people who would maybe be a little bit more like hesitant to do it, like seeing them do it was really big.

For the previous two years, many union educators participating in their locals and state unions had undertaken coordinated advocacy trips and some larger rallies to the capitol to speak with legislators, without response or movement. Many of our narrators noted the February 2018 rally at the capitol, co-organized by the state unions to unsuccessfully push forward a bill to raise educators' wages by five thousand dollars as a tipping point that shifted educators' dispositions toward more confrontational action.

For many educators in Oklahoma, and elsewhere, a culture of personal sacrifice for work is commonplace. As one forty-six-year veteran Stillwater teacher, Sue Hoffman, described of the 1990 strike: "It was so against everything that as a teacher you did. You know, you were in your classroom, you did this, you didn't, no matter whether you had the money for stuff, you did it. And, you know . . . it was so, it was hard." Another veteran educator of twenty-four years, Jody Webber described feeling "selfish" in the lead up to the most recent strike: "I want my kids to have great teachers, but if you don't pay us, they're not going to have great teachers. . . . And I feel a little selfish feeling this because it's not what we're supposed to do as teachers." Even though educators experienced unprecedented public and community support, striking educators described non-educator family members, friends, and online commentators questioning their motives in ways that made them feel defensive or guilty for wanting better wages or working conditions. Stillwater educator Allison Dierlam recalled such questions: "'Are they just in it for the money as opposed to for our children,' or when we'd say we're in it to get fully funded in education, they're like, 'what does that mean?'"

The disciplining narrative of the uncomplaining educator who spends her own paltry salary on school supplies and makes do with what she's provided was made more powerful by prevalent fears of retaliation by administrators. Even in a serious teacher shortage, Oklahoma educators knew they would face consequences for supporting or becoming involved in organizing the strike, and many fears were justified as educators faced repercussions upon their return to their classrooms, including increased surveillance, threats to job security, and online harassment from some parents. In places, especially where educators struck without the support of their school boards or administrators, some educators were fired or experienced increasingly hostile working conditions, as with Cagle in Tulsa Public Schools.

O Stillwater Educators Organizing Via "Extra PLC Meetings"

In Stillwater, while Morejon created the TTN Facebook page and gained a lot of recognition from this, as a relatively new teacher, the local effort in his home city began in earnest with a group of his rank-and-file colleagues at Stillwater Junior High School (SJHS). A fellow teacher at the time, Heather Anderson, described the emergence of this informal group early in the academic year:

> There had been a lot of tensions with some new mandates that administrators had been passing down, paperwork that we had not been previously made to do, common assessments. And so people were frustrated. And we met in PLCs [professional learning communities] to talk about things that we were frustrated with. And sometimes these PLC meetings were very driven by administration and so we were very frustrated with that. It didn't feel like a true PLC community. And so we started having extra meetings, if you will, after school and during our planning periods throughout the week.

While the movement for PLCs arose as a means for in-service teachers in grade-level or departmental teams to meet to grow their pedagogical practice, institutionally implemented PLCs have become, more often, mandated spaces where teachers review and discuss student data (Cochran-Smith). As Anderson described, administrators were unaware of these "extra" PLC meetings. Morejon attended these meetings, which served as a space to air SJHS-specific grievances among young and veteran teachers alike. Eventually these "extra PLC meetings" among the English department grew "organically" to encompass more departments in the school and eventually, teachers from the high school, which shared space with the junior high. As state-level talks of the strike became louder in the early spring, the group grew to include educators from other schools in the district and eventually began meeting at a local Methodist church. Building representatives from the Stillwater Education Association (SEA) stepped up to facilitate the meetings, in communication with the OEA and to coordinate logistics as the strike date loomed.

Anderson explained that the "extra PLC meetings" began with a focus on site-specific grievances and then, "we started to delve into the bigger picture. Like, I, as a teacher, am working way more overtime than any other profession, and I don't have much to show for it. And we've been asked to do these extra duties, and it's really taking time away from my family. And so, when those talks started bubbling, it really started to get more organized and [we started] saying we need to do something about this and now is the time."

Searcy Crow was also a part of these early efforts. A veteran teacher at Stillwater Junior High School (a former colleague of Morejon and Anderson), Crow was born and raised in Stillwater, her father worked for the local newspaper and her mother was a thirty-five-year veteran special education teacher in the district. Her mother, an active unionist, inspired her to become a teacher: "I watched her really, truly enjoy her students and being involved in her students' lives and going to their prom and their games." Her mother's involvement in the union inspired Crow's own political involvement: "She was very involved with OEA. She was very involved in SEA." In 1990, Crow was eleven years old when her mother struck alongside her fellow Oklahoma educators for smaller class sizes, increased funding, and wage increases:

> I do remember that one day she let my sister and I come with her, and we stood in front of the high school and walked back and forth right there at the intersection of Boomer [Ave] and we, you know, held signs and chanted with everybody. And I remember her talking a lot about her hope for [House Bill] 1017 was just smaller class sizes. She had several hopes about 1017 of course, but the biggest one was class sizes.

In 2018, Crow found herself helping to organize many of the same activities, now with her own young daughter in tow. Crow teaches in a "very politically active" building, where many of the teachers are "pretty involved and definitely more aware than a lot of schools about what's going down at the capitol." The issues that motivated Crow to become involved in her local area in the lead up to and during the strike were teacher retention and increased education funding "as a teacher and as a parent, honestly."

As part of our oral history project, Crow was interviewed by another veteran educator, Kristy Self, both English teachers at the junior high and high school, respectively. Self and Crow graduated high school in the same class. Growing up, Self also knew and was influenced by Crow's mother, a person who Self acknowledged "many people have had a chance to look up to," and both recognized the "special bond" they experienced with their teachers as students in the district. While Crow was active in the OEA, Self has spent much of her teaching career working to create educational spaces to ensure that LGBTQ+ students in her small town and across the state could survive and thrive. Self has been instrumental in mentoring educators and students in her school and across the state to form gender and sexuality alliances (GSAs) and, with other LGBTQ+ activists, organized an annual statewide GSA summit.

Crow's and Self's decisions to become educators via the influences of community elders, teachers-as-mentors, and parents is commonplace across our oral history interviews. Like Crow and many others, their parents' (often mothers') union organizing activities and participation inspired them to step up their activities in the 2017–2018 academic year. In Stillwater, Crow, Self, Anderson, Webber, and many other community-rooted educators played pivotal interdependent roles in building up pressure to ensure the support of the school board and superintendent, organizing a network of community organizations to provide childcare and nutritional services to Stillwater students, organizing local picket lines and rallies, recruiting and coordinating donations for food to rally-goers in town and at the capitol, arranging transportation and carpool schedules, and more. For many, their year-round caregiving and community-oriented labor in their church communities, LGBTQ+ activist networks, and their webs of relationships with alum, students, and families served as the basis for their capacity to do so.

For Anderson, her involvement in the early organic emergence of the "extra PLC meetings" helped to ease her fears: "There were some worries about could

I lose my job, that kind of thing. But eventually, whenever I realized that this is a big picture, big movement, I wasn't afraid to jump in anymore and I felt very comfortable speaking up for my profession." Anderson was not new to experiences of risk for taking a stand on the job. For years, she navigated pushback from parents and questions from administrators for teaching about issues of race, Whiteness, and social justice themes. As an illustrative example, Anderson often paired district-required "canon" texts written by, as she stated, "old dead White guys," with literature that challenged such texts as universal perspectives (e.g., pairing Harper Lee's *To Kill a Mockingbird* with Brendan Keily's and Jason Reynold's *All American Boys* to critically engage tropes of White saviorism). Self also pushed the boundaries of expectations for pedagogical neutrality, teaching units that, for example, explored the work of water protectors at Standing Rock and LGBTQ+ people in the military. A year or two prior to the walkouts, Anderson experienced coordinated online harassment from a parent group for organizing a basic White privilege discussion exercise with her grade level team that had created an overwhelming amount of emotional labor on top of her already-intense workload.

According to Anderson, in the immediate aftermath of the strike, many of the Stillwater Junior High School teachers "said, no. You [OEA leadership] don't dictate when it ends, the teachers do. I mean it's not the union that speaks for all of us." Educators used sick days to continue to rally at the capitol the Monday after OEA had called off the strike. Yet, Anderson described what felt like a "threatening" environment on the part of her administration. "You need to be in the classroom or else, that kind of a situation." Stillwater educators felt intensely defeated, exhausted yet required to prep students for standardized testing, and, overall, ready for an end to the school year. While SEA continued to hold meetings at the local church after the strike ended, participation dropped significantly in the immediate aftermath. The justified animosity toward OEA, threatening atmosphere on the part of administration, and educators' feelings of mental and physical exhaustion contributed to the decline of Stillwater educators' organic grassroots organization in the months and years following.

In an interview in early 2021, Self, however, felt that the experiences of educators getting organized and politically active during the 2018 strike led to more robust involvement in SEA in the longer term, and gave them a stronger position from which to advocate for safer and better working conditions during the pandemic that they wouldn't have had otherwise.

O Moore Rank-and-File Educators' Efforts to Wildcat

Like Stillwater, Moore, a city on the outskirts of Oklahoma City, educators attempted to continue to walkout after OEA called off the strike. While Stillwater, along with other major districts in the state, continued to walkout until the OEA officially called the strike to an end on Thursday, April 12, Moore Public Schools Superintendent Robert Romines called educators back to class the day prior to its official end. As the state's third largest district (behind Tulsa and Oklahoma City), many have speculated that Moore's return kicked off a domino effect that contributed to OEA's decision and the decisions of subsequent districts to follow suit.

While the SEA in Stillwater was largely inactive except for contract negotiations, Moore's NEA local, TEAM, was more robust, in part due to the regular activities of its racial justice caucus, CREM, discussed in the previous chapter. TEAM also has its own union hall with a large meeting space. Angel Worth was a second-year educator during the walkouts, a natural organizer and keenly attuned to state and local politics. Growing up in a military and union family, Worth had always been a union person and, with talk of the strike emerging, became active in TEAM and in her building. She attended the capitol rallies every day, and with a group of colleagues, hunkered down in her state representative's offices for much of the two week-strike.

Initially, like many of our interviewees, she felt the walkouts were disorganized and was unsure of the plan once educators arrived at the capitol. After the excitement of the first day or two wore off, she wanted an informed, effective plan of action. She soon realized that she and her colleagues would be responsible for their own activities, and no one would tell them what to do. So, she and her co-workers began to get organized, working with other educators to form a local secret Facebook group for Moore to share information and create talking points. Worth was not the only person to step up, others in their network organized pickets and daily marches from a different school site each day of the strike.

From the start, Worth could sense the superficial charm in her and colleagues' conversations with legislators. Then, things shifted as her group began to become more confrontational and specific in their demands on officials:

> And so, it went from real feel-good, like, "I'm here for education," to, "When are you going to leave?" Like, it almost feels like when you're invited over to somebody's house, and you can tell that they don't want you there anymore. That's kind of what it felt like. There was just this tension that nobody wanted to address that we were past the feel-good emotions and to the point, "Okay. But, are you going to do anything? Is anything going to change?" That's kind of where that shift happened.

Into the middle of the second week, Worth needed a break from the daily slog of occupying her unwilling representative's office space. She decided to attend a legislative session that heard a bill which would legalize discrimination against LGBTQ+ parental adoption. As an educator with strong commitments to LGBTQ+ and intersecting justice issues, Worth described feeling distraught. It was in that moment she learned of her superintendent's call to end the strike:

> And so, I walked into my representative's office because it had been kind of a place of refuge to that point, like despite the fact that I didn't agree with a lot of things that he said and didn't feel like he was doing very much. His [legislative assistant] was amazing, like, love her. And then

that's just where a lot of people from Moore would be. And actually, the [TEAM] union president was in there. So, I remember going in there being like, "[Hey], this thing just happened. I'm so sad." I just remember crying or whatever.

Then within half an hour of being in his office, we got the email that Moore was done. So, I was already in a pretty emotional kind of emotionally fragile state of mind, and then that happened, and then our [state] representative was out of the building on a meeting, which felt really suspicious because our representative has a really close connection with our superintendent. So, a lot of people started saying, "Do you think that he pressured [Moore Superintendent] Romines to pull the plug?" 'cause he wasn't there for us to be like, "What's happening? Why did this happen?"

So, our union president went into [our state representative's] office and shut the door, and he was in there with a couple of other union people, which I understand them wanting their privacy, but it did feel like there was *literally a barrier in division and communication.* This has happened. You have all these teachers out here in this room. You all are in there. We don't know what to do next. And then they opened the door, and then they left, and they didn't talk to us [teachers] or anything (emphasis added).

Immediately afterward, Worth walked to her car and made a Facebook Live video to post to Moore's secret Facebook group calling on educators to continue to walkout the next day, which quickly went viral. Worth and her fellow workers organized a march from Moore to the capitol building with hundreds of educators, parents, and students.

Marches from surrounding districts had been taking place throughout the strike, including in Moore, and these provide an important glimpse into the amount of organizing labor and learning that took place during the strike. The largest was a one hundred ten-mile multi-day march from Tulsa to Oklahoma City, and its organizers underscored the labor necessary to coordinate such an event. Heather Cody and Kate Baker had been active members of TCTA, and through participating in a leadership training, were recruited by TCTA's then-president, Patti Ferguson, to lead an action during the strike—as Baker put it, the "brainchild" of Ferguson and TPS superintendent Deborah Gist—a one hundred ten-mile march from Tulsa to the capitol in Oklahoma City. In the lead-up to the march, Cody took on the bulk of the organizing work: identifying food, lodging, first aid support, and other resources to make the march happen. They held daily assemblies, created group processes for decision-making and information sharing among the hundreds of participants, navigated both outpourings of community support and one evening emergency when a rural community school administration disallowed their group to spend the night in its gymnasium. Another evening, they navigated handling an unknown man who showed up to a group assembly and attempted to take it over. Together, they learned to manage national and international press requests after reporters ignored them initially, in which Cody felt gender played a role in relation to the ease with which Cagle and Morejon had access to media representation. Of the experience, Baker and Cody described forming strong and lasting emotional bonds with their fellow marchers.

Yet, unlike the Tulsa march and others, Moore's was unsanctioned and unsupported by the union or the district administration. Fellow Moore educator, Stephanie Price, recalled the march as a "powerful" moment: "It was a huge group of people. I mean I have this picture saved somewhere of tons of educators and support professionals and parents from Moore all standing on the steps of the building across the street from the capitol. It was just a beautiful protest, and it was very powerful." Worth understood it as, "a really pivotal moment because everybody knew that Moore wasn't supposed to be there. Everybody knew that Moore had pulled the plug and yet here are all these people back the next day." Then, the weekend came and went, and the momentum did not continue as fewer and fewer Moore educators returned the next week. After the OEA pulled the plug soon after, other districts followed Moore to re-open schools and morale and energy dissipated.

On one of the unsanctioned days at the capitol, Worth decided, with the support and prompting of colleagues impressed with her organizing skills and political knowledge, to run against her state representative. Recounting the experience, she described a tense moment when she spontaneously announced to the incumbent her campaign to unseat him in front of an audience of fellow teachers, after she had had enough of his empty rhetoric. He immediately stormed out, and Worth's colleague told her, crying, that she had overheard his angry conversation with TEAM's president in the hallway:

> She's like, she overheard a conversation—this is hearsay, but she overheard a conversation between [Worth's state representative] and our union president, and allegedly, [the state representative] said, "I told you to keep teachers like that out of my office. I don't have to deal with that grandstanding witch."

Many other educators described legislators' talk and tone as inappropriate. In Karly Eden's interview study with Oklahoma educators, she reported that legislators made "derogatory remarks like, 'How come your math scores are so low?,'" cussed and flung papers at teachers, and generally acted angrily and aggressive toward the predominantly women educators (77).

As Worth shifted her energies to focus on the campaign, she began to realize how much work and effort she would have to put in to push her campaign forward, and the severe disadvantage she experienced as a working-class educator in comparison to wealthier candidates like her opponent. She was campaigning, teaching, and, on top of this, she worked as a grocery store clerk on evenings and weekends. She came to understand in a very real way that the game was rigged. In addition to her union president's collaborationism with the superintendent and legislators during the walkout, he also provided TEAM's union hall for her opponent's campaign event that summer–the same representative who had previously (allegedly) called her a grandstanding witch. These experiences caused her to cut ties with her local union and join the AFT, even as it had no real presence in her district. Worth has only grown into her role as an organizer and leader, later becoming active in a short-lived effort among educators across the state affiliated with NEU to push for safe school re-openings during the pandemic. Her activities culminated in the organization of a community protest at a school board meeting determining safety protocols where she delivered a petition with a few thousand parent and educator signatures. Like Anderson and many others, Worth continued to feel a sense of defeat by the culture of fear in her district, the lack of respect, and the constant uphill battle to fight for safe and equitable working conditions.

● Conclusion

While many educators across Oklahoma contributed to sparking the seeds of rank-and-file rebellion in the year or more leading up to the strike, they faced an uphill battle against a collaborationist state union, weakened and centralized in the decades following the 1990 strike by right-to-work legislation and ever-increasing austerity policies that continue to contribute to an exodus of educators from dismal and oppressive working conditions. In OEA's press conference calling off the strike, they were clear about their plan to return to their focus on lobbying (Wendler and LaCroix). While Worth had become disillusioned with her local and the OEA for their undemocratic collaboration with superintendents and legislators, the organizers of TCTA's one hundred ten-mile march, Cody and Baker, were recruited to become staff members for the OEA. The OEA's efforts turned from building the kind of relational and emotionally powerful horizontal modes of organizing (i.e., daily democratic assemblies) that fueled activities like the one hundred ten-mile march and toward "get out the vote" efforts, which became only partially successful that following November, with sixteen of sixty-five educator political candidates elected to the state legislature (Williams and Hosseini).

Rank-and-file Oklahoma educator organizers who undertook much of the relational labor to spark and sustain the strike did not see Cagle or Morejon as their leaders and most felt the OEA and their locals were disconnected from their grievances and patronizing of their efforts. In Oklahoma, many women educators who stepped up to organize in tangible ways in their local areas were often parents worried for their children's educational experiences. Many of the educators we interviewed, like Anderson, Self, Torres, Price, Worth, Waters, and others across the state were agitated and stepped up to organize because they were committed to social justice pedagogies and witnessed, firsthand, the race, class, and gender inequities experienced by their students and families in school and society. They knew, in mundane, everyday ways, how it felt to take a stand for their pedagogical commitments. In Oklahoma, it was largely rank-and-file women's militancy that created the conditions for the strike. Of Morejon's politicking in the months that followed the strike (i.e., photo-ops with education-friendly politicians who sought his endorsement, publicized meetings with the state superintendent), Cody stated, "I don't see them out organizing any effort to make a difference. None of them came and walked with me. Just because you have a large social media presence doesn't mean much." Educators had ample experience being under the thumb of administrators and legislators and were uninterested in Morejon or other social media celebrities taking up the role of spokesperson for the movement.

Like Oklahoma, in West Virginia, no single person or group of revolutionaries oversaw the 55 United movement or mutual aid activities like the food distribution networks that sprang up in the lead-up to the walkouts. In a state with the fourth highest rate of poverty in the nation, food–from distribution to consumption–is political. Education workers inherently understood this political dynamic and developed ad hoc networks to ensure students were well-fed throughout the duration of the walkouts. Teachers at Beckley Elementary, for example, had around three hundred students on free and reduced lunches. Educators there pooled together their funds to set up free lunch at a local grocery store for their students during the walkouts. When businesses heard about this gesture, they donated food and gift cards to offset the cost. At Horace Mann Middle School in Charleston, bagged lunches were sent home in advance of the walkouts, funded and packed by parents and teachers. Those who couldn't donate worked at local food pantries and drove food drop-offs to students' houses. When asked about this outpouring of support, one teacher, unsurprised by these gestures, stated that giving "is basically a fact of life for teachers every day."

As we discuss in more depth in the next chapter, while West Virginia's organization sustained into the following years, Oklahoma's militancy dissipated, in practice, yet not in spirit. Cagle's experience of intense retaliation caused him and other OTU members to shift gears, working via alliances with legislators to push policy changes and efforts to push for a change in union leadership. In 2020, Oklahoma Governor Kevin Stitt attempted to appoint an anti-public education, anti-vaccinations homeschooling mother (with little to no public education experience) to the state school board (Brown and Palmer). OTU members composed a strongly-worded open letter implicating superintendents in the state for their unwillingness to advocate for education. After receiving a call from his district administration, Cagle scrambled to remove the open letter from the internet, not realizing the extent of the edits that had been made by other OTU members. "I have kids in college," he said, "I can't lose my job."

Even as many educators experienced retaliation or threats of retaliation, most of our interviewees expressed that they knew they would have to mobilize again, if anything were to change. Putnam City educator, Crystal Watkins, hoped for a way forward that would not have to rely on statewide action, noting the scales of retaliation experienced across rural, urban, and suburban districts meted out by the legislature in the aftermath: "So, the backlash after the walkout, the grab for control of the school districts. We're losing local control, I feel." In contrast to appealing to state legislators on behalf of public education and educators across the state, Watkins expressed a desire for local union power: "So, we lost–we're starting to lose some of our rights as individual districts. I would like to see that go back even further the other direction where we do have the ability to say as a district, here's what we want to fight for, and we're not going to have to wait for everyone else." For Watkins, local union power might be the antidote to the state OEA's co-optation she felt took place: "[S]ome other authority kind of just took away our morale at the end. It was so wonderful, and then someone just swept in and said it was over."

In Oklahoma and elsewhere, educators' work is cast as women's work, and politicians and legislators made clear what they thought about women stepping out of line via their infantilizing and misogynistic comments. In many places, feminist modes of organizing via relationships of mutual care, distributed leadership, and diva citizens comprised the most powerful and generative instances of rebellion in the context of fomenting and sustaining the strike yet were not necessarily narrated as such in media and scholarly analyses.

Chapter 4. Class, Elections, and Relationship with the State

> Don't let anyone tell us that we–but a small band–are too weak to
> attain unto the magnificent end at which we aim. Count and see
> how many of us there are who suffer this injustice. . . . Ay, all of us
> together, we who suffer and are insulted daily, we are a multitude
> whom no man can number, we are the ocean that can embrace
> and swallow up all else. When we have but the will to do it, that
> very moment will Justice be done: that very instant the tyrants of
> the Earth shall bite the dust.
>
> – *Kropotkin*, An Appeal to the Young

James Miller, a teacher in Louisville, recalled a political shift that took place in
Kentucky after the 2018 walkouts:

> People like to think that debt is a moral failing, but people are starting to
> see through it, that austerity isn't the most moral thing we can do and
> that raising taxes can help. And if we have to do these things and find
> other avenues for revenue, that's acceptable. . . . Political change is hap-
> pening because of the [educators'] movement and because of the pen-
> ny-pinching that's taking place in the state. I think this is a national issue,
> and we would've seen this drawing away from the center even without
> the teacher movement nationally, but I think it's a big part of this.

Many of the so-called "red" states continue to face an uphill battle against
reactionary, Republican lawmakers. According to a February 2019 Gallup poll,
conservatives in Kentucky outrank liberals by twenty percent (Jones), increasing the likelihood of either centrist Democrats taking control or conservative
Republicans maintaining a majority in each election cycle. Miller described,

> Part of it is a cultural factor in Kentucky because they've done such a
> good job of demonizing Democrats and liberals as making them dan-
> gerous people who want to get rid of morality and religion, and people
> think they would rather die than be a Democrat. . . . There are built-in
> disadvantages for people that they can't overcome at the local and state
> level because McConnell and other Republicans have used their power
> to take over in such a way that the national Democratic Party just didn't
> see it coming, and they've pushed this idea that voting is so important,
> but it doesn't take any of this into account.

As the 2018 strikes and the recent resurgence in education union militancy
illuminates, rank-and-file educators, and perhaps the wider public, increasingly

understands the limits of electoralism. For many others, as Miller relates, and as Angel Worth came to understand after her failed state representative campaign (Chapter Three), an emphasis on elections alone may even be a dead end to political organizing: "If you told this tiny football team that if they just practiced enough, they would beat an NFL team, I'm sorry but that's not enough. All these advantages that they have that practicing and rehearsing won't overcome." In Miller's ideal world, however, unions would recognize this inherent disadvantage and find new paths forward external to the established political system: "When you have workers of all trades and all backgrounds, and if they are their allies consistently, 365 days a year, allies in this struggle, then that's how you can build political power during elections at the ballot box and that's how you build collective power against this electoral problem because we can't sue our way out of gerrymandering." For Miller, such an approach would require a "meaningful Left caucus" that could collectively lead the union to fulfill this solidarity unionist vision.

Unlike Miller, others in Kentucky had a different perspective on gaining power. After the strike, Jeni Bolander of the KY 120 social media organization believed that endorsements, get-out-the-vote campaigns, and lobbying potential allies was a smart strategy given the uneasy political terrain in her state. KY 120 committed the summer of 2018 to building a non-partisan electoral campaign that they had hoped would sweep out bad legislators–those that had voted for the Sewer Bill, which would have decimated teachers' pensions, and were unfriendly to the movement–and bring in new legislators more amenable to their line of thinking. "It's about building relationships," KY 120 leader Brewer said in an interview. "We need to create a relationship with politicians that can help us win our fights when we need them."

Bolander likewise believed that this strategy has more upsides than downsides. "Those relationships matter. Build them with your elected representatives whenever you can. Being able to text a representative during a vote and saying, 'Don't you even think about it,' is important. It's a big deal that we can do that and that it gets responded to." The "accidental activists" went from being "just an average, working, tax-paying Kentuckian," as Bolander described herself, to having candidates for governor conducting interviews at her house, seeking an endorsement from KY 120. This seeming shift in power meant turning away from direct action and into electoral political advocacy. Bolander recalled a conversation she had in 2019 as then-candidate for governor, Robert Goforth, was leaving her home after an interview. In Bolander's retelling, Goforth stated that he would now listen to concerns related to public employees much more clearly because they had taken the time to sit down and talk with him, go through their issues with him as potential constituents, rather than showing up at the Capitol to scream during a walkout. "When we're there enough, you can't forget us, because you know we've been advocating," Bolander stated. "If we just show up once a year for a walkout, then we're an angry mob. We're not a teacher, married to a teacher, trying to help protect our families and our pensions."

In previous chapters, we discussed that unionist and movement leaders in each of the states had varying kinds of relationships of solidarity and engagement with non-educator-led social movements in their areas and different forms of (often new, tenuous) rank-and-file-led organizing infrastructure. In Kentucky, educators and educator movement allies rooted in Louisville-based movements for Black Lives had particular analyses of the state and its monopoly on racialized educational and physical violence against the city's Black communities. In many places, and illuminated most starkly in Oklahoma, women-led and feminist-oriented organizing, in and through educators' participation in the strike and their experiences as care workers in their homes and communities, developed key understandings of the state's (hetero)patriarchal devaluation, even derision, of women's decision-making, autonomy, and value as care workers. Many developed strong antagonisms against their business unions' anti-democratic collaborationism and gendered power inequities within rank-and-file groups like TTN and OTU. In both Oklahoma and Kentucky, feminist, queer, anti-racist, and left-worker movements became marginalized as broader rank-and-file militancy became absorbed within state union organizations that operated via centralized, hierarchical modes of representative organization. In Arizona and West Virginia, the formal extra-union or dissident union rank-and-file organizations that had formed during the strikes persisted in the years following in ways unlike Kentucky or Oklahoma yet with differing orientations toward and relationships with their formal unions.

In this chapter, we draw on transnational studies of worker organizing in educator movements to focus our discussion on a key strategic tension illustrated by Miller's and Bolander's differing perspectives. Arguably, this tension lies at the center of the resurgent militancy of contemporary education labor movements in our four states and beyond, as educators think with and practice unionism: To what extent should educators collaborate with and build power through relationships with the state (e.g., via electoral campaigns, relationships with legislators and other elected education leaders)? To what extent should educators build power through collective organization and direct action?

By "the state," we mean, generally, the webs of state institutions, political actors and parties, and governing bodies at the local, state, and national levels. As Hopland importantly notes, understanding the state also requires a deeper understanding of capitalism, and the ways in which state governance is entwined with and influenced by wealthy corporate interests (e.g., West Virginia coal baron Governor Justice's tax avoidance schemes for his private companies are interrelated with his interests in disinvesting from public education). Rather than answer this question prescriptively, we approach it descriptively, trying to understand with critical generosity and in-depth contextualization how and why certain collaborationist or pressure-oriented (or both) approaches to the state emerged as predominating or marginal during and in the aftermath in each of the so-called "red" state strikes. By considering these in relation to and learning from various transnational movement contexts, we pose it as a dynamic, ongoing question that educators and unionists might regularly engage through critical and situated reflection.

● The Question of the State: A Transnational Perspective on Theories of Power and Change

In his case study analysis of contemporary education labor movements in Toronto, New York City, and Mexico City, Paul Bocking writes, "The key strategic political question is still how to deal with the state" (390). Since the long 1970s of militant educator unionism, as M. Murphy noted of the early histories of teacher unionism in the US, professionalism had become a strong discourse for state collaboration and against worker militancy during the 1980s and 1990s. In the US and Mexico, emerging market-based, neoliberal reforms aiming to deprofessionalize the work of teaching through an emphasis on datafication and privatization of public education, leaders of the NEA, AFT, and Sindicato Nacional de Trabajadores de la Educación (SNTE), Mexico's national teachers union, and influential academics "argued for a turn away from militancy and the defense of contractual rights, to embrace new forms of teacher evaluation as a mark of professionalism, alongside teacher voice in school budgeting, teacher evaluation, hiring and firing decisions, implicating union members in managerial decision-making" (Bocking 51). Alternatively, Bocking writes, during this period Canada's educator unions largely avoided the pitting of teacher professionalism against workplace concerns.

In Mexico, SNTE has historically had a more direct and intimate relationship with the state, given its emergence and relationship with the Institutional Revolutionary Party (PRI), a party that ruled the nation for seventy-one years until 2000 (Bocking). While major educator unions in the US and Canada are relatively independent of the state, they have long, often complex histories of engaging in electoral party politics (Weiner, "The Future of Our Schools"), and all three nation's educator unions are subject to public sector labor laws and interventions that have sought to constrain worker militancy. As Bocking writes, collaboration with the state without an emphasis on union democracy and building collective power among union members, as it occurred in this era of neoliberalization, diminishes the power of a union overall:

> [T]his work considerably reduces the opportunity for union officers to work directly with groups of members. In this environment, the markings of a union leader are fluency in a technocratic form of policy and quasi-judicial knowledge. A technocratic union becomes autocratic when these specific forms of expertise become unchallengeable by rank-and-file members, leading to their apathy and demobilization. (391)

Thus, a singularly state collaborationist approach without meaningful participation of members has extraordinary limitations, as the terms of engagement are set by state actors (politicians and their interests). Alternatively, for anti-collaborationist and confrontational (militant) approaches, the terms of engaging in negotiation are set by workers themselves. Their ability to enforce the terms of negotiation (their power) is earned not from electoral political allies, rather from the strength of their collective organization. As we discuss via examples, social movements that prioritize meaningful and horizontal grassroots participation have undertaken strategies that work with and within state institutions/political parties and without and beyond the terms of electoral politics.

Union leaders' collaboration with the state to the detriment of meaningfully addressing educators' working conditions throughout previous decades were (and continue to be) sources of agitation that have spurred dissident militant rank-and-file union organizing transnationally. As the "global education reform movement" seeks "the transfer of public education funds to the private education sector, a growing industry estimated to be worth over US$6 trillion," educators across the globe have responded and informed one another's' efforts (Stark and Spreen 234; see also Bocking; Stark). For example, the Trinational Coalition to Defend Public Education is an organization composed of educator unions and unionists from Canada, the US, and Mexico that formed in 1993 to protest the North American Free Trade Agreement, part of a hemispheric coalition to fight against corporate capitalist incursion into public education. The organization holds regular convenings to share movement knowledge. In Stark and Spreen's review of recent global educator movements, "educators across the globe systematically challenged neoliberal austerity policies in 2018 and 2019" in Zimbabwe, Morocco, New Zealand, Brazil, Iran, Chile, Argentina, Mexico, the UK, Tunisia, Poland, Costa Rica, the Netherlands, Guyana, Jordan, Canada, the US (including Puerto Rico), and more (245).

Transnational educator and social movements have long grappled with the question of the state. In Mexico, the Coordinara Nacional de Trabajadores de la Educación (CNTE) emerged in the southern states in the 1970s as a grassroots, radically democratic, and militant alternative to the state-controlled SNTE. In the US, social justice caucuses emerged in many major urban centers as educators envisioned rank-and-file-led union movements that could attend to educational and intersecting justice issues affecting their students' and communities' lives.

Further, social movements, like Brazil's Landless Workers' Movement (MST) and its educational "real utopias" (Tarlau "Occupying Schools") or Mexico's Zapatista movement offer further insights into both the possibilities and limitations when labor and social movements collaborate with or confront the state—or engage purposeful strategies that undertake both to try to achieve their visions and demands. In our discussion of these North and South American examples, we highlight how movements' various relationships to the state have evolved through specific historical and political conditions and offer a transnational lens for understanding this question in the context of the 2018 strikes.

● Social Movements and Dual Power Institutional Participation

Rebecca Tarlau, in *Occupying Schools, Occupying Land: How the Landless Workers Movement Transformed Brazilian Education*, engaged a multi-year political ethnography within the Movimiento dos Trabalhadores Rurais Sem Terra (MST), or Landless Workers Movement, in Brazil. She recounts the movement's thirty-year "long march through the institutions" (5). Emerging in Brazil's rural countryside, the MST initially aimed to redistribute land through occupation and reform with three main principles situated within a broadly anti-capitalist and socialist politics: land reform, agrarian reform, and social transformation. To address the latter aim, the MST first turned its energies to popular education efforts. As the MST grew (from a few rural regions in the 1980s to twenty-three of Brazil's twenty-seven states currently) and collaborated with state institutions, the movement shifted and broadened to transform public education. The movement demanded "communities' right to participate in the governance of these schools, with the purpose of promoting alternative pedagogical, curricular, and organizational practices" and to create schools as sites that could grow and sustain their movement (5).

MST, as one of the largest social movements in Latin America and the globe, comprises a large network of regional and statewide collective leadership bodies across the nation. In the context of its educational struggle, the MST engages in movement-expanding pedagogical work via "teacher trainings, conferences, bachelor's degree programs, nonformal educational offerings, and other initiatives that teach activists and teachers about the movement's pedagogical and agrarian vision" (Tarlau 212). The question of the possibilities and limitations for movements' engagement with state institutions has a long history of analysis and insight within social movement literature. In the book, Tarlau challenges and aims to nuance prevalent theories within this literature, including Frances Piven and Richard Cloward's influential perspective that "movements inevitably become more conservative and less effective as they institutionalize" (7). Tarlau engages a Gramscian theory of the state as "an assemblage of organizations, institutions, and national and subnational government actors that often have contradictory goals" and which rely on political hegemony (or the consent of civil society) to govern (5). As an illustrative example, many public education systems have the contradictory goals of both "labor market preparation and democratic citizenship," even as, under neoliberalism, these have become increasingly conflated (Lipman 14). Contradictions exist, also, at various scales of governance, as various parties and actors engage in the everyday practice of translating these goals within their specific local and institutional contexts.

Tarlau argues that activists can utilize their social vision within the framework of state institutions while recognizing these contradictions, as those in the MST have. Further, various local and state governing bodies may be weaker or stronger and may have more or less sympathetic politicians in office that can determine the movement's strategies for engaging in collaboration or confrontation. MST's practice of "contentious co-governance" involves a multi-directional relationship between the movement from below, collective leadership, and institutional engagements to implement and experiment with ("prefigure") the movement's social vision ("Occupying Schools" 5). In such a framework, social movements, like the MST, combine a strong grassroots organization with strategic institutional participation (e.g., partnerships with state institutions or organizations, electoral campaigns).

For the MST, co-governance is possible because of its strong social movement infrastructure and decades of cumulative movement knowledge. Even so, as Tarlau describes in-depth, contentious co-governance prefiguration, or the practice of strategic engagement with state institutions is messy, uneven across different geographic scales and political contexts, and complex. Further, it is situated within specific political and historical conditions. In Brazil, the MST had long had a relationship with the Worker's Party (Partido dos Trabalhadores or PT) a Marxist and socialist political party that maintained a hold of Brazil's presidency from 2002–2018 until its shift right with the ousting of PT's Dilma Rousseff and election of the ultra-right Jair Bolsonaro as president. The left-coalitional PT party emerged out of opposition to the Fifth Brazilian Republic, a brutally repressive military dictatorship that governed the nation from 1964–1985. Out of the movements that emerged to form PT, among other social movements, Brazilian municipalities have a history of participatory budgeting and governance that have created specific conditions for MST's engagement in strategic, contentious co-governance (Tarlau, "Occupying Schools").

Social movement scholars like Sonia Alvarez use the phrasing dual strategy, where movements work simultaneously against, within, and without the state. As a major example, throughout two decades, MST developed and sought the strategic institutionalization of a national educational proposal for public education in rural Brazil, Educação do Campo. In the late 1980s, the call for the movement to support education came from families occupying land in camps and settlements who desired formal access to schooling (73). Throughout the 1990s and 2000s, MST's education sector evolved through its local, regional, state, and national collective decision-making bodies to advocate for educational policy and through the development of university partnerships to develop bachelor's degrees in "geography, agronomy, and pedagogy" (153). A proposal emerged that sought to expand these initiatives.

As Tarlau writes, "The phrase 'Educação do Campo (Education of the Countryside)' was deliberate, indicating a proposal not simply in the countryside or for rural populations but, rather, a proposal of those rural populations, implemented by them according to their realities" (164). As the proposal was adopted to become the Brazilian Ministry of Education's official approach to rural education, Tarlau details the challenges and limitations of MST's efforts over time. The official proposal was a far cry from the MST's and other coalition groups', including unions and other civil society actors, original vision rooted in a

Freirean-socialist framework. In large part, this had to do with the ways in which MST's institutionalization of the proposal expanded quickly, providing opportunities for key institutional actors to co-opt movement leaders and demobilize movement participation in the effort. However, Tarlau writes that even as the proposal lost its connection to a socialist agrarian development model (to that of one supported by capitalist agribusiness), Educação do Campo made a significant impact on rural communities' access to quality education and "legitimize[d] the idea that rural schools should have a differentiated educational approach than urban schools and create[d] dozens of educational programs specifically designated for rural populations" ("Occupying Schools" 216–217).

● Horizontalist, Anarchistic Structures of Power and Anti-Collaborationism

As Tarlau notes, activists and movement thinkers have debated the efficacy of state institutional participation. The histories and ongoing social movement efforts and organization of Mexico's grassroots democratic teachers' movement, CNTE, and the Zapatista Army of National Liberation (EZLN) offer a different perspective on the question of state power. Both the democratic teachers' movement and the EZLN emerged from the longer histories of social movements in Mexico's southern states. The EZLN of Chiapas and CNTE, which emerged from and remains the strongest in the states of Oaxaca and Chiapas, both have roots within Indigenous peasant, land struggle, and rural militant labor movements in the 1960s and 1970s (Cook; Vergara-Camus). Unlike the MST, both organizations within different social contexts have taken far more left-libertarian approaches to organizing and perspectives on the role of collaborating with and/or collectively pressuring state power in achieving their respective social visions.

Often, EZLN is compared to the MST as an example of a movement that went in the opposite direction, rejecting any state or institutional participation and seeking to build counter-institutions beyond the state (Tarlau "Occupying Schools"). As Vergara-Camus explains regarding the differences in approach between the MST and EZLN, in particular, "[F]or these social movements, the question of state power is a very practical one. It is a question to be approached by taking into consideration the actual history of national state formation and the concrete experience of each movement with the state" (430). Whereas MST was formed and coalesced under similar conditions as PT and found within PT an opportunity for contentious co-governance, the EZLN had a very different history with state repression. "After forty years of broken promises and betrayals from state officials, Indigenous subsistence peasants have come to see the state as the main class enemy. . . . The Zapatistas rejection of state power and their decision to build forms of self-government derives as much from this experience as from an ideological reflection on how best to radically transform society" (431). MST's power, according to Vergara-Camus, relied on the state to expropriate land for their agrarian reform demands. While MST has confronted the state in the past, it must continue to negotiate alongside it at other times, always working within and without/against the system.

The EZLN began in 1994 as a guerrilla organization in the remote Lacandona jungle. Whereas Brazil's transition from dictatorship to liberal democracy included a left-wing political party that was, at least initially, relatively accountable to the social movements that brought it to power, in Mexico there was no such equivalent. Mexico was in effect a single-party state for seven decades as the Revolutionary Institutional Party (PRI) maintained control over the political system of the nation. By 1988, a split occurred within the PRI among the neoliberal camp and the nationalist camp. The nationalist camp, led by the popular Cuauhtemoc Cardenas, broke with the PRI to build the Democratic Revolution Party (PRD), and by the close of the decade, most other left-wing parties had been subsumed within it (Vergara-Camus). Although the PT in Brazil emerged as a result of popular struggle against the military dictatorship, combining social movements with militant labor struggles, the PRD did not emerge from similar circumstances and thus lacked a popular basis of support among the diverse groups within Mexico. The PRD's electoral route dominated the party, and its leaders co-opted grassroots organizers that had helped galvanize its initial break from the neoliberal PRI.

Initially, the EZLN attempted to work with the left-leaning PRD in its resistance to the PRI's Ernesto Zedillo administration (1994–2000). In their "Third Declaration of the Lacandona Jungle," the EZLN organized resistance with the PRD through their creation of the National Liberation Movement (MLN). This proposal refused to recognize Zedillo's government and sought a constituent assembly to replace it, governed by the masses in their localities. Within a year, the MLN had fallen apart. The PRD watered down proposals of insurrection and downplayed the calls for revolution. The party's goals were limited to opposing neoliberalism in form but not in function. In response to the MLN, Zedillo's neoliberal government provided a salve that pacified the PRD and broke its relationship with the EZLN. Zedillo announced that he would enact electoral reform, giving public funds to electoral campaigns, thus aiding the PRD in its future as a political party (Vergara-Camus). Ironically, Zedillo's government would most likely not have made this reform had it not been for the temporary alliance that brought EZLN and the PRD together, yet it was this compromise that ended up splitting the two. The PRD believed this compromise would give them an opportunity to undermine Zedillo and the neoliberal PRI. They redoubled their efforts at the ballot box and became further estranged from the EZLN in the process.

The following year (1996), EZLN pressured Zedillo into a series of negotiations known as the San Andres Accords. The Accords were intended to lay the groundwork for the constituent assembly that was the initial demand of the MLN. In it, EZLN demanded greater rights for Indigenous peoples in southern Chiapas, including rights to culture, women's rights, and an end to hostilities with the Mexican state. Indigenous scholars from across Mexico attended the

R&C

Accords meetings, and at the time, it appeared that EZLN's move to work as an outside force agitating for more liberal reforms would be successful. The Zedillo government signed the San Andres Accords and by the end of 1996, draft legislation from the meetings were being created to protect Indigenous rights and autonomy of the land. One month later, in December 1996, Zedillo rejected the legislative drafts and used the power of his office to quell EZLN negotiations between themselves and other Indigenous movements during negotiations. Zedillo cut EZLN off from the rest of Mexico in effect. Their goals were seen as limited to the Indigenous peoples of Southern Mexico. By 1998, EZLN had outright rejected the institutional political path towards social change, instead opting for a combination of insurrection and peasant organizing to force the federal government's recognition of the Accords (Vergara-Camus).

CNTE and the democratic teachers' movement, likewise, emerged out of the specific political-historical relationship with the state-controlled national teachers union, SNTE. At the time of its formation in the 1980s, rural normal schools (teacher education institutions) comprised a significant percentage of Indigenous bilingual students in training to become teachers, many with strong connections to and histories with social movements. In 2010, Elba Esther Gordillo, president of the SNTE and major PRI politician, called these rural normales "guerrilla seedbeds" and efforts had been underway since the 1960s to close or restructure them (Padilla 24). The Mexican government considered them "leftist political centers" (Bocking 91). Like the EZLN, CNTE's approach to the question of the state has been decidedly anti-collaborationist, instead seeking to build a "sustained capacity for disruptive protest while avoiding electoral engagement, fearing co-option and a loss of autonomy" (Bocking 390).

In the US and Mexico, the 1980s through the 2000s saw a sharp decline in unionization. While Canada's relative culture of social democracy contributed to the maintenance of its overall union membership, in all three countries, union militancy declined, and transnational neoliberal policies took hold. CNTE offers an important exception, orchestrating one of Mexico's largest national educator strikes in history in 1989. Educators struck and protested from across the southern states (Oaxaca, Chiapas, Michoacan, and Guerrero) where CNTE has historically held the most participation and influence. Significantly, educators in Mexico City joined the action, led by women primary school educators of SNTE's Section 9, its largest local (Bocking; Cook). While in more recent years, the CNTE has had more limited participation and influence in Mexico City, urban social movements for housing rights emerged from the poor state response to a devastating 1985 earthquake, creating a new culture of dissidence toward the ruling neoliberal PRI. During the 1989 national strike, educators occupied city streets and the SEP offices, and won twenty-five percent wage increases, and in Section 9, Oaxaca, and Chiapas, free and fair elections for state education executives (Bocking 108; Cook).

While it has lost its influence in Mexico City, CNTE continues to remain strong in the southern states. Scholar of the movement, Maria Lorena Cook, argues that CNTE's longevity and successes has been its commitment to participatory, democratic processes that helped maintain the momentum of a mass movement and mitigated the corrosive effects of internal conflicts. "The development of functioning school and district-level committees which elect delegates to state assemblies, helped ensure the movement could continue to function were it to lose control of the formal machinery of the union. This is how the CNTE functions in states where it has the support of a critical mass of teachers but lacks institutional control of the local" (paraphrased by Bocking 109; Cook 193–196, 216–265).

After CNTE's successful 1989 strike, Elba Esther Gordillo was appointed the president of the SNTE and became a strong advocate of neoliberal educational policy, including "datafication," limiting the professional autonomy of teachers in the classroom and teacher educators in the nation's normales. Gordillo worked to curb the militancy of CNTE, specifically in Mexico City, by "welcom[ing] many Mexico City dissident leaders into full time union positions for Section 10 and at the national office. Others were vaulted above the standard career steps into school directorships" (Bocking 110).

These unique circumstances in both Brazil and Mexico during the period of intense neoliberalization shaped the collective experience of Indigenous rights organizations in their relationship to state power. Brazil's MST worked within and within/against state institutions to enact social movement aims yet experienced neoliberal incursions. Coming out of the military dictatorship, both the PT and the MST worked in coalition periodically to achieve democratic reforms that benefited poor peasants in their efforts at land reform. The victory of the PT was tied to the social and labor movements of Brazil in ways that the left-leaning PRD in Mexico never truly was (Vergara-Camus). In Mexico, when the PRD reneged on their promises to work alongside EZLN, the latter found that the state would be in perpetual class war with the peasant class and thus sought alternative modes of organizing resistance. MST's trajectory towards co-governance and institutional participation emerged through its historical relationship with the Marxist-socialist-leaning PT. Meanwhile, EZLN's trajectory towards anarchistic structures of power outside the state and, similarly, CNTE's refusal to collaborate with the state emerged from specific histories and experiences with electoral reforms (Vergara-Camus). For each, its orientation and relationship to the state is premised on the strength of its grassroots, collective organization beyond the state and its responsiveness to its participants and members.

● Contemporary Education Labor Movements in the US: Grappling with Questions of Power and Change

Different than in either Brazil, Mexico, or Canada, the US has been the primary exporter of neoliberal policy experiments, as "many of the key actors, including philanthropists and corporations promoting the for-profit education industry, come from the United States" (Stark and Spreen, 234). In the US, for Shelton, the decline of (relative) state support for robust labor unions (labor liberal capitalism) and the rise of neoliberal capitalism (individual competition in a free market) were premised on a confluence of specific factors that shaped urban places during the height of educator militancy amidst the political and economic crises of the 1970s (Shelton). In urban places during the 1970s, Shelton argues that US teacher strikes in deindustrializing cities facing declining tax revenues "exacerbated an already overwhelming sense of crisis in the decade" (195). During this sense of crisis, "political networks from the right . . . tapped into long-standing racial conflict, cultural assumptions about 'productive' citizenry, anxiety about shifting gender roles, and the beliefs of much of the White working and middle class that the state victimized them during a tough economic climate" (195). With waning Democratic investment in labor in the decades since, neoliberal educational policy and governance has generally had bipartisan support among both Democratic and Republican politicians. Republican- and Democrat-controlled states have pushed for school choice and privatization, high stakes standardized testing and curricular regimes that punish under-resourced schools and communities, teacher merit pay reforms, and more (Buras; Lipman).

Values that took hold and undergird the common sense of neoliberal policy suggest that "those who worked the hardest and produced the most deserved the most rewards," and "only individual competition in the marketplace—not collective organization or social policy—could provide it" (Shelton 195). Shelton argues the decline of educator militancy in the 1980s and 1990s is intimately connected to many (White) worker's internalization of producerism—and that producerism is inextricably entwined with the construction of Whiteness. Weiner adds that the predominance of paternalistic and hierarchical business unionism has created barriers to rank-and-file voice and power within their unions. For Weiner,

> [D]espite their all-too-glaring problems, teachers unions are the main impediment to the neoliberal project being fully realized. Even when unions don't live up to their ideals, teacher unionisms' principles of collective action and solidarity contradict neoliberalisms' key premises—individual initiative and competition. Neoliberalism pushes a "survival of the fittest" thinking. Labor unions presume people have to work together to protect their common interests. ("The Future of Our Schools" 9)

For Weiner, social movement unionism requires rank-and-file democracy, solidarity with (and deep understandings of the interrelatedness of) entwined social justice movements, and, importantly, an internationalist approach. "Neoliberalism's devastation of public education is a global epidemic that requires a global cure" ("The Future of Our Schools" 53).

Many scholars trace the resurgence of educator militancy in the past decade or so to the emergence of social justice or movement unionism, or a form of unionism that seeks to understand the relationships between schools and racial, economic, gender, immigrant, and other forms of justice. Social movement educator unionists have engaged deeper questions about what issues their unions should fight for. Through doing so, they have challenged producerist ideologies in public education and beyond.

An emerging body of literature on the rise of, particularly, urban social movement educator unionism and activism since the 1990s has sought to capture the conditions and internal organizing under which, in particular, urban social justice caucuses formed to challenge the prevalence of collaborationist unionism that has enabled the neoliberal turn and its impacts on public education (Asselin; Benson; Bocking; Brown and Stern; Maton; Morrison; Shiller; Stark; Stark and Maton; Uetricht). Stark's four-year militant ethnography documenting the formation of the United Caucuses of Rank-and-File Educators (UCORE) from 2015–2019 provides key insights into the ways in which U.S. urban educator activists and organizers have sought to build a national movement to revitalize and transform their unions, schools, and society along social justice principles.

Stark traces the emergence of social justice caucuses, or groups of educators within (or even outside) a union that work to steer its priorities and resources, to a 1994 meeting of the National Coalition of Education Activists (NCEA), out of which emerged a document that detailed key principles of social justice unionism, "committed to a bottom-up, grassroots mobilization—of teachers, parents, community, and rank-and-file union members" (Peterson, "A Revitalized Teacher Movement" 16). Models of social justice or movement unionism had been underway in different places previously in the 1980s and 1990s and cohered and found new articulation in the context of the NCEA meeting. Stark writes that the influential NCEA document drew on past traditions of social movement and community-based unionism:

> [The NCEA document] mirrored some of the strategies and tactics of more radical teachers' unions, including the democratic governance and economic justice work of the Chicago Teachers Federation (CTF) under Haley, the racial justice pedagogies and common good demands of Black educators in the pre-Brown South, the anti-racist community organizing of New York's Teachers Union (TU), and the militancy of rank-and-file organizing in the "long seventies." (20)

In the decades since, the NCEA principles have foregrounded those of educator organizers in emerging social justice caucuses and caucus networks.

In the past few decades, social justice caucuses formed in Chicago, Seattle, Los Angeles, Oakland, Newark, Philadelphia, Baltimore, New York, and more. In each of these contexts, social justice caucuses were commonly born out of educators' involvement and training within local social movements and educational struggles. In Chicago in 2008, CTU members organized in solidarity with the Kenwood Oakland Neighborhood Organization's struggle against school closures in predominantly Black neighborhoods and the pushout of educators of color. Finding intransigence within the larger union to support the efforts, educator organizers formed CORE (Stark 25). They drew on their experiences in the struggle to engage in a community-based, grassroots strategy for mobilization that led to their success in winning the leadership of CTU in 2010. In Oakland, the social justice caucus, Classroom Struggle, emerged out of the education committee for the city's Occupy movement in 2011, which occupied Lakeview Elementary School (slated for closure) and organized more than twenty percent of educators to participate in a one-day general strike and march (Stark 29). In each of the cities, these caucuses shaped their efforts around fighting against resonant neoliberal reforms that continue to reshape, resegregate, and displace Black, Brown, Indigenous, and working-class communities in urban places (Lipman).

Stark found that, while social justice caucuses engage in various situated strategies and practices, organizers emphasized common collective approaches, like building democratic rank-and-file power. As Massachusetts' Educators for a Democratic Union (EDU) caucus describes: "union power manifests primarily in the organizing activities of empowered rank-and-file members, not through lobbying elected officials" (123). Further, caucuses have emphasized building rank-and-file power via "community collaborations," locally and within school buildings (125). Social justice caucuses also tend to find common purpose in transforming their unions to "fight" for their members and for schools that communities deserve (126). Finally, social justice caucuses work toward "advancing justice in their schools, whether through grassroots organizing, labor struggles, policy advocacy, or progressive pedagogies" (129).

Stark illuminates that key tensions exist among organizers around how to engage or understand state institutions in their work. Caucus organizers engage tensions between union democracy, within unions that, in most places, comprise predominantly White educators, and social justice principles. Within caucuses, organizers may disagree on what social justice issues are education or caucus issues (e.g., policing and police brutality (Asselin)). Without serious engagement, such tensions can lead to the marginalization or push-out of educators and communities of color, as Louisville, Kentucky educators experienced after disagreements about the significance of the Gang Crime Bill to the educator movement. As many social justice caucuses have run and/or won slates of candidates for their union's leadership, they grapple with tensions between union democracy and conceptions of social justice on a broader scale with the wider union membership. As Asselin has documented in her study of MORE and WE, these tensions can be opportune sites of pedagogical engagement—whether undertaken internally via educator study and inquiry groups or meetings, or externally through the discursive and educative work of caucuses' activities and campaigns (e.g., caucus organizing for the National Black Lives Matter at School Week of Action).

The development of social justice caucuses offers important context for a growing disillusionment with the concessionary business models that still predominate most educator unions. Through caucus networks and meetings, educator organizers have learned with and from transnational educator movements. Yet, as Stark describes, there are important regional differences in contemporary educator movements in the US that suggest the importance of understanding the militant educator movements in West Virginia, Kentucky, Oklahoma, and Arizona. While educators in these states pushed for demands that emphasized economic justice, "only strikes in urban, left-leaning locals such as OEA [Oakland Education Association] (led in part by members of the Classroom Struggle caucus) and UTLA (led by the Union Power caucus) emphasized racial justice demands" (Stark 140). While the major urban strikes in 2018 and 2019 were tied to collective bargaining, the statewide strikes were tied directly to specific state legislation and were undertaken with the tacit support of most public school administrators and school boards. In the "red" states, major political and geographic differences exist in the relationship between more progressive, racially and economically diverse, yet smaller urban areas and with generally more conservative-leaning, predominantly White- and conservatively-governed rural communities. While urban social justice caucuses tend to understand collective bargaining as a means, rather than the end, to organizing for social justice and the common good, the "red" state strikes emerged in places with strong anti-union legislation that has weakened unions' capacity to bargain, if they have a legal right to do so at all.

These differences, among others, offer important context for how different educator movements have engaged, implicitly or explicitly, the question of the state, and require a more sustained analysis, as we turn to next.

● West Virginia United: Syndicalism and Anti-Electoralism

West Virginia had been a blue state until only recently. Democrats controlled both houses of the state legislature from 1933 until 2015, and the governorship from 2001 to 2017, the year that Jim Justice switched his political party back to Republican. Between 1950 and 2010, a majority of U.S. House of Representatives members from the state were Democrats. "Democrats have been in control for eighty years and look where it got us," said educator organizer Jay O'Neal about the political impact of the 2018 walkouts. "Union leadership tells us to 'Remember in November' and everything but yeah, we might not have as many direct attacks, but we wouldn't be in a teaching Mecca because Democrats are in power." O'Neal's statement about the disconnect between union leadership's perception of power and the perception of WV United, the social justice caucus that emerged from the 2018 strike, explains the difference in these two approaches to the state. Whereas union leadership returned to business unionist approaches and elections post-strike, O'Neal thought the caucus could better spend its early and limited time by building rank-and-file power.

Every West Virginia educator we interviewed stated that the walkouts did, in some way, awaken a political consciousness in the state's teaching workforce. "People are paying a lot more attention now," Emily Comer said.

Teachers in my building are reading the news more and paying attention to education issues, and that's just not something that happened before the strike last year, at least not until the lead up to it. Teachers rarely talked politics at work, but now it's something that happens all the time. Teachers in my hallway now know who the individual legislators are and that's really cool, there's a big difference there now.

Similarly, West Virginia educators, Adam Culver explained,

Being a teacher, you realize that most teachers are not political. State Senator Ojeda said it to us flat out in Cabell County that, "I know you got into this job thinking you had the least political job out there, but you actually have the most political job out there." Most teachers think they just have their content area they teach because that's what they enjoy the most, and they don't think about the politics of it all, they're focused on the content of what they teach but not the politics of how they're teaching.

Within our interviews, descriptions of educators' political awakenings encompassed a range of implicit meanings, from their awareness of legislative policy impacts on educators' work to learning from experiences of collective struggle how power operates and social change works.

In *Cultures of Solidarity*, Rick Fantasia argues, "Solidarity is created and expressed by the process of mutual association. Whether or not a future society is consciously envisioned, whether or not a 'correct' image of the class structure is maintained, the building of solidarity in the form, and in the process, of mutual association can represent a practical attempt to restructure, or reorder, human relations" (11). The forming of labor unions and the use of rank-and-file organizations within unions expresses inherently anti-capitalist beliefs since capitalism has individualized our notions of self and self-interest. Yet, educators' willingness to transform society through acts of associated bonding is no less meaningful. Cultures of solidarity supports workers to see in the system a flawed relationship (e.g., labor laws intended to negotiate peace) and to see within themselves the capacity to enact more liberatory modes of relating in the world.

Ohio County Education Association President Jenny Craig found that the walkouts awakened a sense of worker consciousness, rather than simply a trade union consciousness. She stated,

Now teachers are seeing themselves as part of a larger whole, that we're workers and that we have something more in common with one another. You saw that after the strike because we started to collaborate with other unions more and we were more a part of the community, which is why we have been so successful. . . . Teachers didn't see each other as a key part of that larger whole, that all workers need that solidarity, and when the [WV United] caucus came to be, I think that really came to be a driving force for locals to understand how to make community allies and be purposefully a part of the community and other labor groups.

At the end of the 2018 West Virginia walkouts, the Communications Workers of America (CWA) Local 142 in West Virginia went on strike against Frontier Communications. Fourteen thousand union employees struck for three weeks protesting a contract that would reduce full-time employment, increase temporary employment, and increase health insurance costs. The strike was successful, and a new contract ensured layoff protection for one hundred percent of Frontier's employees (Young). Simultaneously, two separate unions at Technocap, a metal enclosure manufacturing plant in Glen Dale, struck over contract disputes around health insurance premiums (Garland). Members of the Ohio County Education Association bought gift cards and stuffed backpacks of supplies for striking workers. This forged a sense of solidarity and bonding between the strikers and the community. "The teachers went down to help with the Technocap workers," Craig stated, "brought them gift cards, talked with them, and that wouldn't have happened without the walkouts. And now a lot of parents have this feeling of, 'I get it, this is systemic and we need to help one another.'" Chris, a Frontier worker, shared, "If all the teachers band together, and the same for us, if all the communication workers band together, there's no fight we can't win. All we want here is to take care of our families, and provide them with great, affordable health care."

The purpose of building up this labor movement via acts of solidarity was not to transform the electorate, but to shift the power between government, businesses, and workers. In the 2018 midterm elections, Republicans retained control of both houses of the state legislature and all three U.S. House races were won by the GOP in landslide victories. Only Democrat Joe Manchin won his race by a slim margin. Comer reflected on the midterm elections and the caucus' role in this fight:

> The outcome showed less for us and more for the Democrats who ran, because more people probably would've voted for the Democrats if they had a reason to, if they had actually spoken to people about issues they cared about, and I don't think they did. So for us putting pressure on them, that can play a part in that. I don't think the caucus should be in the business of getting Democrats elected. We're here to make sure PEIA is funded and that we smash any legislation related to privatization or charters and that we're defending public schools. It's not our role to get Democrats elected; it's Democrats' job to get Democrats elected.

As new power players in the grand political scheme, WV United could have chosen the route of electoralism. Similarly politically-motivated educators had chosen to do this when, in the months following the 2018 walkouts, a group of educators formed the "Future of 55 Political Action Committee," whose mission is to support and elect pro-education political candidates through endorsements, lobbying, and fundraising. A debate began soon after about what role the newly-formed caucus should play in the upcoming election. Some believed that an endorsement from the caucus would help get some of the newly-minted, pro-education Democrats elected, and flex the muscles of the caucus as a legitimate organization. Others, however, believed that endorsements and traditional political campaigns were an unnecessary use of caucus time.

"A campaign is a time suck," O'Neal said, "and there's no guarantee that you're going to win, and almost always, people here will be Democrats, but they'll never have the funding that the Right has so you'll always be outspent, and it just felt like there would be a better use of our time to be organizing our co-workers and building strength that way." Remaining outside of the electoral sphere proved to be the best option for the caucus, ultimately. "I think it helped that we didn't formally jump in as a caucus to any kind of campaign or endorsing candidates," O'Neal said. "That made us a little more independent in some ways and allowed us to jump in with a different focus and really push that."

After the election and the realization that the Republicans would maintain control of the legislature, WV United's independence from the Democrats made an impact. A second strike was in the works. Many of the issues facing educators in 2018—a permanent fix to the PEIA and significantly higher wages over several years to compete with neighboring states—never materialized. Everyone interviewed for this project from West Virginia stated that, in hindsight, educators should have stayed out longer in 2018 to ensure that these issues were resolved through legislation, not promises. But the failed promises of the elected elite provided fodder for the next round of walkouts.

By January 2019, WV United had worked out a plan for building power leading up to the next legislative session. The caucus began to frame the next fight around increased mental health supports for students. One-third of children in West Virginia are raised by their grandparents, what some have termed "grandfamilies." Grandfamilies make $20,000 less than the average median household income in the state, increasing the state's generational poverty. In counties where more than eighty percent of children are raised by grandparents, there is a correspondingly higher rate of opioid addiction. Nationally, West Virginia ranks forty-sixth for child poverty and fiftieth for child poverty for those under the age of six (Gutman). West Virginia schools have been severely understaffed to deal with the complex experiences and realities faced by students with little access to nutritious food, stable housing, among many other hardships. At the beginning of 2019, schools were operating at a sixty-six percent efficiency standard for student-to-counselor ratios. Likewise, public schools were at an abysmal twenty-three percent efficiency standard for student-to-psychologist ratios (Gutman). Considering that more than one in four students in West Virginia have suffered from some form of childhood trauma (Gutman), WV United educators sought to address these disparities directly.

Eventually, WV United members came to realize that the push in 2019 needed to center their demands against the legalization of charter school development when Senator Patricia Rucker, a former Tea Party activist and ALEC-sponsored legislator, was appointed as the Senate Education Chair despite having no previous teaching experience in public schools. The first task in shaping this fight toward social justice was to hold statewide walk-ins on the first day of the legislative session. Twenty of the fifty-five counties participated in the State of Our Schools walk-ins. "The walk-ins related to charters and privatization were really important [that] year," stated Comer, "because I think that at that point most people didn't know what was going on with charter schools. That was happening around the same time as the UTLA strike, but our caucus did a good job of educating people about what was happening in LA and what charter schools were doing to LA and what UTLA was doing to fight back, but also why we couldn't let charters enter West Virginia."

As happened in 2018, the unions held several rallies in advance of an impromptu two-day strike that shut down fifty-four of the fifty-five counties. The House of Delegates voted to permanently table SB 451, the bill that would have allowed charter school development, and the strike ended quickly. Comer stated, "The walk-ins and awareness that our caucus brought to the issue of charter schools played a huge role in defeating charter school legislation through the strike. I don't think that would've happened without the caucus." Brian Bowman, another West Virginia educator, stated similarly,

> I remember posting something asking people about what charters were, and most people said they didn't [know], and that continued for educating people about what these issues were and the work that Terri [a member of the caucus] does, about what charters do, what ALEC does, what the Cardinal Institute [a Koch-funded think-tank in West Virginia] is, how these companies will benefit from these privately-owned and operated entities is instrumental. And it's important to push for a walkout and organize and sharing what corruption is happening within the unions when poor decisions are made. And this brings in new members who are disaffected and angry at what they're seeing. They want an open and democratic process, and they see a lack of that in the unions.

In lieu of endorsing candidates who could have defeated SB 451, WV United believed that building independent worker power was of primary concern. As Bowman's statement above suggests, membership concerns were more precisely targeted at building dual power, or rank-and-file organization as a caucus within the union, to combat both the intransigency of union leadership as well as the ineffectiveness of politicians and elected officials to block charters long-term.

Independent, autonomous groups began organizing food projects to ensure low-income students did not go hungry during the duration of the 2018 walkout. In 2018, the WVPEU group had no centralized leadership, dictating actions or coordinating mass efforts across the state. Countywide groups were set up as impromptu methods of coordinating actions locally, and schoolwide groups developed alongside this to provide similar efforts within individual schools. Local presidents were often at the mercy of the majority, as was shown in the wildcat action that took place following Governor Justice's "cooling off" day, which took union leadership and elected officials by surprise.

The WV United caucus, then, built off these efforts and designed their caucus to reflect the strength of local, horizontal organizing methods. Refusing an endorsement process was the first move that the caucus made to avoid an approach to building power that relied on relationships with the state. "I think it's a good goal to get politicians behind your concerns," Bowman shared, "but when it comes to endorsements from the caucus, it's extremely important to keep an organization like the caucus as non-partisan as possible. I'm not saying it isn't impossible because we wade into those casual conversations, but I have always said that if we bring in people of various political viewpoints then that'll make us much stronger." Secondly, the caucus relied on locals to set up their own process for walk-ins at the beginning of the 2019 legislative session. Individual organizers with or without ties to union leadership could set up a walk-in at their school. This process reinforced the belief that the caucus instilled early on that every member is an organizer, and every organizer can do the work of the union.

When union leadership formally called the 2019 walkouts in protest of SB 451 (Student Success Act), workers had been educated in their rights to demand direct action via the 2018 wildcat strike and the political education work of WV United. Once again, the southern coal counties had voted right away to endorse a statewide walkout. The walkouts centered around issues that developed organically from the base to the union leadership. Yet again, the strike succeeded because workers knew their fight could unite educators against the efforts of a retaliatory legislature.

Decentralized leadership within locals and school sites were key for educating the public about the effects of charter schools and their ties to neoliberal policies of privatization and defunding of public resources. WV United's steering committee provided resources for others to use but acted more as a general clearinghouse of information that they could disseminate to others, including infographics, videos, and written reports. Through this process, the caucus relied on the pre-established structure that had been created in 2018 to share information rapidly and democratize actions in the lead-up to another statewide strike. The caucus gained legitimacy by encouraging others to take actions they felt were necessary.

WV United engaged in practices that resonate strongly with traditions of anarcho-syndicalism, developing out as it did in a horizontal and democratic movement. According to Immanuel Ness, common features of syndicalist unions include that workers: advance actions, rather than union officials or bureaucrats; oppose collaboration with management; exert independence from electoral politics and political parties; form a culture of worker solidarity within the job itself as well as local communities; commit to and practice horizontal and democratic union structures; withhold their labor as a "principal strategy" to transform their conditions; and oppose collective bargaining agreements that prohibit workers from taking direct action (5–6).

Political education on the significance of direct action became important. Matt McCormick believed this process served multiple purposes:

> We need to be able to keep people informed enough at the ground level, and if it gets bad and we need to walk, we need to walk, and if we're

together at the grassroots level, we can shut it down and effect change. It doesn't matter who is in power, friendly or hostile, if they're doing something against public education, we can shut it down. . . . This is the best tool we have. This also shows that this is a bigger issue than a teacher or non-teacher issue, so we need to keep calling meetings where we open up meeting spaces to all educators, regardless of membership or non-membership. It transcends the petty politics of what the state-level unions try to do. . . . At the end of the day, we have to be ready to say we don't care what the state leaders want but our members know what we need and we will do what our members want and what our members need. The same kind of grassroots movement that led us on a grassroots strike [in both years] is the same type of organizing that'll help us against a state leadership that we can't always trust.

Red for Ed days, described in Chapter One, highlights the class politics of the caucus in its early stages. Signals of worker solidarity predominated in both 2018 and 2019 as education workers donned shirts, buttons, and posted pictures of their schools coming together as one either in support of bread-and-butter concerns (2018) or in opposition to charter schools (2019). Through this, the sense of community involvement grew and expanded, with social and economic justice union politics becoming a mainstay in the caucus' organizing principles.

Given that West Virginia is a right-to-work state and public employees have no legal right to collectively bargain a contract, any concessions made by the state to public employees must be done through lobbying or direct action. WV United's reliance on direct action over lobbying was a political decision as much as it was a strategic one. Hostile Republican majorities in both houses and the Governor's mansion in 2018 and 2019 meant that lobbying would have weakened and diverted grassroots mobilizations when other actions were necessary. As O'Neal so aptly put it, "Strikes work! Direct action works!"

SB 451 was ultimately defeated, due again in no small part to the rapid mobilization of everyday workers across all fifty-five counties and a two-day state-wide walkout. It would, however, be resurrected in a watered-down form over the summer during a special session of the legislature. HB 206, an education omnibus bill that established local protocols for the creation of charter schools, passed successfully despite intense pressure from the unions. "We learned that rallies are one thing," O'Neal stated, "and strikes are another. The legislature will get mad when they see people showing up *en masse*, but they don't fear them. That's the difference between a rally and a strike."

WV United organizers reflected on the limitations of allowing union leaders to make the call to strike. "We should've stayed out [in 2019]," argued educator Josh Russell prior to the passing of HB 206. "I think that the state leadership did learn from the membership [in 2019] whereas last year [in 2018] they were trying to dictate to us, but lessons learned, I think we really should've stayed out but we got divided when the day two came and people didn't know whether to stay out, or go back, and that's the lesson we need to remember over the summer and fall."

"The strength of the union is not the number of members or the number of members who show up to a rally," O'Neal said, "but the number of members who withhold their labor and shut shit down. That's the power of a union and I feel like our union leadership has not had that set in. We don't have collective bargaining and they're not thought of as that type of union and we saw that briefly in 2018 and somewhat in 2019, and I want them to stay in that mindset, rather than focusing on rallies."

In the summer of 2019, the education unions held several high-profile rallies at the capitol in their attempt to block HB 206. While the caucus was hoping for a pre-emptive call by union leadership for an August strike, as a bargaining chip against Republican tactics to pass an unpopular bill at a time when a strike was impossible to put into effect, leadership opted for calls to "Remember in November." State AFL-CIO President Josh Sword at a rally that summer proclaimed, "Elections have consequences." The notion that greater electoral gains would have halted charter schools long-term was the prevailing belief among union leadership, but for the caucus, elections mattered less than the strength built up through rank-and-file power and direct action.

The summer rallies illustrate the differences in how union leadership and the caucus understood power. At each successive rally, union leadership would send out a call for members to make the tedious trip to Charleston, day after day, without attempting to mitigate travel costs or subsidize housing to provide easier access for members traveling from across the state. Rallies began to have a set procedure to them during and after the 2018 walkouts that continued into the summer of 2019: leadership would call a rally and expect members to find their own transportation to the capitol, members would arrive early and enter the capitol building to either give testimony to the legislature or rally inside the capitol building, return outside for a short prepared speech by the leadership of various unions, and then be told to go home and rest so that they could return the following day for the same process.

Caucus members, on the other hand, understood rallies as opportunities to meet with the rank-and-file, gather contact information, and listen to and understand their concerns instead of dictating to them what they thought they needed to hear. "I think the leadership still has a very top-down way of looking at things," O'Neal said,

> I think they took the idea from the 2018 strike that we could change things with so many people at the capitol, and I remember when the first omnibus bill was coming out and people were talking about it but both AFT-WV and WVEA were saying, "We need a bunch of red shirts at the capitol," when in reality it was that we withheld our labor *en masse*, but I think they still go to that idea of rallies and things, but it's top down because there's someone talking to you and telling you what

to do. But you flip the script when you go around and hear people's concerns and hear what's most important to them.

The unions' positioning of themselves as the legitimate heirs of the walkouts conflicted with the caucus' growing militant base, nowhere more evident than in the summer of 2019. The caucus had conceded the decision to call for a fall walkout to union leadership and witnessed the effect of this concession: Without pressure from below, union leadership fell back to its conservative strategies.

"The old strategies aren't working," O'Neal emphatically said at the end of his interview with Brendan, "[direct action] is the way to make change."

● KY 120 and JCPS Leads: A Conflict in Power

The 2018 Kentucky walkouts had the possibility of building power with and for BIPOC communities of Louisville, the state's largest city and the oft-target for hatred by then-Governor Bevin. Described in Chapter Two, however, divergent ideas about how to proceed at the end of the 2018 legislative session with regard to the racist Gang Crime Bill resulted in a clash between Jefferson County educator-activists and the members of KY 120. The former demanded a continuation of the walkouts to block this harmful bill that would criminalize many of Kentucky's students and the latter siding with the KEA in calling off the strike indefinitely. The 2018 sickouts ripped open old wounds between organizer-leaders that had been simmering for years prior.

In Kentucky, divergent opinions of class power fell along racial lines. Black educator-organizers in Louisville and their allies, while favoring some components of electoralism, focused their activism on social justice unionism and actions that built alliances across grassroots, community-based organizations. These individuals often sided with the group JCPS Leads, a group that formed in 2019 after hundreds of Jefferson County educators critical of KY 120's handling of a one-day sickout in 2019 were removed from KY 120's social media and the ongoing marginalization of their racial justice concerns within KEA. Educator-organizers outside Louisville and their allies affiliated with KY 120, which emerged as a grassroots organization that later became functionally affiliated with the KEA. KY 120 eventually focused their activism on relationship-building with elected officials. The intersecting components of race and class discussed in Chapter Two influenced the contrasting theories of change that inform each group in practice.

Tensions between the role and extent to which each group should commit to election work grew out of the conditions each group saw in their own district. As Jeni Bolander stated in our interview, "... we realized that if we wanted some of the problematic legislators gone, we had to play the hand we were dealt. This meant putting forth educationally-friendly Republicans to run and friendly Republicans already in the legislature to help by giving us information or help us from the inside, and we found several." After the 2016 election, Republicans controlled sixty-two of the one hundred seats in the state House of Representatives, twenty-seven of the thirty-eight seats in the state Senate, the Attorney General's office, and the Governor's mansion.

Throughout the 1990s, the Democratic Party held trifecta control over the state government, much like in West Virginia. It wasn't until 2000 that Republicans gained control of the Senate, and for a brief time between 2004–2008 for Governor as well. The "Trump effect," however, gave Republicans trifecta control for three years from 2017–2019. If we break down for demographics where Democrats won their elections after 2018, fifteen of the thirty-eight Democratic House seats are in Jefferson County where Louisville is located. Another seven are in Fayette County, home to Lexington, the second largest city in the state. In total, fifty-eight percent of Democratic House seats come from the two major urban centers in Kentucky. This calculation contributed to KY 120's understanding that working alongside Republicans was necessary, as an organization that had most of its membership outside these areas.

In the midterm elections, KY 120 endorsed sixty-eight individuals for state legislature races, including four Republicans. Of the sixty-eight endorsed candidates, twenty-one won. The concept of endorsements and lobbying was, for KY 120, a way to shift the balance of power within the legislature. "For us," Brewer said, "it's about respect. If we can get legislators who will think, 'What will Nema say if I vote for this,' elected, then that's a win." Brewer and, consequently, KY 120's understanding of politics relied on a give-and-take, quid pro quo approach. Candidates for office would come to KY 120, request an endorsement, present their answers to any questionnaire they had, and then publicly support one another during the election. When asked how they would keep politicians honest after the election, Brewer stated that, "We remember people who worked with us and people who screwed us, and I don't forget. You work against us, and that's it, we won't work with you after that."

Functionally, KY 120 worked to take on the role of the KEA during and after the election as an unofficial representative of public employees. The legitimacy that they had gained during the 2018 walkouts carried over into the summer when district leaders met to decide the endorsement process for candidates. Candidates who received the KY 120's endorsement could expect a large social media presence, which had been established during that year's series of walkouts, and volunteer canvassers. Bolander believed the biggest success of this endorsement process was that it brought in so many new people to the political process, who would have otherwise been uninvolved in a midterm year. "You saw teachers getting involved by canvassing and making phone calls for political candidates," she stated. "I knew plenty of people who started doing this for the first time; it was for me."

Tyra Walker's experience after the 2018 walkouts was very different from that of those involved in KY 120. As discussed in Chapter Two, Black educator-organizers, like Walker, were effectively cut out of much of the decision-making process for ending the strike. Their efforts to advance racial justice were characterized as "divisive," part of a longer history of marginalization within KEA

(Edison and Rovira). As Jefferson County educators, Edison and Rovira, write, "But racism is pretty divisive, too!" (120). In 2019, Kentucky educators faced another uphill battle over their pension. Republicans were planning to attack the Kentucky Teachers Retirement System (KTRS) as the session was winding down, much as they had done in 2018. KY 120 called for a statewide sickout in protest of this bill, shutting down several school districts, including Jefferson, Fayette, Bath, Boyd, Carter, Letcher, Madison and Marion counties, in a one-day protest (McLaren). The bill, HB 525, sought to change the composition of the KTRS board by limiting KEA's seats and turning those seats over to other educator and administrator non-union professional organizations, like the Kentucky Association of Professional Educators (Desrochers). The JCTA did not support the sickout, and the divisions sowed in 2018 between Jefferson County educators and KY 120 remained strong.

Walker's experiences shaped her understanding of unionism and its relationship with political parties. The series of wildcat strikes damaged the relationship between Jefferson County educators and the rest of KEA. Every year, KEA holds a delegate assembly where elected representatives from across the state meet to pass new business items that will shape the union for the rest of the year. Walker was a delegate at the KEA Delegate Assembly only a few short weeks after West Virginia's and Kentucky's 2019 strikes. As she attempted to put forth a new business item to deal with Kentucky's racialized educational disparities, the other delegates sidelined her. Every proposal that Jefferson County educators put forth was shut down by the rest of the state's delegates.

Walker believed that KY 120 was responsible for blocking much of the work coming out of Jefferson County that year. "[KY 120 leaders] pretty much blocked us from getting anything done at the assembly," Walker related in her interview.

> For instance, there was a new business item for our comprehensive school support priority schools, and schools that need extra assistance and smaller classroom sizes, but because it was Jefferson County pushing for it, they [the delegates] said "no." And even someone else came up and helped me reword it and they still shut it down because those other counties retaliated against us due to the [2018] sickouts. It was brought to my attention by another white teacher that the other counties were mad about the sickouts and wildcats and because KY 120 didn't lead it.

Race and Whiteness featured prominently in how Jefferson County's educators related to others in KEA. In 2018, educator-organizers stood together in unison. Black Lives Matter, Save Our Schools Kentucky, and Kentucky Alliance all worked together to shut down the state. "And when [KY 120] came out and told everyone to shut it down this time [2019]," Walker stated, "it didn't work because you didn't go out to everyone who helped you last year."

Edison had a similar experience at the 2018 Delegate Assembly. While there, Edison was told by KEA's president that everything had been done to resolve the pension issue that year and they should be prepared to call off the strike. "How did they get that conclusion?" Edison wondered. "Everyone was looking for [KY 120 leaders] to tell them what to do, that's just how teachers are; we wait for someone to tell us what to do." When Edison returned to Louisville that weekend, she met with other BLM activists at a local coffee shop and prepared to keep the schools shut down if need be. The wave of teacher strikes rocking the nation was momentum enough for Louisville's organizers to feel the wind at their backs and believe that they could keep the state shut down for one more week. Confusion followed.

Governor Bevin had come out and vetoed the state's revenue bill and the budget bill, an unexpected turn for many educators. "The Democrats were happy because those bills were going to tax the working class," Edison explained,

> They had all voted "no" on this bill, but then, all of a sudden, the unions told us to push our legislators to override the veto. They started calling out some of the Democrats that were happy that Bevin had vetoed the bill, and again, that threw a lot of red flags at us, because we're looking at these Democratic legislators who are supportive of us, and our union leadership is calling them out because they were okay with the budget being vetoed.

Jefferson County was facing the threat of a state takeover and many teachers began to panic. Higher rates of arrest, suspension, and lower standardized test scores were being trod out by the superintendent to make the argument that the county wasn't performing at the level it should. KEA's president approached Edison, as chair of the Black caucus, and asked her to make a statement about how the Black caucus was opposed to the state takeover. Instead of reaching a consensus about how to do this, however, union leadership, "stole my profile picture and added my statement to show why Black and Brown kids won't be made better by this bill. That was totally unprofessional and uncalled for and had me angry at my own union."

Edison believed that her union's handling of the situation during the sick-outs, coupled with its unwillingness to aid in shaping a racial justice-oriented narrative for many Black and Brown parents in Louisville led to a breakdown in trust between community members and the education unions. KEA's opposition to the state takeover was undemocratic, but Edison knew that this campaign would not resonate with parents. "They're not going to care about that," Edison relayed. "All they're going to see is that the county has been failing Black and Brown students for years and we needed to at least admit that we've failed, that we're going to do something to make this better, make them feel like they're at the center of your agenda, but they [KEA] said no, they're not going to do that."

Mistrust between community activists and unions spilled over as KEA and the emerging KY 120 began working in tandem to push electoralism and a monolithic image of what the union should be. BLM activists came up with an innovative way of reaching the community about the problems with a state takeover. A planned march at the Kentucky Derby at Churchill Downs was in the works and the unions were informed about this idea for direct action. However, at the last minute, KEA backed out and shut down the planned action. "It got really bad between BLM and the unions because they're corporate unions, they're not trying to do social justice work, but we're social justice folks that work in the community, so this non-intersectionality work going on meant that a lot of bad blood was going to start," Edison said.

In 2019, wounds from the previous year's walkouts reopened. Edison had been working with Emerge KY, a Democratic women's group that helps women run for office, for a few years. In 2019 she knew what it looked like to commit to community organizing, union organizing, and electoral organizing all at once. That year, Edison believed that she knew what to expect from the legislature in a year where Governor Bevin would have to face off against strong challengers within and outside his own party. The difference was that the intersections of race and geography altered the landscape in such a way that relying on her union was no longer a possibility. "There was a problem by now of Louisville activists and a lot of White teachers who didn't see all of this backdoor stuff," Edison explained, "and most of them didn't know all of this because they weren't at the table with membership, and most of this information wasn't being said to the membership." When the call went out for another round of sickouts in response to the pension board bill, HB 525, KY 120 had ensured members that the superintendents would support the action. After the one-day sickout, superintendents informed local association presidents that they would not back a strike over the bill. KY 120 called everyone to return to the classrooms, but Louisville educators were keen to respond to bills targeting Jefferson County in particular.

One such bill was a site-based decision bill that would take away the ability for Jefferson County's school board to determine curricula and hire principals and would inhibit community involvement in decisions affecting their schools. Coupled with that was a voucher bill that would've allowed for publicly-funded private schools, which could further starve the already cash-strapped public school system in Jefferson County. "So now," explained Edison, "all of these [Louisville] teachers are looking at Nema [KY 120 leader], who are mad because this is a repeat of 2018 where she tells people to go on strike and then they go back before everything is resolved, and everyone doesn't agree with her because this isn't leadership." Black Lives Matter in Louisville soon became suspicious of KY 120 and questioned why such relatively like-minded activists would call off a powerful strike before all education-related bills had been resolved.

Soon thereafter, hundreds of Jefferson County members who questioned this decision were kicked out of the main KY 120 discussion page. This led to the formation of the group JCPS Leads, and within a single day its social media group boasted nearly four thousand members. "[W]e realized our unions weren't doing anything to stop [poor legislation], and we realized that KY 120 wasn't going to have our backs, so we just stood up and said we'll do it ourselves," Edison said. During the previous year's sickouts, community support coupled with social media allowed non-education workers and parents to stay informed about the sickouts, why they were taking place, and what the demands from educators were. In 2019, however, this did not happen. The one-day sickout was hastily called without using the same channels that had existed in 2018. Anxious about what would happen to striking teachers, the call to return was heeded by all except Jefferson County. When JCPS educators went on a wildcat strike several days later, union leaders did not take it well. JCTA's president, Brent McKim, condemned the strike on the official JCTA social media page. McKim refused to meet with members who traveled to Frankfort in protest, opting instead to meet with the county superintendent and informing them, according to Edison, that schools could reopen if a delegation from each school could come to Frankfort and negotiate on their behalf.

Edison questioned this decision. "Who said this was our plan? Why do you think you can keep speaking on our behalf?" By continuing to shut down the schools and working alongside BLM to educate parents about this decision, "we showed the governor that he [McKim] had no power over his members . . . he didn't have power over us." McKim had been distrusted for some time by many educators. When Democrats controlled the legislature, McKim could negotiate with more amenable legislators. However, the deals struck were not always the best for members. Edison recalled that, for the past decade, money was being pulled from the public employees' pension fund to prevent the state from having to raise taxes.

> That is his [McKim's] house up there. He's been at the capitol because he's one of our lobbyists there. And when the stock market dropped [in 2008], our pensions were depleted because they had borrowed all this money, and this new governor [Bevin] said, "I'm not paying this back, we're going to have to find out how to deal with this without paying it back," that's why we're here, because of these past ten years or more. . . . [T]his whole time we're preparing to strike because of these bad bills, and we didn't even know until later that our union president had been pushing it behind the scenes.

The relationship that had developed between KEA, JCTA's leadership, and KY 120 made it tough for racial justice-oriented educator-organizers like Edison, Walker, and Rovira to trust their union to protect their interests. Mistrust, split along racial lines, became exacerbated through a series of actions that pitted an electorally-minded, reformist agenda against a more militant, localized one. Refusal on the part of JCTA and KEA union leaders to endorse the actions led by rank-and-file educators in Jefferson County, coupled with the cold shoulder many delegates felt during both years at the annual delegate assembly, solidified fears that the unions in and of themselves could not be trusted to protect their members. According to our interviews and Edison's and Rovira's written reflections, organizing alongside community activists, like BLM, was the only route to fight for public education for Louisville students.

Unlike the enthusiasm that the KY 120 group enjoyed after the election, shifting the balance of power as they saw it away from anti-public education politicians, Hancock, an organizer for the public employees Facebook page, KY

United We Stand (precursor to KY 120), was more pessimistic about the concept of "relationship building" with elected officials:

> I just saw that [KY] 120 was getting this insider information on what was happening at the legislature, and I don't want to discount that that isn't valuable, it is. . . . It's that it seems like they're tolerating them to get something out of the situation rather than accepting them and wanting to see things change. That's my concern with the relationship building. Is this a true relationship or a symbiotic relationship?

Distrustful of this strategy as Hancock was, she felt there was little else KY United We Stand could do to block harmful legislation or change the electoral map of Kentucky. There was less of an organizational structure built within KY United We Stand prior to the walkouts, and this led to KY 120 becoming a more mobilized offshoot. Those who had been most active in KY United We Stand joined KY 120, placing more time and energy into building it and working to complete its mission. KY United We Stand's non-partisan, nebulous structure meant that online-to-on-the-ground actions could only materialize at times of intense crisis (e.g., 2017 special session announcement, 2018 walkouts, midterms), with each successive crisis draining member capacity or diverting it into KY 120's structure. Finding a middle ground between electoral activism and direct-action activism is challenging. KY United We Stand opted to become the educational resource for Kentuckians who could stay up to date about issues related to public employees. Lacking structure or timed call-to-actions that can bring in new members into building this project, members became distant observers on social media rather than active participants.

As Walker noted of the ineffective KY 120-led 2019 sickout, the success and energy of the 2018 walkouts were significantly rooted in the coalitional relationships among educators and community-based organizations and activists, particularly in Kentucky's urban areas. Edison and Rovira write,

> Our goals, as educators in the public school system, should be restoring the promise of public education by insisting that "common good" issues, like the conditions enabling the school-to-prison pipeline, be negotiated alongside typical bread-and-butter issues, like wages and benefits. Whatever your color, if you truly love your job and molding young minds into productive citizens, then you definitely should be striking–or disrupting business as usual and putting your bodies on the line, as earlier generations did for humanity in the 1960s! Those not standing in solidarity with us spin a narrative; they call us "divisive" to cover up their own apathy. (125)

Edison's and Rovira's orientation to the state and collaborationism–one premised on rank-and-file power and coalitional relationships with community-based movements–stands in stark contrast to KY 120's electoral emphasis and hierarchical structure. While KY 120 and the KEA sought to repress dissent with the removal and marginalization of Jefferson County educators, KY United We Stand did not have the organizational structure or base to do more than moderate discussion on social media. Without such rank-and-file power, Hancock's perspective offers the only other, rather narrow and individualized, option educators and public employees feel they have to effect change: "The only superpower you have is to vote, and even if you're not voting for who I want you to vote for, I still want you to vote. I won't tell anyone who to vote for, but I will tell them they need to get out and vote because our turnout is terrible."

● Oklahoma and Arizona: Divergent Paths

The experiences of West Virginia and Kentucky rank-and-file educators as they navigated during and in the aftermath of the 2018 strikes provides insights into the different contexts that contributed to educators' and educator organizations' approach to electoralism and its consequences in the short term. As we turn to consider Arizona and Oklahoma, we aim to illuminate the differences in each state's emerging rank-and-file-led educator movement and their divergent relationships to their state unions.

O Oklahoma: Desires for Union Democratization

United Sapulpa Educators (USE) president, Carla Cale, experienced the statewide walkouts in 1990 as a new teacher. Cale remembered becoming involved in her union as soon as she began teaching, an ethic she had internalized from her teacher education program. Growing up in Sapulpa, a town southwest of Tulsa, Cale recalled the 1990 walkouts had some support among the Sapulpa school board and community, though not as widespread as in 2018. After USE, a local affiliated with OEA, voted overwhelmingly in favor of walking out, Cale recalled a contentious school board meeting: "I remember a local community member, a very active community member, speaking up and wanting us all terminated at that board meeting." The few other educators we interviewed who had participated in the 1990 walkout responded similarly of their experiences—community members demanding teachers fired *en masse*, vitriolic legislators, and much less supportive administrators and school boards.

Prior to the 1990 strike, an OEA delegate assembly strike authorization vote in 1988 had pushed the legislature to author an emergency bill to address dismal education funding, rapidly expanding class sizes, and educators' paltry wages. By April 11, 1990, the State Senate had failed, by a handful of votes, to add the emergency clause to HB 1017. Within twenty-four hours, OEA was on strike and rallied at the Capitol on April 12, 1990. They held out for four days until HB 1017 was passed. Educators won $6,000 wage increases and hundreds of millions of dollars in increased funding for schools (Oklahoma Education Association). At the time, the Speaker of the House, Steve Lewis, said of the action: "It was a simple outpouring of physical demonstration, of commitment and concern. It was just something that you had to see to understand. And just the thought of professional people by the thousands standing out in the rain to try to show their concern and commitment, it made the difference" (Jones). Such praise in the aftermath aimed to situate educators as "professionals," distinguishing their actions from trade unionists and common workers.

Oklahoma legislators had long been trying to pass right-to-work legislation that would drastically restrict unions' ability to recruit dues-paying members and the protection of unionized workers from termination. As one of the largest public sector unions in the state at the time, it is not hard to imagine (and in line with Shelton's thesis) that this action contributed to Oklahoma's eventual 2001 passage of a right to work law, which was voted on by state question (Oklahoma Historical Society). This meant that ordinary voting residents ensured Oklahoma became the twenty-second "Right to Work" state. The new laws had a dramatic effect on public sector unionism. In 2001, Oklahoma union members counted 119,000 and by 2005, just 77,000 (Layden). OEA, the largest educator union in the state, lost forty-four percent of its members between 1993 and 2019 (Carter).

Cale stated one of the most current pressing issues facing Oklahoma public education is "keeping people politically engaged. Education employees, educational supporters. . . . Parents, community members, every human being that supports education needs to stay politically engaged at all times, not just during walkout times." In 1990, educators relied primarily on news media and their unions for information concerning the walkouts. The walkout had been authorized by a vote of union members—Cale recalled her angst in voting "yes" back then, fearing losing her teaching job. In 2018, while union members were polled, the determination for the walkouts arose from informal, rather than formal, decision-making processes only after OEA leaders had come to understand the widespread support and inevitability of increased confrontation. Since right-to-work, no vote to authorize a strike was technically necessary (as it was in 1990) because they were not "legally" allowed to strike in the first place. With fewer resources and members, state union leaders worked to cultivate and maintain relationships with elected leaders and understood the strike as a potential threat to this work.

Social media provided an important space for information sharing, both on the larger Facebook pages (TTN and OTU) and in the many locally organized secret groups. Cale's experience as a local union leader provides a window into the differences in how the union operated in its communication and connection to members between the 1990 strike and that of 2018:

> [In 2018, a] lot of the information was passed on through building reps, which is United Sapulpa Educators. We have building rep[resentative]s in each of our building sites. For every ten members we have in a building, they're allowed to have a building rep, which is a voting member, and their voice within our local association. We also had mass communications going out to every district employee from administrators to our support staff via emails. And there were a lot of meetings that were hap-

pening between myself as the leader of our organization and our district leadership in the weeks leading up to the walkout. And those meetings that happened between our superintendent [and] our assistant superintendent, were very positive meetings. And that made my job as president of United Sapulpa Educators a little bit easier, a little less stressful.

Like many unions, while educators may be allowed one building representative per ten members, many buildings struggle to find educators willing to serve in the position and levels of engagement in the larger union vary widely across locals in the state (Weiner, "The Future of Our Schools"). Unlike the 1990 walkout, union leaders collaborated closely with more supportive administrators, and much of the informational flow was uni-directional–from the union leadership (in conversation with superintendents and elected officials) to the members.

Nikki Rice, an educator in Broken Arrow, a wealthier suburb of Tulsa, received nearly all her information from either the OEA newsletters and emails and from social media: "They would send out newsletters and emails. And Facebook. There was a lot of stuff on Facebook." She, and most of her colleagues, did not attend any union meetings during the lead up to the action, and she did not recall much discussion among her colleagues. "Leading up to the walkout? You know I don't really remember having very many conversations because it was kind of like well if it happens it happens. I don't know if it will happen. Maybe it will; maybe it won't, just kind of wishy-washy type stuff and I honestly don't think that the teachers thought it would happen." Alternatively, in Putnam City, educators benefited from active building representatives. As educator Crystal Watkins described: "We have two really active people that are in our part of the district, the north side of the district that are really active with PCACT [Putnam City Association of Classroom Teachers], which is our district union. . . . They were always going to meetings and bringing us back information, which was really helpful." Far from one representative for every ten educators, PCACT maybe had one or two per school, and Watkins happened to be at a site with a very active rep.

Watkins had experienced "grumblings" in Putnam City throughout the year prior and even earlier after the failure of the 2016 penny sales tax, she thought.

> It was already in the works. It was already something that was going to happen. West Virginia, I think the feeling was that we were so angry that we'd been wanting something to happen for a long time. And we're like, "Well, West Virginia just did it." It wasn't like a catalyst, but it was like a, "See, someone is doing something. We can do the same thing. Why do we keep pushing this back?"

Watkins said educators at her Putnam City school, adjacent to Oklahoma City, turned over at nearly fifty percent each year, facing large class sizes, increasing workloads, and low pay. Some educators lamented the town's shifting racial and class diversity as Black and Latinx families moved in from the city. For educators who remained, Watkins described the general sentiment: "We've got empty rooms with no teachers in them and kids practically stacked on top of each other in certain grades and core subjects. So, that's really what got us going was like, 'We can't just keep every year starting from zero.'" Largely because of the experience of union mentors, Watkins and her co-workers were actively engaged in pushing for and organizing the walkout:

> We had a lot of coalition meetings, if you will, leading up to that. Just a lot of checking in. Our reps would constantly be gauging how we felt about things.... Our reps would have meetings with us and say, "What do we need to do? What needs to happen in order for us to feel like we can keep, retain, and get quality teachers? How can we get our classroom numbers down?" Basically, they would just check in. I'm going to do air quotes here for "list of demands." And they would go back to the larger group and report back to all the other schools [in the district].

In these coalition [site-based PCACT] meetings, Watkins described how educators in her local were pushing for a much earlier date, even at the end of the fall semester and the beginning of the spring: "I feel like we as in teachers set a date, and we were going towards that goal, and the whole thing was co-opted by OEA, and they changed the date [to April 23], and we were set on an earlier date."

In the aftermath of the strike, union and non-union members alike grew incensed at the ways in which the OEA, in communication with legislators and the state's superintendents, called off the walkout. On the day the union called off the walkout, union staff had sent a poll to members. However, with many members at the Capitol and little access to reception, many did not receive it. Many of our interviewees did not recall receiving it at all. Mid-Del City educator, Tessie Curran described a common sentiment in response to the decision: anger. "I was so mad because it was at that point where I felt like we were getting somewhere, and I felt like we were so close to understanding everything that was going into what we were fighting.... I didn't know how quickly everything was just gonna go back to normal. I couldn't deal with that. It was very difficult. I was very angry."

As Watkins' and Rice's experiences illuminate, educators had vastly different experiences with the strike and their local and state union organizations. Rice stated the best thing to come out of her experience in the walkouts was the ways in which she was able to develop closer relationships with her fellow educators, people she hardly knew before. They would keep each other informed, have political discussions, and stay up to date. Although she already felt that was waning a year and a half later. Rice felt she was mostly a passive participant, following the direction of OEA and local union leaders. For Watkins and others, while spaces of union democracy were made possible through the energy and commitment of active building representatives, the state union's top-down "co-optation" left a sore feeling for many. While Larry Cagle's OTU made clear its aim to make a change in the leadership of OEA in the aftermath of the strike, the issues with the union's structure and modes of accountability to its members were organizational in nature, rather than simply a problem of individual leaders. OEA's diminishment in membership and union structures after right-to-work created a sense that a (quite one-sided) lobbying relationship with legislators was the only way to push for pro-public education policies. In the absence of stronger, democratic union movements to challenge this orientation from within the union, OEA leaders chose to try to preserve their legislative relationships rather than continue to confront the state via striking.

As studies of social justice caucuses have illuminated, a shift in union leadership is not the only ingredient necessary for union democratization and to push unions to fight for working conditions and the common good. In both Asselin's study of MORE and WE and Stark's study of caucuses in the UCORE network, when social justice caucuses win union leadership by putting forth slates of their own candidates, the caucus can wield more substantive influence in the union (as with CORE). However, it can risk limiting caucus organizers' energy for building active caucus members, site-level unionists, and engaging in community-based relationship-building. These kinds of activities are what have made many social justice caucuses successful in their efforts to steer the priorities of their unions. Likewise, as Arizona demonstrated in their soon-to-follow walkout, business union-oriented leaders respond most strongly to organized rank-and-file power.

O Arizona Educators United and Grassroots Organization

As AEU organizer, Rebecca Garelli describes in her contribution to the edited volume, *Strike for the Common Good: Fighting for the Future of Public Education*, soon-to-be organizers for AEU, "camped out on other states' 'United' pages for quite some time. We lurked in the background, watching and learning how other states were organizing" (103). AEU organizers drew on West Virginia's and Oklahoma's strategy "tracking and counting the counties, districts, and schools that had mobilized–and from Oklahoma–like updating lists and making them public" (103). However, they engaged these strategies not only to visualize and track local support but also to build the infrastructure of their grassroots organization, and "so all members of the group could see what districts and which schools had a volunteer liaison" (103). Erin's interview with AEU organizer Vanessa Arrendondo shed light on the amount of administrative and relational work that had to take place in order to develop and maintain these volunteers. AEU core organizers, at the time, were few in relation to overall numbers of educators in the state. While Arrendondo and others managed the organization and visualization of the liaison network, liaison communications, and requests for input via various kinds of social media and texting technologies, liaisons benefited from in-person trainings conducted by the state union. The AEA had the infrastructure and resources to do so. Such training combined with AEU's organizational independence allowed them to facilitate and participate in escalating actions in the lead-up to the strike, like "Red for Ed" days, where educators showed up together wearing red and "walked-in" to school all together as a show of force and organization.

AEU organizers also learned from Oklahoma, and other states, in the ways they structured their social media. While Oklahoma had massive, centrally moderated Facebook pages controlled by just one, two, or a few people, AEU had developed a network of linked local Facebook pages, which dispersed decision-making and coordination activities among local organizers. The core AEU organizers balanced the engagement of liaisons by both providing clear directions and meaningful resources for what liaisons could/should do in their local places and engaged several processes to develop their five main demands from the ground up. "We hosted a series of polls in the main AEU Facebook page that allowed teachers to offer suggestions for demands and vote on what was most important to them. Ultimately, these polls developed what became the five demands of the movement" (Garelli 109).

Garelli writes that AEU organizers had "built a strong and respectful relationship with our statewide union," noting that this relationship was much different than more contentious relationships in Oklahoma and Kentucky (108). "The AEA understood that our grassroots group, AEU, included the 'drivers of the bus,' and union leadership understood that educators' voices needed to be out in the forefront" (108). Oklahoma's OTU educator organizer, Larry Cagle, said that he felt that AEA had learned from the experiences of OEA after seeing the extreme backlash the state union had experienced over how the walkout ended, a sentiment similarly felt by many other Oklahoma educators. By the end of the 2017/2018 school year, the OEA dropped in membership by 1.7 percent and KEA membership in Kentucky had also fallen 1.7 percent (Antonucci). Alternatively, educator union membership in state-level NEA associations increased in West Virginia and Arizona, by 3.8 percent and 10.3 percent, respectively (Antonucci).

Karvelis recounts that AEU struggled to become differentiated from the state union, which endorsed candidates, unlike AEU. As a result, AEU began to become increasingly associated with the Democratic Party and, he theorizes, created a kind of political legibility that had not existed in the early days of the movement: "Due to the #RedForEd movement's status as a new entity outside of the typical patterns of contention and political logic in Arizona, it was difficult for established power structures to identify and react to the movement" (Karvelis, "Towards a Theory of Teacher Agency" 2). Cagle stated similarly of his experiences in conversation with legislators. He recalled a conversation with a state legislator, who told him that the legislature remains scared of teachers. During the walkouts, Cagle reported the legislator said, "we didn't know who to negotiate with at first." As things progressed, they locked onto OEA to negotiate an end to the strike and succeeded on terms less than favorable to educators.

Karvelis argues that the broader Red for Ed movement in the state, including AEU, became more institutionalized after the walkouts as they sought to advance the Invest in Ed policy agenda through canvassing for political candidates who would support the measures. He writes, "[A] deep fracturing of the movement occurred as partisan lines were further developed, and focus shifted from collective demands and towards standard models of electoral activism" (4). He argues this shift impacted the possibilities that had emerged from the democratically-driven solidarity actions during the strike: "the ability to claim the unoccupied spaces in Arizona's political landscape and to exploit the gaps that previously existed disintegrated" (4).

For AEU organizers, as Arrendondo articulated, the movement's shift away from its five main demands, constructed through the early efforts of AEU organizers to develop and cohere a statewide network of local organizing, was a significant contributor to the loss of three quarters of site liaisons after the walkouts ended. When asked what she wished they had done differently, Arrenondo said:

> I would keep bringing everything back to the members. The one thing would be to just go back to the members and ask "what do you want?" Ultimately, we were able to undertake the statewide walkout because all of these members came together. Not just because we said, as leaders, "Okay, we're going to do it." Members were in it for the long run, and they believed in the cause. They believed in the five demands. (Karvelis, "Rural Organizing" 101).

For AEU organizers, these kinds of questions around movement strategies, institutionalization, and grassroots organizing are dynamic and ongoing. Unlike Oklahoma's organizations, AEU continues to organize, building upon its movement knowledge. While some core organizers stepped back or left teaching, others remained—like Arrendondo and Garelli. AEU has, most recently, been active in its efforts to fight for a safe return to in-person schooling during the pandemic, supporting several sickouts in local districts in the state. AEU has also inspired a national network of statewide rank-and-file educator organizations in Washington, Virginia, Indiana, New Jersey, and Arizona under the banner of NEU. Garelli, among others, have been instrumental in developing this network while continuing to organize within AEU.

● Conclusion

In this chapter, we began our discussion of the question of the state via studies of transnational educator and social movements, examining both how different movements take up the question of whether and how to collaborate with the state within their national contexts and how these movements exist in conversation. Educator movements are interstate and transnational movements. They exist in conversation at the level of the grassroots, via labor conference meetings and through study (Bocking; Stark; Stark and Spreen). They necessarily exist in conversation as many neoliberal policy strategies that have wrought the most damage on global public education originated with US corporate and state interests. Such policies have and continue to be implemented across the globe as the education industry becomes increasingly profitable for private business and politically useful for the state under capitalism.

A significant challenge, as Bocking writes, is scale. Neoliberal policies have been and continue to scale up across the US, as West Virginia educators experienced and mobilized against in 2019 with the introduction of pro-charter school policies, and across the globe. In response, so have union movements attempted to scale up. In his study of teachers' unions in New York, Ontario, Canada, and Mexico, Bocking writes, "To varying degrees in all three cases, it appeared that the strongest scalar advantage was afforded to teachers at the local district level. Teachers' unions are trying to reconsolidate themselves at higher scales but face much stronger government authorities at the state/provincial or national level than locally" (387). Further, Bocking argues for the importance of unions' strong school-site presence, as educators feel these policies in their lives most directly within their classroom practice and everyday work. As our analysis of West Virginia, Kentucky, Oklahoma, and Arizona suggests, educators participated in (or became alienated from) their state's struggles to the extent they identified with and had meaningful access to participate in the movement's formation and decision-making. Likewise, such grassroots participation is a foregrounding principle of longstanding and formidable social movements, like the MST, EZLN, and Mexico's democratic teachers' movement.

As the experiences of Kentucky's Jefferson County educators suggest, movements' decision-making is always fraught, contingent upon the various ways educators understand the roots of the issues impacting their and their students' and communities' lives and how these issues are felt in the classroom and beyond (also see Asselin; Stark). West Virginia educators constructed a social justice-oriented caucus informed by the emerging worker consciousness of its members. This consciousness and orientation to their work was bolstered by the experience of a successful wildcat strike unsanctioned by its state union in 2018. The experiences of educators across Kentucky during and in the aftermath of their major strike illuminates the significant impacts of White supremacy and racism on educator solidarity. While educators in Jefferson County had built strong coalitions among racial justice community organizations which contributed to the energy and participation of the 2018 strike, KY 120 and KEA favored centralization. Such centralization enabled KY 120 and KEA leadership to avoid and repress serious conversations about the educational issues facing Kentucky's urban communities in favor of catering to its White, conservative, and/or rural members, engaged primarily via social media. As a result, its KY 120-led 2019 sickout lacked the strength of force of the more grassroots-mobilized 2018 strike. While Arizona rank-and-file educators organized a robust grassroots network of local organizing, Oklahoma educators' organizing was more nebulous, organizationally disconnected across localities, and contingent. The most visibly articulated leaders in the news and social media were not recognized by most educators as such, and the state union was able to claim control over ending the action before most were ready.

The 2018 strikes took place at a statewide scale. In the aftermath of winning partial demands that were both impactful locally and statewide, in each state, retaliatory legislation sought to repress future actions. For example, in 2019, Oklahoma legislators introduced a bill (which later died in committee after strong backlash) that would permanently revoke a teacher's state license for engaging in a future walkout or protest (Yan). And, despite their 2019 strikes, West Virginia eventually passed a school privatization bill during the next summer break. It seems fair to say that none of the emergent educator movements may yet have the kind of strength of collective and grassroots organization that would enable them to engage in strategic and contentious co-governance. In different ways, each of the state educator movements under study illuminates the risks of state collaboration and the significance of building strong, intersectional, queer and feminist, and democratic power fueled by cultures of solidarity. For Tarlau, such cultures of solidarity are necessarily prior to co-governance. In places like Jefferson County in Kentucky, like CORE in Chicago and other social justice caucuses, coalitional relationships with and for community and social movement organizations provide important sources of power and resources for advancing the most impactful, relevant demands for educators, students, and communities. In all the "red" states, educators with experiences participating in social movements and labor struggle were and continue to be at the forefront of organizing most forcefully in their local districts and state contexts and were the backbone of the strikes in the first place (see Dyke and Muckian-Bates).

As all these struggles teach us, scaling up to the state level and beyond cannot shortcut local, grassroots organizing. And such local, grassroots organizing is rooted in, as we have elaborated in other chapters, the specific histories and contexts of local places. These histories and geographies require movements' concerted engagements with intersecting relations of power and oppression along the lines of race, gender, and class, and how these relations shape the conditions of education and struggle, locally and beyond.

Epilogue

The resurgence of militancy that ignited in West Virginia in 2018 spread rapidly across several other states. One week after West Virginia education workers struck, adjunct faculty at Virginia Commonwealth University struck as well, winning a twenty-five percent pay increase for adjunct instructors. Both Oklahoma and Kentucky educators struck on the same day, April 2, and by the end of the month, educators in Arizona and Colorado also struck along with bus drivers in Dekalb County, Georgia. In 2018, at least thirteen additional strikes by graduate students, contingent faculty, and non-academic employees occurred at universities across the country, more than any year prior in recent history (Herbert and Apkarian). The following year, in 2019, massive strikes by educators in Los Angeles, Oakland, Chicago, and Denver continued the Red for Ed revolt, in addition to another two-day strike in West Virginia and periodic sickouts in Kentucky.

In one way, the two years show similarities in the demands and victories made by education workers. Decades of austerity had cut public employees' pensions and benefits. Salaries for educators had become stagnant while funding for public education remained low. In 2018, West Virginia's education workers won a five percent pay increase for all public employees in the state, a freeze to any changes in their health insurance increases, and a year later, temporarily defeated a charter school bill from becoming law. Kentucky's educators managed to draw attention to the pension changes in the dreaded Sewer Bill and apply enough pressure to legally challenge, and then overturn, it. Oklahoma educators won significant wage and funding increases, even if far below their initial aims. Arizona educators won a nineteen percent pay raise for educators and laid the groundwork for the passage of a bill that increased education funding in the state by hundreds of millions of dollars two years later.

In another way, however, the strikes' differences between 2018 and 2019 were contingent upon a variety of factors. Central Appalachia's demographic characteristics and the relationship between lawmakers, union officials, and rank-and-file educators made the strikes and their aftermath in Kentucky and West Virginia quite different. West Virginia's rank-and-file formed a progressive caucus, WV United, dedicated to continued grassroots organizing, oftentimes in opposition to their state or local union leadership. The 2018 wildcat action created tensions between union leaders and the rank-and-file, contributing to WV United's commitment to independence from electoralism and old guard union leaders. Kentucky, however, was split between Black educators and their allies in Jefferson County, their unions, and the statewide organization KY 120. While many Jefferson County educators sought to push for a community-based social movement unionism, predominantly White leaders of the statewide groups sought, more often, to shut down discussions of demands and tactics they feared might alienate the state's rural and predominantly White educators and residents. Their desire to return to a pre-Governor Bevin era meant that educator-organizers focused their energy on electing supportive political candidates rather than organizing independently of them. The relationship that became established between the state's union leaders and the new leaders of KY 120 hindered the development of an autonomous rank-and-file-led statewide caucus or organization.

In Oklahoma, the 2018 walkouts had been building in momentum since at least a year prior, stalled by hesitant state union leadership. Like most other state-level unions in each state, the OEA participated in and supported the rank-and-file-mobilized effort after it became clear walkouts were inevitable. While the threat of the strike forced the state legislature to partially concede to educators' demands, the OEA's surreptitious directive to educators to go back to work before any additional gains could be made, in collaboration with legislators and superintendents, created deep antagonisms that led many educators to leave the union. The rank-and-file statewide, predominantly online, groups tended to be led or moderated by only a few louder voices. Educators have had little recourse or movement to continue to advance their aims or halt retaliatory legislation at the state level, at least. Alternatively, learning from the experiences of previous states, Arizona educators' formation of an aspirationally democratic, rank-and-file-led statewide organization tipped the balance of power in their collaboration with their state union. The infrastructure of their organization enabled their continued efforts to increase funding for public education and inspired similar statewide organizations in other states. Even so, in the aftermath of 2018, AEU organizers contended with demobilization and tensions between electoral strategies and direct-action approaches.

● What the Red State Educator Organizing Can Teach Us

Throughout the book, we have aimed to illuminate the significance of and intertwinement of horizontalism and union democracy, rank-and-file power, and community-based educator organizing that is attentive to the ways in which educators' working conditions are necessarily shaped by racial, heteropatriarchal, and settler colonialist capitalism (Weiner, "Education Reforms and Capitalism"). While these latter terms may feel abstract, we have tried to show, through tracing longer histories of educator organizing and educator unions, these forces are tangible even if differently experienced in each situated place.

During the red state strikes and beyond, so many folks undertook extraordinary actions in defense of their fellow workers and the common good. Many rank-and-file educators in West Virginia, Arizona, Oklahoma, and Kentucky were able to take on significant roles in their movements because many of them had long-haul roots in social and labor movements: Rebecca Garelli's experience in the 2012 CTU Strike, Jay O'Neal's labor organizing, Stephanie Price's racial justice work with her local union's racial and ethnic minority caucus, Kristy Self's LGBTQ+ organizing and advocacy efforts, Petia Edison's long time efforts to fight for Black youth in and beyond her union, to name just a few (also see Dyke and Muckian-Bates). Many educators were directly plugged into the work of grassroots organizing in their workplaces and within the broader community for years prior to their statewide strikes, whether in their local unions, community organizations, or in social movement organizations. The strikes in and of themselves produced notable gains, but most importantly, they provided outlets for educators to connect with one another around shared grievances and continue the work they had been doing, although this time in a more concerted and direct way. Their efforts to continue this work after the strike wave deepened and strengthened their relationships, connecting them to similarly oriented educators across the country. They began coordinating efforts to refuse to return to schools during the COVID-19 pandemic, with local, national, and international communication networks in place from the previous round of walkouts.

The usefulness and challenges of digital organizing offers one important lesson from the strikes. In their study of West Virginia educators' use of social media, Crystal Howell and Caleb Schmitzer found that the secret statewide Facebook group created an important space of information-sharing, empowerment, solidarity, and connected members to the wider labor movement in important ways. However, they write, the social media group, unlike the later-developed WV United caucus, was not a formal democratic organization in and of itself. In some places, social media groups with tens or hundreds of thousands of members may have felt to many in the moment like a strong show of rank-and-file power, the power of these groups was precarious without democratic structures and relationships simultaneously in place. Administrators of the groups, as with KY 120 and JCPS teachers in Kentucky, could unilaterally remove posters who they felt were divisive for seeking demands that centered racial and social justice. In Oklahoma, most educators who organized actions and activities in their local districts found Alberto Morejon's sole-moderated TTN limited in its usefulness and Morejon prone to disapproving posts he did not like. AEU organizers reflected that their liaison and communication network across the state of Arizona were critical to the success of their organizing.

Second, in each state, the strikes came to fruition after rank-and-file educators galvanized their hesitant state unions to direct action. In the book, we've drawn on labor and educator union history to illuminate how labor law acts to manage peace between workers and management from early labor law to recent right-to-work legislation, and labor-electoral coalitions have presented challenges for rank-and-file militancy and power. Business or service unionism predominates most educator unions, and rank-and-file efforts to democratize and transform their unions have faced significant challenges (Hagopian and Green; Stark).

One major way rank-and-file educator organizations have aimed to address the intransigency of business unionism and the narrowed electoral strategy is through rank-and-file organizing. The term "organizing" pervades labor movement writing yet it is often used in ways that tend to presume the transparency and clarity of its meaning. The truth is, it has no singular meaning in and of itself, and must be understood as a practice within the ideological context of its use. Our ideological orientation is firmly rooted within the traditions of solidarity and social movement unionisms.

Most educators know all too well the pitfalls of externally imposed standardized curriculum in the classroom. Just so, there is no standardized set of steps for organizing that educators can follow to ensures success. As in teaching and learning, organizing for rank-and-file-led union democracy and social justice is premised on the strength of relationships among organizers (and potential organizers), attention to differences in power and vulnerability in organizational structures and interpersonal practice, and the embrace of discomfort as people are challenged by one another to think and act in new ways that might challenge previously held understandings. Anyone can become an organizer (as so many did during the 2018 strikes and beyond). Yet, like teaching, organizing skills and knowledge are earned from practice, experience, and reflective study.

Maton and Stark write of the need to understand the centrality of political education for educator organizing in social justice caucuses.

> Political education activities are integrated throughout the work of many unions and grassroots organizations (e.g., Bocking, 2020; Foley, 1999; Riley, 2021; Taylor, 2001). Such activities have been found to serve a range of purposes, including: attracting and retaining members (e.g., Foley, 1999), fostering new and deepened connections among people and ideas (e.g., Chovanec, 2009; Maton, 2016a; Riley, 2021), strengthening the reflexive organizing capabilities of learners (e.g., Freire, 2004), and contributing to the design of more resilient and responsive activist organizations (e.g., Chovanec, 2009; Maton, 2018; Stark, 2019; Tarlau, 2014). As such, political education is fundamental to the daily operations and longevity of grassroots movements pushing for social and economic change. (3)

In their study of social justice caucuses across the US, Maton and Stark created a typology of political education that is useful for making visible the work of developing and sustaining strong rank-and-file organizations:

> We find that political education takes five main forms in teachers' grassroots social justice caucuses—structured, situational, mobilized, relational and networked forms. *Structured political education* involves participation in intentionally-designed and -created activities with an explicit agenda of political education. *Situational political education* is

comprised of contextually-situated personal, organizational or institutional experiences of policies that tend to reap negative emotional
responses among educators. Such experiences are not intended by
policymakers to be educational, and yet facilitate political education.
Mobilized political education refers to the ways in which political learning occurs through involvement in explicit political action, such as a
strike or rally. *Relational political education* positions relationships as
the central component in supporting the growth of a particular political viewpoint. Finally, *networked political education* involves personal
or organizational participation in formal networks, alliances and/or
partnerships that support political education. (11)

Maton and Stark's typology is useful in that it makes visible the sites of learning and relationship-building necessary for growing democratic participation in
educator movements. In our interviews, educators recounted how much they
learned by spending time on picket lines and at rallies with their co-workers
making sense of the issues, witnessing the power of the rank-and-file as bus
drivers and school cooks refused to cross the line and aided in shutting down
hesitant districts. Importantly, educators shifted from feelings of isolation to
solidarity as they came to better understand the systemic nature of public education disinvestment. During the strikes, mobilized political education became
widespread and fueled educators' actions. In quieter times, other forms of political education become ever more important (Niesz).

As in our state contexts under study, tensions between union democracy and
social justice among a teaching force that is predominantly White and women is
common and necessary to learn from. In Stark's study of the UCORE network,
which emerged in the years after the 2012 CORE-led strike in Chicago, she notes
tensions in organizing that arise between union democratization and racial and
social justice. These tensions largely emerged between predominantly White
educators and educators of color, and among teaching and support staff (which
tend to have more diverse class and racial compositions than certified teachers)
who held quite different understandings and analyses of justice issues and their
intersections (138). In instances where caucuses have won leadership in their
larger unions, tensions between democracy, broader union support, and racial
and social justice issues can come more prominently to the fore. Stark provides
two key examples:

[D]uring an extraordinarily intersectional one-day strike led by the
Chicago Teachers Union, the Fight for $15, and leaders from the Black
Lives Matter movement in 2016, CTU leaders in the CORE caucus faced
a backlash after an invited speaker from the Black liberation organization Assata's Daughters ended an invited speech with chants against
the police (field notes, April 1, 2016). While the strike was overwhelmingly supported by members, caucus and union leaders needed to nego-

tiate whether to publicly affirm their community partner or the officers she condemned. These tensions can also emerge in bargaining, as organizers determine whether to set their bargaining model and demands based on the democratic input of members or in alignment with the priorities of organizers. In Seattle's SEE caucus, for example, organizers debated whether pursuing a democratic Bargaining for the Common Good model would support or undermine the caucus's work for racial justice, given the disproportionately white demographics of the teaching staff and broader city. (138–39)

Similarly, Asselin notes the ways in which racial and criminal justice issues can create, in her words, "fault lines" among social justice caucus members (184). While caucus members in MORE and WE found consensus in taking stances around issues of economic justice and immigrant justice, issues surrounding police and police unions had been far more contentious. Some members sought to avoid taking stronger stances of solidarity against police brutality because they believed they would lose members and power, and others held pro-police stances and felt the caucuses' discussion and engagement with the Black Lives Matter movement was distracting them from the "real" educational issues their caucus should focus on.

Asselin found, however, that many organizers felt "union democracy" and "social justice" did not need to be dichotomized, and, in practice, MORE and WE found pedagogical opportunities within these tensions to develop caucus members' collective analyses of the "real" issues–that are always-already raced, classed, and gendered. As one caucus organizer, Sonia, describes:

I think one example is talking about hiring and firing practices in our contract . . . specifically looking at populations of teachers of color, which have gone down in the last 10–20 years . . . And then a lot of that was attached to school closures in the last 10 years and that even though technically if the school closes those teachers aren't necessarily fired, they go back to the pool, it still forces many people into retirement. It encourages people to look elsewhere and then those kind of closures targeted more veteran teachers of color that are among the most valuable educators in our district and they are lost . . . On the surface many people go, "Oh, it's just school closures, it's about managing your resources, it's about funding," and people don't automatically look at it through a racial justice lens or a social justice lens. And that our work seeks to put it through that lens and encourage people to think about it in that way. (197)

As Asselin writes, "In response to crises, MORE and WE have attempted to solve the extension dilemma by adapting their internal structures and creating spaces where they can organize in the tensions that allow for the both/and [union democracy and racial justice] rather than either/or" (24).

In many social justice caucuses, educators have engaged in radical learning communities (i.e., book study groups), to develop these lenses and engage tensions as opportunities (Maton; Morrison; Riley). For example, in her participatory study of an activist inquiry group composed of WE members, Maton describes how educators shifted and transformed their understanding of school reform in Philadelphia from a relatively colorblind economic analysis of neoliberalism to one that centered structural racism. For members who undertook this shift in "problem framing," it created more strategic clarity for their ongoing efforts to build strong relationships with existing community and social movement organizations.

As our "red" states demonstrate, issues of race are not unique to major urban areas. For example, race was not *not* an issue in predominantly White West Virginia. Rather, the state's longer history of colonization, slavery, White-only property ownership laws, and out-migration for survival shaped the intensification of poverty for the state's fewer Black persisters. Multi-racial worker organizing shaped the state's earliest and most violent labor battles (see Chapter Two). In the more diverse Oklahoma (like many places), rank-and-file educators are predominantly White because desegregation policies pushed out so many Black teachers, despite the efforts of the state's Black educator association to fight for wage parity and their right to teach. In Arizona and Oklahoma, public education disinvestment and privatization schemes from conservative lawmakers seek to redistribute resources away from the majority-racial minority public education system, doubling down on segregation.

In every state, patriarchal outrage spewed from legislators at predominantly women striking educators. In Kentucky, Governor Bevin accused educators of leaving children vulnerable to sexual assault while they struck (Stracqualursi), and in Oklahoma, educators were accused of acting like teenagers who wanted a new car. Militant educators became infantilized, cast as misbehaving, and accused of enabling deviance. Militant educators challenged the devaluation of care work through, in many instances, caring practices of relational organizing.

Some educators may understand that gender is a salient factor shaping their dismal working conditions (Russom). In their study of the social justice caucus, WE, in Philadelphia, Brown and Stern write that analyses that engage the intersections of race, class, gender, and sexualization are necessary in new educator movements yet often siloed or understood as in-tension rather than mutually constitutive, and more so among White educators. While educator organizers in their study often drew on feminist traditions of organizing without naming them as such, e.g., horizontalism, distributed leadership, understanding dissent as productive rather than inefficient, consensus-based decision-making, they tended to frame their political orientations toward union democracy and anti-racism. Brown and Stern argue White supremacy and heteropatriarchy are inextricably intertwined with and make possible neoliberal and neoconservative market-based school reform movements. They write, "Making the gendered analysis more audible and a central part of public and organizing discourse might create a connective tissue that links together movements by illuminating and legitimating the forces that create precarity among diverse, but often overlapping, communities" (192).

● Beyond 2019: The Pandemic and Continued Organizing Efforts

We write still in the midst of the pandemic. There is certainly much more to learn and understand from this tumultuous era of educator organizing. Yet, we think there might be some preliminary insights to glean. The lessons learned from the strike wave in each state directly impacted crucial organizing efforts to keep schools shut down during COVID-19 until adequate public health safety measures could be implemented. In West Virginia, WV United had the opportunity to test out their solidarity unionist model during the early days of the pandemic. In the beginning of 2020, the caucus put forth a slate of candidates for leadership positions in WVEA. Jay O'Neal ran for president of the union, Nicole McCormick for vice president, and three other educators ran for open positions on the state executive board. It was the first contested election for WVEA president since Dale Lee took office in 2008 and one of the few times in recent memory when the union experienced serious contention for executive positions.

The caucus slate faced significant challenges. WVEA uses a delegate system for statewide offices, meaning that delegates are allocated based on local membership. Not every local sends its full list of delegates to the annual delegate assembly, in part because of low membership participation. The first and most pressing challenge the caucus faced was finding contacts in each of the fifty-five counties who would support their insurgent campaign. The skills O'Neal, McCormick, and others learned from striking helped immeasurably in this endeavor.

Due in no small part to the building of the WVPEU Facebook page, the caucus was able to quickly find at least one sympathetic WVEA member in most counties. From there, the caucus slate went to task, returning to their organizing roots of holding one-on-one conversations with members, asking about their concerns, what they would like to see their unions do in the near future, and how they could continue fighting for a fix to PEIA. Candidates knew from the events that led to the 2018 wildcat strike that there was at least some residual resentment to the old guard's tactics.

On the two-year anniversary of the strike, the caucus held a large gathering in Charleston with former assistant secretary of education turned public education advocate and educational historian, Diane Ravitch. The event was a watershed moment for the caucus just ahead of a heated election. Ravitch's support for many of their overall goals—uniting both AFT-WV and WVEA into one union, spending less time on lobbying and more time on grassroots organizing, emphasizing a social justice agenda in union work—was central to explaining to membership that the so-called radical goals the caucus had formulated were indeed achievable and reasonable.

However, COVID-19 hampered many of the caucus' plans for getting out their message. O'Neal, who had scheduled tours across the state to meet with WVEA members, had to cancel those events in favor of a digital organizing strategy. Educators already swamped with the new reality of teaching during a global pandemic, with tools they were unfamiliar with, and in an ever-changing environment, forced many to prioritize their own personal well-being.

For their part, Lee and his slate of candidates emphasized the message of "steady leadership in unsteady times." Lee and his supporters claimed that it had been the elected leaders of WVEA who weathered the storm of the 2018 strike successfully, and only this group of candidates could chart a path forward amid pandemic-related uncertainties. Convention had also been moved from the in-person, politicking-heavy setting to a one-day, online event. This, again, put the caucus on the defensive, relying on supporters and fellow WVEA members to convey their platform to other locals in advance.

When the votes were tallied, the progressive slate of candidates garnered an impressive forty percent of the vote. Not enough to win but enough for the caucus to make their mark. The defeat was a bittersweet moment for WV United. On the one hand, it was hard to reconcile the energy and passion of rank-and-file members in 2018 with the results in 2020. Indeed, the wildcat strike was a referendum on conservative leadership and evidenced a desire for change. Organize 2020, the North Carolina Education Association's rank-and-file caucus, won their election for union president only a few short years after forming their caucus. And, unlike the work of CORE in Chicago, West Virginia's rank-and-file education workers took the reverse course of action—engage in militant organizing, go on strike, and then work to take over union leadership.

Electoral emphasis in Kentucky fared no better in 2020 than it did in 2018. Republicans achieved a nearly five percentage point increase in proportion of votes in the House of Representatives races between the two years, from 59.59 percent in 2018 to 64.46 percent in 2020. Similarly, Kentucky Republicans went from having a 61–39 majority in the state House of Representatives in 2018 to a 75–25 majority in 2020. The hated Governor Bevin had narrowly lost re-election in 2019 by 0.4 percent (KY State Board of Elections). This was perhaps the most impressive victory between the years outlined here. During the lead-up to the election, KY 120 once again flooded their social media pages with state endorsements, information about how to vote during the COVID-19 pandemic, and reminded viewers of their success in ousting Governor Bevin one year prior. Much of the information their social media page shared came directly from recently elected Lt. Governor Jacqueline Coleman's (D) or Governor Beshear's (D) pages, solidifying the ties, however informal, between KY 120's politics and those of the highest-ranking elected officials in Kentucky.

Despite these connections with the governor's office, Kentucky school districts were no safer when they returned from summer break than when they shut down earlier that year. District superintendents could determine whether to reopen in-person or remain virtual as students returned to classes in September. It wasn't until Governor Beshear's executive order on November 23, 2020, that all public and private middle and high schools were forced to remain remote or virtual until at least January 4, 2021. Likewise in West Virginia, Governor Justice allowed schools to reopen for in-person instruction in September if counties met a convoluted and changing requirement on his much-derided color-coded infection tracking system. No official executive order closed schools for in-person instruction as they shifted into the next calendar year.

In Oklahoma, Republican governor and ardent Trump supporter, Kevin Stitt was elected in 2018 after former governor Mary Fallin's handling of the education walkouts decimated her public image. Since he began office, Stitt has maintained vocal support for state control of local education, vouchers for religious and private education, and the privatization of public education. He made national news for his disapproval of mask mandates and, during the initial deadly surge of COVID-19 infections, encouragement of residents to dine in at restaurants and "support local business" (S. Murphy). While some independent organizing took place among educators, vocal conservative and predominantly White parents engaged in public protest, brought lawsuits against local school boards to force their full re-opening, and shamed educators at school board meetings for their selfishness for asking for basic public health precautions.

The dynamics that emerged and intensified between many rank-and-file educators and OEA continued, as the union initially hesitated to come out as a forceful voice for safe working conditions, opting for a more conciliatory tone. Later, OEA took a stronger rhetorical stance in press conferences yet did not put forward any clear demands for school safety, opting to serve more as an information hub and legal resource for educators. Mirroring the language of the State Board of Education and state leaders, OEA engaged language that highlighted the necessity to make decisions at the local level. While not the same, "local control" rhetoric had been a go-to for Stitt to justify his refusal to make a statewide mask mandate during the height of the pandemic.

In Arizona, AEU led the fight for safe re-openings, engaging similar but more robust and further reaching escalating efforts, including social media campaigns and motorcade demonstrations. By December, rank-and-file educators in Gilbert and Chandler had organized sickouts for January 2021 (while their union locals distanced themselves publicly from organizers and refused to endorse the actions (Hernandez)). As Garelli described in our interview, before the walkouts, educators she talked to about their shared poor working conditions felt resigned to their lack of power. Now, educators in suburban districts felt empowered to organize work stoppages to protest for health and safety.

● When We Fight, We Win

As many writers and thinkers have illuminated, the crises many of us are experiencing in the pandemic are not solely, or perhaps mostly, the result of the virus, but rather the absence of social policy to mitigate transmission and protect the health and economic well-being of all people, especially those most vulnerable. If any moment calls for educators to engage the intellectual traditions and practices of solidarity and social movement unionisms, it is certainly now. The 2018 and 2019 strikes had widespread public support. In the pandemic, parents' feelings toward reopening were much more starkly divided along race and class lines (Halloran et al.), and educators' calls to "refuse to return" until schools were safe(r) was more controversial than "more education funding now!"

Much research and writing has documented the disproportionate impact the pandemic has had on mothers and women, as they manage caregiving and waged work, even as they make up most frontline workers (Rabinowitz and Rabinowitz). Many have also accused educators and unions for shirking their responsibility to do what is best for the children, framing their resistance to unsafe working conditions as an unwillingness to work (Strunk). In many, especially working-class predominantly Black, school districts, pre-pandemic building safety has *already* been an ongoing fight, made much worse by the pandemic. For example, the Philadelphia Federation of Teachers in coalition with community-based justice organizations had long been fighting for their district to address issues of asbestos and other environmental hazards, which have been linked to student and teacher illness, even death (Ruderman and Graham).

As we have aimed to illuminate in the four preceding chapters, simply having a militant presence in the workplace is insufficient to develop the capacity for massive labor actions. And, while strikes are the most important tool, they do not on their own necessarily portend sustainable movements or big wins for labor. The role of politicians, regardless of their politics, play little role in this either. Rather, from the perspective of our study and related literature, the most successful education labor movements undertake the ongoing work of connecting social movement demands to labor demands, deepening analyses of how gender, race, class, and settler colonialism shape education work and unions, and building radically democratic rank-and-file organizations that practice a healthy wariness of recuperation by business unionism or electoralism. Easier said than done!

We end by acknowledging and honoring the collective labor involved in realizing this book. From the many educators who shared their stories with us to the many education union, labor, and social movement thinkers—in K–12 and higher education, in and with social justice caucuses, in university labor organizing, and the Industrial Workers of the World—who have informed our study. Even so, readers should understand our story of the spring 2018 strikes is by no means definitive but one retelling. So many more educators' stories—educators who organized and continue to organize in their local places—are not included on these pages. No doubt their experiences would further deepen how we understand the significance, challenges, and possibilities of the educator movements that have taken shape in these so-called "red" states.

In her memoir, historian and Okie Roxanne Dunbar-Ortiz writes that, in Oklahoma, "red" historically signifies much more than just right-leaning. "Red" conjures a painful and submerged history of Oklahoma's thriving communist and socialist past, the violence of Indigenous forced migration and genocide, and, for her, the red soil of Canadian County in which her mixed heritage family labored in poverty as tenant farmers during the Dust Bowl era. The strikes and the wider Red for Ed movement suggests the struggle for political hegemony and historical consciousness in these states are active, contingent, and ongoing.

Works Cited

Abowitz, Kathleen Knight, and Kate Rousmaniere. "Diva Citizenship: A Case Study of Margaret Haley as Feminist Citizen-Leader." *Counterpoints*, vol. 305, 2007, pp. 233–255, https://www.jstor.org/stable/45136063.

Acosta, Curtis. "Dangerous minds in Tucson: The banning of Mexican American Studies and critical thinking in Arizona." *Journal of Educational Controversy*, vol. 8, no. 1, 2014, article 9. https://cedar.wwu.edu/jec/vol8/iss1/9.

Agba, Christopher Belken. *Developing a Marginalized and Segregated Community: Case Study of a West Virginia Neighborhood*. 2020. West Virginia University. Ph.D. Dissertation. *The Research Repository at WVU*, https://researchrepository.wvu.edu/cgi/viewcontent.cgi?article=8605&context=etd.

Albisetti, James C. "The feminization of teaching in the nineteenth century: A comparative perspective." *History of Education*, vol. 22, no. 3, 1993, pp. 253–263, https://doi.org/10.1080/0046760930220305.

Ali, Arshad Imtiaz, and Tracy Lachica Buenavista, editors. *Education at War: The Fight for Students of Color in America's Public Schools*. Fordham UP, 2018.

Alvarez, Sonia E. *Cultures of Politics/Politics of Cultures: Revisioning Latin American Social Movements*. Routledge, 2018.

Antonucci, Mike. "Mixed Results from New NEA Membership Numbers Pre-Janus Ruling, Post 2018 Teacher Walkouts in W. Va., Okla. and Ariz." *The 74 Million*, 19 June 2019, https://www.the74million.org/article/mixed-results-from-new-nea-membership-numbers-pre-janus-ruling-post-2018-teacher-walkouts-in-w-va-okla-and-ariz/.

Anyon, Jean. "Social Class and the Hidden Curriculum of Work." *Journal of Education*, vol. 162, no. 1, 1980, pp. 67–92. https://www.jstor.org/stable/42741976.

Asselin, Chloe. *Tensions, Dilemmas, and Radical Possibility in Democratizing Teacher Unions: Stories of Two Social Justice Caucuses in New York City and Philadelphia*. 2019. City University of New York. Ph.D. Dissertation. *CUNY Academic Works*, https://academicworks.cuny.edu/gc_etds/3433.

Bacharach, Samuel, et al. "Professionals and Workplace Control: Organizational and Demographic Models of Teacher Militancy." *ILR Review*, vol. 43, no. 5, 1990, pp. 570–586. https://doi.org/10.1177/001979399004300505.

Bailey, Phillip M. "Gang Bill Critics Say Targets Black Men and Children Passes Kentucky Legislature." *Courier Journal*, 13 April, 2018, https://www.courier-journal.com/story/news/politics/ky-legislature/2018/04/13/kentucky-senate-moves-gang-bill-forward-rejects-racial-impact-study/515293002/.

Bailey, Jason. "PFM Report Uses Exaggerated Claims to Justify Harsh, Counterproductive Cuts." *Kentucky Center for Economic Policy*, 28 Aug. 2017, https://kypolicy.org/pfm-report-uses-exaggerated-claims-justify-harsh-counterproductive-cuts/.

Bailey, Lucy E., and Karen Graves. "Gender and Education." *Review of Research in Education*, vol. 40, no. 1, 2016, pp. 682–722. https://doi.org/10.3102/0091732X16680193.

Baker, Scott. *Paradoxes of Desegregation: African American Struggles for Educational Equity in Charleston, South Carolina, 1926–1972*. Univ of South Carolina Press, 2006.

——. "Pedagogies of Protest: African American Teachers and the History of the Civil Rights Movement, 1940–1963." *Teachers College Record*, vol. 113, no. 12, 2011, pp. 2777–2803. https://doi.org/10.1177/016146811111301206.

Bartell, Tonya, et al. "Teacher Agency and Resilience in the Age of Neoliberalism." *Journal of Teacher Education*, vol. 70, no. 4, 2019, pp. 302–305. https://doi.org/10.1177/0022487119865216.

Bauer, Louise Birdsell. "Professors-in-Training or Precarious Workers? Identity, Coalition Building, and Social Movement Unionism in the 2015 University of Toronto Graduate Employee Strike." *Labor Studies Journal*, vol. 42, no. 4, 2017, pp. 273–294. https://doi.org/10.1177/0160449X17731877.

Bellei, Cristián et al. "The 2011 Chilean Student Movement Against Neoliberal Educational Policies." *Studies in Higher Education*, vol. 39, no. 3, 2014, pp. 426–440. https://doi.org/10.1080/03075079.2014.896179.

Berkshire, Jennifer, and Gordon Lafer. "When the 1% Run Our Schools: A Conversation with Jennifer Berkshire and Gordon Lafer." *YouTube*, uploaded by Network for Public Education, 23 Oct. 2017, https://www.youtube.com/watch?v=0ta7kPrgLBY.

Berry, Joe. *Reclaiming the Ivory Tower: Organizing Adjuncts to Change Higher Education.* Monthly Review Press, 2005.

Berry, Joe, and Helena Worthen. "Waves of Contingent Faculty Organizing Sweeps onto Campuses." *Labor Notes.* 8 Oct. 2014, https://www.labornotes.org/blogs/2014/10/wave-contingent-faculty-organizing-sweeps-campuses.

Bhattacharya, Tithi. "Why the Teachers' Revolt Must Confront Racism Head On." *Dissent*, 1 May, 2018, https://www.dissentmagazine.org/online_articles/why-teachers-strikes-must-confront-racism.

——. "Women Are Leading the Wave of Strikes in America. Here's Why." *The Guardian.* 10 April 2018, https://www.theguardian.com/commentisfree/2018/apr/10/women-teachers-strikes-america.

Billington, Monroe. "Public School Integration in Oklahoma 1954–1963." *The Historian*, vol. 26, no. 4, 1964, pp. 521–537.

Blanc, Eric. "Rank-and-File Organizing and Digital Mobilizing in the Red State Revolt." *Strike for the Common Good: Fighting for the Future of Public Education*, edited by Rebecca Kolins Givan and Amy Schrager Lang, University of Michigan Press, 2020, pp. 91–101.

——. *Red State Revolt: The Teachers' Strikes and Working Class Politics.* Verso, 2019.

——. "Betting on the working class." *Jacobin*, 29 May 2018, https://jacobin.com/2018/05/west-virginia-teachers-strikes-militant-minority-healthcare.

Blee, Kathleen M., and Dwight B. Billings. "Race Differences in the Origins and Consequences of Chronic Poverty in Rural Appalachia." *Social Science History*, vol. 20, no. 3, 1996, pp. 345–373. https://doi.org/10.1017/S0145553200018708.

Blount, Jackie M. *Fit to Teach: Same-Sex Desire, Gender, and School Work in the Twentieth Century.* SUNY Press, 2006.

Bocking, Paul. *Understanding the Neoliberalization of Education Through Spaces of Labour Autonomy.* 2017. York University, Ph.D. Dissertation. *YorkSpace*, http://hdl.handle.net/10315/34487.

Bousquet, Marc. *How the University Works: Higher Education and the Low-Wage Nation.* NYU Press, 2008.

Bowles, Samuel, and Herbert Gintis. *Schooling in Capitalist America: Educational Reform and the Contradictions of Economic Life.* Haymarket Books, 2011.

Bradley, Ann. "Legislative Plan Ends 12-Day West Virginia Teacher Strike." *Education Week*, 28 Mar. 1990, https://www.edweek.org/teaching-learning/legislative-plan-ends-12-day-west-virginia-teacher-strike/1990/03.

Brandt, Elizabeth. "Teacher Strikes, Work Stoppages, and Interruptions of Service: NEA Research Memo." *National Education Association*. Aug. 1970, pp. 1–13. https://files.eric.ed.gov/fulltext/ED070157.pdf.

Brecher, Jeremy. *Strike!* PM Press, 2014.

Brogan, Peter. "Getting to the CORE of the Chicago Teachers' Union Transformation." *Studies in Social Justice*, vol. 8, no. 2, 2014, pp. 145–164. https://doi.org/10.26522/ssj.v8i2.1031.

Brown, Autumn. *Organize, Activate, Liberate: Luper, Fisher, Davis and the Quiet Resistance of Radical Pedagogy in Oklahoma City During Civil Rights.* 2022. Oklahoma State University. Ph.D. Dissertation.

Brown, Karida L. *Gone Home: Race and Roots through Appalachia.* Univ of North Carolina Press, 2018.

Brown, Amy E., and Mark Stern. "Teachers' Work as Women's Work: Reflections on Gender, Activism, and Solidarity in New Teacher Movements." *Feminist Formations*, vol. 30, no. 3, 2018, pp. 172–197. https://doi.org/10.1353/ff.2018.0046.

Brown, Trevor, and Jennifer Palmer. "Stitt's New Board of Education Pick Spread Disinformation, Conspiracy Theory." *The Oklahoman*, 6 Dec. 2020, https://www.oklahoman.com/story/news/politics/2020/12/06/stitts-new-board-of-education-pick-spread-misinformation-conspiracy-theories/315857007/.

Buhle, Mari Jo, and Peter Buhle, editors. *It Started in Wisconsin: Dispatches from the Front Lines of the New Labor Protest.* Verso, 2012.

Buras, Kristen L. *Charter Schools, Race, and Urban Space: Where the Market Meets Grassroots Resistance.* Routledge, 2014.

BWST Staff. "Gilcrease Elementary Faces Possible Closure." *The Black Wall Street Times*, 28 Feb., 2019, https://theblackwallsttimes.com/2019/02/28/gilcrease-elementary-faces-possible-closure/.

Cameron, Alex. "A Look Back at the 1990 Teacher Strike in Oklahoma." *News 9.* 1 April 2018, https://www.news9.com/story/5e349028527dcf49dad7d3cd/a-look-back-at-the-1990-teacher-strike-in-oklahoma.

Cantrell, Paul [@inthehands]. "They've Hidden That Debt Off the Balance Sheets." *Twitter*, 11 Mar., 2022, 10:12am, https://twitter.com/inthehands/status/1502316495610724352.

Carter, Ray. "OEA Membership Down 16 Percent Over 5 Years." *City-Sentinel*, 12 July 2019, https://city-sentinel.com/2019/07/oea-membership-down-16-percent-over-five-years/.

Casey, Betty. "The Broad Foundation Lands at TPS: Should Parents Care?" *Tulsa Kids*, 8 July, 2016, https://www.tulsakids.com/the-broad-foundation-lands-at-tps-should-parents-care/.

Catte, Elizabeth et al., editors. *55 Strong: Inside the West Virginia Teachers' Strike.* Belt Publishing, 2018.

Chatterjee, Piya, and Sunaina Maira, editors. *The Imperial University: Academic Repression and Scholarly Dissent.* U of Minnesota Press, 2014.

Clark, Paul F. *The Miners' Fight for Democracy: Arnold Miller and the Reform of the United Mine Workers.* ILR Press, 1981.

Clayton, Leonard. *A History of Black Public Education.* 1977. University of Oklahoma. Ph.D. Dissertation.

CNN Wire. "Kentucky Governor Said Teachers' Strike Left Children Vulnerable to Sexual Assault." *Fox News 8*, 14 April 2018, https://tinyurl.com/3mt8ytf9.

Cobble, Dorothy Sue, editor. *The Sex of Class: Women Transforming American Labor.* Cornell UP, 2007.

Cochran-Smith, Marilyn. "Teacher communities for equity." *Kappa Delta Pi Record*, vol. 51, no. 3, 2015, pp. 109–113. https://doi.org/10.1080/00228958.2015.1056659.

Colby, Glenn, and Chelsea Fowler. "Data Snapshot: IPEDS Data on Full-Time Women Faculty and Faculty of Color: An In-depth Look at the Makeup and Salaries of Full-time Faculty Members in US Higher Education." *American Association of University Professors*, Dec. 2020, https://www.aaup.org/sites/default/files/Dec-2020 _Data_Snapshot_Women_and_Faculty_of_Color.pdf.

Commission on Educational Reinvention. *Reinventing the African-American Child's Academic Experience: A Cultural Shift for A Strategic-systemic Transformation of Tulsa Public Schools.* Citizens United for a Better Education System, 2015.

Cook, Maria Lorena. *Organizing Dissent: Unions, the State, and the Democratic Teachers' Movement in Mexico.* Penn State Press, 2010.

Cowen, Joshua M., and Katharine O. Strunk. "The Impact of Teachers' Unions on Educational Outcomes: What We Know and What We Need to Learn." *Economics of Education Review*, vol. 48, Oct. 2015, pp. 208–223. https://doi.org/10.1016/j.econ edurev.2015.02.006.

Da Silva, Chantal. "After Florida Shooting, West Virginia Governor Jokes to Teachers: 'Nobody's Going to Shoot At Me, Right?'" *Newsweek*, 27 Feb. 2018, https://www .newsweek.com/after-florida-shooting-west-virginia-governor-jokes-students -nobodys-going-821466.

D'Amico Pawlewicz, Diana, and Jenice L. View. "Social Justice and Teacher Profession-alism in the United States in Historical Perspective: Fractured Consensus." *Handbook on Promoting Social Justice in Education*, edited by Rosemary Papa. Springer, 2020, pp. 1279–1297. https://doi.org/10.1007/978-3-030-14625-2_130.

Dandala, Saturnin. "Teacher Social Justice Unionism and the Field of Industrial Relations in the United States." *Journal of Labor and Society*, vol. 22, 2019, pp. 571–84. https://doi.org/10.1111/wusa.12426.

Del Valle, Gaby. "Teachers Often Have to Crowdfund for Classroom Supplies. Some Districts Are Banning the Practice." *Vox*, 29 Mar. 2019, https://www.vox.com/the -goods/2019/3/29/18286095/donors-choose-crowdfunding-ban-school-districts.

Desrochers, Daniel. "How a Little-Known Feud Between Two Teacher Groups Fueled Last Week's Sickout." *Lexington Herald-Ledger*, 5 Mar. 2019, https://www.kentucky. com/article226976139.html.

Dobbie, David, and Ian Robinson. "Reorganizing Higher Education in the United States and Canada: The Erosion of Tenure and the Unionization of Contingent Faculty." *Labor Studies Journal*, vol. 33, no. 2, 2008, pp. 117–140. https://doi.org/10.1177 /0160449x07301241.

Doe, Sue et al. "What Works and What Counts: Valuing the Affective in Non-Tenure-Track Advocacy." *Contingency, Exploitation, and Solidarity: Labor and Action in English Composition*, edited by Seth Kahn et al., The WAC Clearinghouse and UP of Colorado, 2017, pp. 213–34. https://doi.org/10.37514/PER-B.2017.0858.2.14.

Douglas-Gabriel, Danielle. "Labor Board Withdraws Rule to Quash Graduate Students' Right to Organize as Employees." *The Washington Post*, 12 Mar. 2021, https://tinyurl .com/4p9vyzr3.

Dunaway, Wilma A. *Slavery in the American Mountain South.* Cambridge UP, 2003.

Dyke, Erin, and Brendan Muckian-Bates. "Social Movements Gave Rise to the "Teachers' Revolt," Not Bernie." *New Politics*, 6 Nov. 2019, https://tinyurl.com/43cx9f33.

Dyke, Erin et al. "Introduction: Understanding the 2018 Statewide Walkouts." *Critical Education*, vol. 13, issue 2, 2022, pp. 56–58, https://doi.org/10.14288/ce.v13i2.186727.

Dyke, Erin et al. "Beyond Defeat: Understanding Educators' Experiences in the 2018 Oklahoma Walkouts." *Critical Education*, vol.13, no. 2, 2022, pp. 77–95. https://doi.org/10.14288/ce.v13i2.186610.

Dunbar-Ortiz, Roxanne. *Red Dirt: Growing Up Okie.* University of Oklahoma Press, 2006.

Eberhart-Phillips, Jason. "School-Strike Injunction Sought." *The Arizona Daily Star*, vol. 137, no. 236, 3 Oct. 1978. https://tucson.com/oct-3-1978-tusd-teachers-strike/article_2e2dd7f8-f688-11e9-9c4f-43aa98099da4.html.

Ebert, Joel. "Bill to Allow Charter Schools Passes Senate." *Charleston Gazette-Mail,* 2 Mar. 2015, https://www.wvgazettemail.com/news/education/bill-to-allow-charter-schools-passes-senate/article_27c941e2-e8b6-5696-a4d1-ce1d8f30351b.html.

Eden, Karly D. "'No ifs, no buts, no education cuts': analyzing teacher experiences and participation in the 2018 Oklahoma teachers' strike." 2020. Kansas State University. Master's Thesis. *K-State Reseearch Exchange*, https://krex.k-state.edu/handle/2097/40804.

Edison, Petia, and Ivonne Rovira. "The Antiracist Struggle in the Kentucky Teacher Strike." *Strike for the Common Good: Fighting for the Future of Public Education*, edited by Rebecca Kolins Givan and Amy Schrager Lang, University of Michigan Press, 2020, pp. 117–126.

Education International. "Zimbabwe: Teachers Strike over Pay as Currency Crisis Deepens." *Education International*, 1 Sept. 2019, https://www.ei-ie.org/en/item/22717:zimbabwe-teachers-strike-over-pay-as-currency-crisis-deepens.

Edwards, Haley Sweetland. "War on Teacher Tenure: How Silicon Valley Wants to Fire Bad Teachers." *TIME*, 30 Oct. 2014, https://time.com/3533556/the-war-on-teacher-tenure/.

Eger, Andrea. "Teacher Shortage Milestone: New Record Set for Nonaccredited Teachers Given Emergency Certification in Oklahoma." *Tulsa World*, 29 Oct. 2021, https://tinyurl.com/yrka538y.

Fantasia, Rick. *Cultures of Solidarity: Consciousness, Action, and Contemporary American Workers.* University of California Press, 1989.

Feffer, Andrew. *Bad Faith: Teachers, Liberalism, and the Origins of McCarthyism.* Fordham Univ Press, 2019.

Friedman, Ellen David. "What's Behind the Teachers' Strikes?" *Labor Notes*, 22 May 2018, https://www.labornotes.org/blogs/2018/05/whats-behind-teachers-strikes.

Frost, Linda. *Never one nation.* University of Minnesota Press;, 2005.

Garelli, Rebecca. "Educators United Online." *Strike for the Common Good: Fighting for the Future of Public Education*, edited by Rebecca Kolins Givan and Amy Schrager Lang, University of Michigan Press, 2020, pp. 102–111.

Garland, Max. "Technocap Workers Continue Strike Near Wheeling." *Charleston Gazette-Mail*, 17 June 2018, https://tinyurl.com/2335ywjh.

Goldstein, Dana. *The Teacher Wars: A History of America's Most Embattled Profession.* Anchor, 2015.

Golin, Steve. *The Newark Teacher Strikes: Hopes on the Line.* Rutgers UP, 2002.

Grumet, Madeleine R. *Bitter Milk: Women and Teaching*. Univ of Massachusetts Press, 1988.

Gstalter, Morgan. "Oklahoma Teachers Jingle Keys, Chant 'Where's My Car?' at Governor." *The Hill*, 5 April 2018, https://www.newson6.com/story/5e35e39f2f69 d76f62020110/gov-fallin-angers-teachers-%20over-teenage-kid-comment-in-cbs -interview.

Gutman, David. "Census Report: 1 in 4 W.VA. Kids Live in Poverty." *Charleston Gazette-Mail*, 27 Oct. 2017, https://www.wvea.org/content/more-1-4-wva-kids-live-poverty.

Hagopian, Jesse, and John T. Green. "Teachers' Unions and Social Justice." *Education and Capitalism: Struggles for Learning and Liberation*. Edited by Jeff Bale and Sarah Knopp, 2012, pp. 141–75.

Hale, Jon N. "On Race, Teacher Activism, and the Right to Work: Historicizing the 'Red for Ed' Movement in the American South." *West Virginia Law Review*, vol. 121, no. 3, 2019, pp. 851–882.

——. "'The Development of Power is the Main Business of the School': The Agency of Southern Black Teacher Associations from Jim Crow through Desegregation." *The Journal of Negro Education*, vol. 87, no. 4, 2018, pp. 444–459. https://www.muse.jhu .edu/article/802653.

Halloran, Clare et al. "Pandemic Schooling Mode and Student Test Scores: Evidence from US States." *National Bureau of Economic Research*, working paper no. w29497, 2021. https://doi.org/10.3386/w29497.

Haney, James E. "The Effects of the Brown Decision on Black Educators." *The Journal of Negro Education*, vol. 47, no. 1, 1978, pp. 88–95.

Hardiman, Samuel. "Hundreds of Edison Students Walk Out of Class to Protest Deteriorating Culture at School." *Tulsa World*, 15 Feb. 2018, https://tinyurl.com/3hc8xsm3.

Herbert, William A., and Jacob Apkarian. "You've Been with the Professors: An Examination of Higher Education Work Stoppage Data, Past and Present." *Employee Rights and Employment Policy Journal*, vol. 23, no. 2, 2019, pp. 249–277. https://ssrn .com/abstract=3439730.

Hernandez, Rocio. "Chandler, Gilbert Schools Districts Preparing for Teacher Sickouts on Tuesday." *KJZZ*, 4 Jan. 2021, https://kjzz.org/content/1647487/chandler-gilbert -schools-districts-preparing-teacher-sickouts-tuesday.

Hopland, Macks. "Who Has the Real Power and Where Does That Power Come From." *Facebook*, 21 Mar. 2022, https://www.facebook.com/profile.php?id=3423295.

Howell, Crystal, and Caleb Schmitzer. "Online and on the Picket Line: West Virginia Teachers' Use of an Online Community to Organize." *Critical Education*, vol. 13, no. 2, pp. 59–76. https://doi.org/10.14288/ce.v13i2.186613.

Huber, Patrick. "Red Necks and Red Bandanas: Appalachian Coal Miners and the Coloring of Union Identity, 1912–1936." *Western Folklore*, vol. 65, no. 1/2, 2006, pp. 195–210. https://www.jstor.org/stable/25474784.

Hudock, Megan. "Governor Jim Justice Holds Town Hall Meeting in Morgantown." *12WBOY*, 27 Feb. 2018, https://tinyurl.com/kpyu6xxm.

Jaffe, Sarah. "Work Won't Love You Back: What Teachers Can Teach Us About Work." *The Progressive*. 21 Mar. 2022, https://progressive.org/magazine/teachers-teach-us -about-work-jaffe/.

Jankov, Pavlyn, and Carol Caref. "Segregation and Inequality in Chicago Public Schools: Transformed and Intensified under Corporate Education Reform." *Education Policy Analysis Archives*, vol. 25, no. 56, 2017, pp. 1–35.

Jarovsky, Ben. "You Can Thank Karen Lewis for the National Wave of Teacher Insurrections." *Chicago Reader*, 5 April 2018, https://chicagoreader.com/blogs/you-can -thank-karen-lewis-for-the-national-wave-of-teacher-insurrections/.

Jarvis, Jake. "Thousands of Teachers Rally in Charleston in First of Two-Day Strike." *WVNews*, 22 Feb. 2018, https://www.wvnews.com/news/wvnews/thousands-of -teachers-rally-in-charleston-in-first-of-two-day-strike/article_4629bdb2-52bc-5bf8 -b237-6d2fe74a2106.html.

Jenkins, Jeff. "Justice Vetoes Budget by Unveiling Bull Manure." *WV Metro News*, 13 April, 2017, https://wvmetronews.com/2017/04/13/justice-vetoes-budget-by -unveiling-bull-manure/.

——. "Some Education Workers Return to Capitol, Upset with Deal to End Strike." *WV Metro News*, 28 February, 2018, https://wvmetronews.com/2018/02/28/some -education-workers-return-to-capitol-upset-with-deal-to-end-strike/.

Jones, Jeffrey M. "Conservatives Greatly Outnumber Liberals in 19 States." *Gallup*, 22 Feb. 2019, https://news.gallup.com/poll/247016/conservatives-greatly-outnumber -liberals-states.aspx.

Kahn, Seth. "From Solidarity Invoked to Solidarity Built." *Works and Days*, vol. 69, no. 35, 2017, pp. 251–262.

——. "We Value Teaching Too Much to Keep Devaluing It." *College English*, no. 82.6, 2020, pp. 591–611. https://library.ncte.org/journals/CE/issues/v82-6/30805.

Kahn, Seth et al. *Contingency, Exploitation, and Solidarity: Labor and Action in English Composition.* The WAC Clearinghouse and UP of Colorado, 2017. https://doi.org /10.37514/PER-B.2017.0858.

Karp, Stan, and Adam Sanchez. "The 2018 Wave of Teacher Strikes." *Rethinking Schools*, vol. 32, no. 4, 2018, https://www.rethinkingschools.org/articles/the-2018-wave-of -teacher-strikes.

Karpinski, Carol F. *"A Visible Company of Professionals": African Americans and the National Education Association During the Civil Rights Movement.* Peter Lang, 2008.

Karvelis, Noah. "Towards a Theory of Teacher Agency: Conceptualizing the Political Positions and Possibilities of Teacher Movements." *Berkeley Review of Education*, no. 9.1, 2019, pp. 1–7. https://doi.org/10.5070/B89146418

——. "Rural Organizing, Institutionalization, and 'Getting Back': An Interview with Red for Ed Organizer Vanessa Arrendondo." *Critical Education*, vol. 12, no. 2, 2022, pp. 96–102. https://doi.org/10.14288/ce.v13i2.186550.

Kennedy, Kevin. "Arizona Educator Reflects on When Her Parents Joined a Teacher Strike in 1971." *12News*, 25 April 2018, https://www.12news.com/article/news /education/arizona-educator-reflects-on-when-her-parents-joined-a-teacher-strike -in-1971/75-545855808.

King, Farina. *The Earth Memory Compass: Diné Landscapes and Education in the Twentieth Century.* University Press of Kansas, 2018.

Krutka, Daniel G. et al. "Eight Lessons on Networked Teacher Activism from #OklaEd and the #OklaEdWalkout." *Contemporary Issues in Technology and Teacher Education*, vol. 18, no. 2, 2018, pp. 379–391. https://www.learntechlib.org/primary /p/183635/.

KY State Board of Elections. "2020 General Election." *Commonwealth of Kentucky.* Accessed 4 Mar. 2023, https://elect.ky.gov/results/2020-2029/Pages/2020.aspx.

Larimer, Sarah. "They Have Had It": West Virginia Teachers Strike, Closing All Public Schools." *The Washington Post*, 22 Feb, 2018, https://tinyurl.com/mwbdwdrb.

Larimer, Sarah. "West Virginia Teachers Expected to Return to Classrooms Thursday as Governor Jim Justice Announces Deal." *The Washington Post*, 27 Feb. 2018, https://tinyurl.com/mrx2akc8.

Layden, Logan. "A Decade After Right-to-Work, Bitterness Remains in Oklahoma." *State Impact*, 5 April 2012, https://stateimpact.npr.org/oklahoma/2012/04/05/many-remain-bitter-about-right-to-work-in-oklahoma/.

Lesko, Nancy. *Act Your Age!: A Cultural Construction of Adolescence*. Routledge, 2012.

Lipman, Pauline. *The New Political Economy of Urban Education: Neoliberalism, Race, and the Right to the City*. Taylor & Francis, 2013.

Litvinov, Amanda, and Mary Ellen Flannery. "The High Cost of Education Budget Cuts." *NEA Today*, 16 July 2018, https://www.nea.org/advocating-for-change/new-from-nea/high-cost-education-budget-cuts.

Lomawaima, K. Tsianina, and Teresa L. McCarty. *"To Remain an Indian": Lessons in Democracy from a Century of Native American Education*. Teachers College Press, 2006.

Lynd, Staughton. *Accompaying: Pathways to social change*. PM Press, 2012.

Maton, Rhiannon M. "From Neoliberalism to Structural Racism: Problem Framing in a Teacher Activist Organization." *Curriculum Inquiry*, vol. 48, no. 3, 2018, pp. 293–315. https://doi.org/10.1080/03626784.2018.1474711.

Maton, Rhiannon M., and Lauren Ware Stark. "Educators Learning through Struggle: Political Education in Social Justice Caucuses." *Journal of Educational Change*, 4 Oct. 2021, pp. 1–25. https://doi.org/10.1007/s10833-021-09444-0.

McCormick, Nicole. "Owning My Labor." *Strike for the Common Good: Fighting for the Future of Public Education*, edited by Rebecca Kolins Givan and Amy Schrager Lang, University of Michigan Press, 2020, pp. 112–116.

McLaren, Mandy. "Teachers Group Calls for Statewide Sickout as JCPS, Other Districts to Close." *Courier Journal*, 27 Feb. 2019, https://www.courier-journal.com/story/news/education/2019/02/27/ky-120-united-calls-sickout-over-pension-board-issue/3010332002/.

Meiners, Erica R. "Disengaging from the Legacy of Lady Bountiful in Teacher Education Classrooms." *Gender and Education*, vol. 14, no. 1, 2002, pp. 85–94. https://doi.org/10.1080/09540250120098861.

——. *Right to be Hostile: Schools, Prisons, and the Making of Public Enemies*. Routledge, 2010.

Meyerhoff, Eli. *Beyond Education: Radical Studying for Another World*. U of Minnesota P, 2019.

Millam, Jeffrey F. et al. "Arizona Minority Report." *Arizona Minority Education Policy Analysis Center*, 2016, https://highered.az.gov/sites/default/files/16%20MSRP%20Report.pdf.

Moattar, Daniel. "How Graduate Unions Are Winning–and Scaring the Hell out of Bosses–in the Trump Era." *In These Times*, 29 Nov. 2018, https://inthesetimes.com/article/graduate-student-unions-trump-nlrb-columbia-brown.

Mochaidean, Michael. "The Other West Virginia Teacher Strike." *Jacobin*. 9 April 2018, https://www.jacobinmag.com/2018/04/west-virginia-teachers-strike-1990-unions.

Morrison, Dana. *Organized: An Exploration of Teachers' Engagement in Grassroots Organizing*. 2018. University of Delaware. Ph.D. Dissertation. *UDSpace*, http://udspace.udel.edu/handle/19716/24212.

Musgrave, Nick. "Black Coal: The African American Miners of West Virginia's Southern Coalfields." *Expatalachian*, 12 Feb. 2019, http://expatalachians.com/black-coal-the-african-american-miners-of-west-virginias-southern-coalfields.

Mummolo, Burt. "Tulsa Public School Teachers Protest Low Wages." *KTUL*, 25 Jan. 2018, https://ktul.com/news/local/tulsa-public-school-teachers-protest-low-wages.

Murphy, Brian. "Governor Uses a Plate of Real 'Bull-You-Know-What' as a Prop While Vetoing Budget." *The Kansas City Star*, 13 April 2017, https://amp.kansascity.com/news/nation-world/national/article144513494.html.

Murphy, Marjorie. *Blackboard Unions: The AFT and the NEA, 1900–1980.* Cornell UP, 1990.

Murphy, Sean. "Oklahoma Declares Emergency After Tweet Backlash." AP News, 15 Mar. 2020, https://apnews.com/article/small-business-virus-outbreak-health-oklahoma-ok-state-wire-bda618402858426a612d58910e36911d.

Nero, Donnie. "The Oklahoma Association of Negro Teachers." *Shades of Oklahoma*, vol. 2, no. 3, 31 Dec. 2017. https://www.shadesok.com/blogs/news/the-oklahoma-african-american-educator-s.

Ness, Immanuel. *New Forms of Worker Organization: The Syndicalist and Autonomist Restoration of Class Struggle Unionism.* PM Press, 2014.

Newfield, Christopher. *Unmaking the Public University: The Forty-Year Assault on the Middle Class.* Harvard UP, 2011.

News on 6 Staff. "Gov. Fallin Angers Teachers Over 'Teenage Kid.'" *News on 6*, 4 April 2018, https://www.newson6.com/story/5e35e39f2f69d76f62020110/gov-fallin-angers-teachers-over-teenage-kid-comment-in-cbs-interview.

Novotney, Steve. "Gideon and the Governor." *100 Days in Appalachia.* 2018, February 28, https://www.100daysinappalachia.com/2018/02/gideon-and-the-governor/.

Nuñez, Isabel et al. *Worth Striking for: Why Education Policy is Every Teacher's Concern (Lessons from Chicago).* Teachers College Press, 2015.

Ogren, Christine. *The American State Normal School: An Instrument of Great Good.* Springer, 2005.

Oklahoma Education Association. "1990 Oklahoma Teacher Walkout." (Film). *YouTube*, uploaded by Oklahoma Education Association, 19 Feb. 2011, https://www.youtube.com/watch?v=-K4xdzWx3a4.

Partelow, Lisette. "What to Make of Declining Enrollment in Teacher Preparation Programs." *Center for American Progress*, 3 Dec. 2019, https://www.americanprogress.org/issues/education-k-12/reports/2019/12/03/477311/make-declining-enrollment-teacher-preparation-programs/.

Patterson, G. "Alt-Country Rhetorics: Relearning (Trans) Activism in Rural Indiana." *Activism and Rhetoric*, edited by JongHwa Lee and Seth Kahn. Routledge, 2019, pp. 65–77.

Pen America. "Educational Gag Orders: Legislative Restrictions on the Freedom to Read, Learn, and Teach." *Pen America*, 18 Jan. 2022, https://pen.org/report/education-al-gag-orders/.

Peterson, Bob. "A Revitalized Teacher Union Movement." *Rethinking Schools*, vol. 29, no. 2, 2014, pp. 13–21. https://rethinkingschools.org/articles/a-revitalized-teacher-union-movement-reflections-from-the-field/.

——. "Survival and Justice: Rethinking Teacher Union Strategy." *Transforming Teacher Unions: Fighting for Better Schools and Social Justice*, edited by Bob Peterson and Michael Charney. Rethinking Schools, 1999, pp. 11–19.

PFM Group. "Interim Report #1: Transparency and Governance." *Commonwealth of Kentucky.* 30 Dec. 2016, https://tinyurl.com/3jxbtpbf.

PFM Group. "Interim Report #2: Historical and Current Assessment." *Commonwealth of Kentucky.* 22. May 2017. https://tinyurl.com/4a7hrtjt.

PFM Group. "Interim Report #3: Recommended Options." *Commonwealth of Kentucky*. 28 Aug. 2017. https://www.ktia.com/assets/mmlk/pfm%20briefing.pdf.

Picower, Bree, and Edwin Mayorga. *"What's Race got to Do with It?": How Current School Reform Policy Maintains Racial and Economic Inequality*. Peter Lang, 2015.

Piven, Frances Fox, and Richard A. Cloward. "Normalizing Collective Protest." *Frontiers in Social Movement Theory*, edited by Aldon D. Morris and Carol McClurg Mueller. Yale UP, 1992, pp. 301–325.

Podair, Jerald. *The Strike that Changed New York: Blacks, Whites, and the Ocean-Hill Brownsville Crisis*. Yale UP, 2002.

Pollard, Kevin M. "'A New Diversity': Race and Ethnicity in the Appalachian Region." *Appalachian Regional Commission*, Sept. 2004, https://www.arc.gov/wp-content/uploads/2020/06/ANewDiversityRaceandEthnicityinAppalachia.pdf.

Powers, Jeanne M. "From Extralegal Segregation to Anti-Immigrant Policy. Reflections on the Long History of Racial Discrimination and Colorblindness in Arizona." *Aztlán: A Journal of Chicano Studies*, vol. 38, no. 2, 2013, pp. 191–205.

Prison Policy Initiative. "Oklahoma Profile." *Prison Policy Initiative*, Accessed 26 April 2023. https://www.prisonpolicy.org/profiles/OK.html.

Quinn, Therese, and Erica R. Meiners. *Flaunt It!: Queers Organizing for Public Education and Justice*. Peter Lang, 2009.

Rabinowitz, Loren G. and Daniel G. Rabinowitz. "Women on the Frontline: A Changed Workforce and the Fight Against COVID-19." *Academic Medicine: Journal of the Association of American Medical Colleges*, vol. 96, no. 6, 2021, pp. 808–812. https://doi:10.1097/ACM.0000000000004011.

Raby, John, and Michael Virtanen. "Striking West Virginia Teachers Return to Class Thursday." *KSL Broadcasting*, 27 Feb. 2018, https://www.ksl.com/article/46269899.

Reed, Lindsey D. Teacher Unrest in West Virginia, 2018–2019. 2020. Marshall University. Ph.D. Dissertation. *ProQuest*, https://www.proquest.com/docview/2442205448?pq-origsite=gscholar&fromopenview=true.

Reilly, Katie. "'I Work 3 Jobs and Donate Blood Plasma to Pay the Bills.' This is What It's Like to Be a Teacher in America." *TIME*, 13 Sept. 2018, https://time.com/5395001/teacher-in-america/.

——. "How Republican Governor Matt Bevin Lost Teachers and Lost Kentucky." *TIME*, 7 Nov. 2019, https://tinyurl.com/284zrzru.

Riley, Kathleen. "Reading for Change: Social Justice Unionism Book Groups as an Organizing Tool." *Penn GSE Perspectives on Urban Education*, vol. 12, no. 1, 2015. https://urbanedjournal.gse.upenn.edu/archive/volume-12-issue-1-spring-2015/reading-change-social-justice-unionism-book-groups-organizing-.

Robnett, Belinda. *How Long? How Long?: African American Women in the Struggle for Civil Rights*. Oxford UP, 2000.

Roediger, David. *The Wages of Whiteness: Race and the Making of the American Working Class*. Verso, 1999.

Roediger, David R., and Elizabeth D. Esch. *The Production of Difference: Race and the Management of Labor in U.S. History*. Oxford UP, 2012.

Rottmann, Cindy, et al. "Remembering, Reimagining, and Reviving Social Justice Teacher Unionism." *Teacher Unions in Public Education: Politics, History, and the Future*, edited by Nina Bascia, Palgrave Macmillan, 2015, pp. 53–67.

Rousmaniere, Kate. *Citizen teacher: The Life and Leadership of Margaret Haley*. SUNY Press, 2005.

——. "White Silence: A Racial Biography of Margaret Haley." *Equity & Excellence in Education*, vol. 34, no. 2, 2001, pp. 7–15. https://doi.org/10.1080/1066568010340202.

Ruderman, Wendy, and Graham, Kristen. "A Dying Wish for Schools." *The Philadelphia Enquirer*, 8 May 2020, https://www.inquirer.com/education/a/philadelphia-schools-asbestos-problems-lea-dirusso-lawsuit-20200508.html.

Ruelas, Richard, and Ricardo Cano. "Ducey Says Protestors are 'Playing Games', as Teachers Rally Outside of Phoenix Radio Station." *The Republic.* 10 April 2018, https://tinyurl.com/bdzmhn3j.

Russom, Gillian. "The Teachers' Strikes of 2018–2019: A Gendered Rebellion." *Strike for the Common Good: Fighting for the Future of Public Education*, edited by Rebecca Kolins Givan and Amy Schrager Lang, University of Michigan Press, 2020, pp. 172–182.

Sakai, J. *Settlers: The Mythology of the White Proletariat from Mayflower to Modern.* PM Press, 2014.

Saltman, Kenneth. *The Gift of Education: Public Education and Venture Philanthropy.* Springer, 2010.

Savage, Tres. "Alberto Morejon Charged with Messaging Minor About Oral Sex." *NonDoc*, 22 May 2020, https://nondoc.com/2020/05/22/alberto-morejon-charged-messaging-minor/.

Schapira, Michael. "The University Is a Battleground: An Interview with Zach Schwartz-Weinstein." *Jacobin.* 26 May 2019, https://jacobinmag.com/2019/05/graduate-worker-unions-nlrb-history.

Schell, Eileen. "Foreword. The New Faculty Majority in Writing Programs: Organizing for Change." *Contingency, Exploitation, and Solidarity: Labor and Action in English Composition*, edited by Seth Kahn et al., The WAC Clearinghouse and UP of Colorado, 2017, pp. xi–xx. https://doi.org/10.37514/PER-B.2017.0858.1.2.

Shelton, Jon. *Teacher Strike!: Public Education and the Making of a New American Political Order.* University of Illinois Press, 2017.

Silver, Jonathon D. "Unhappy with 3.5 Percent Pay Raise, Some West Virginia Teachers Strike." *Pittsburgh Post-Gazette*, 14 Mar. 2007, https://tinyurl.com/aycufrt9.

Smith, Barbara Ellen. "De-gradations of Whiteness: Appalachia and the Complexities of Race." *Journal of Appalachian Studies*, vol. 10, no. 1/2, 2004, pp. 38–57.

Smith, Sharon. *Subterranean Fire: A History of Working-Class Radicalism in the United States.* Haymarket Books, 2018.

Stark, Lauren. *"We're Trying to Create a Different World": Educator Organizing in Social Justice Caucuses.* 2019. University of Virginia. Ph.D. Dissertation. *LibraETD*, https://doi.org/10.18130/v3-z4wy-gb48.

Stark, Lauren Ware, and Rhiannon Maton. "School Closures and the Political Education of U.S. Educators." *Shuttered Schools: Race, Community, and School Closures in American Cities*, edited by Ebony M. Duncan-Shippy. Information Age Press, 2019, pp. 287–324.

Stark, Lauren, and Carol Spreen. "Global Educator Movements: Teacher Struggles against Neoliberalism and for Democracy and Justice" *Strike for the Common Good: Fighting for the Future of Public Education*, edited by Rebecca Kolins Givan and Amy Schrager Lang, University of Michigan Press, 2020, pp. 234–252.

Stealey III, John Edmund. "Slavery and the Western Virginia Salt Industry." *The Journal of Negro History*, vol. 59, no. 2, 1974, pp. 105–131.

Stern, Mark, et al. "Educate. Agitate. Organize: New and Not-So-New Teacher Movements." *Workplace: A Journal for Academic Labor*, vol. 26, 6 Jan. 2016, pp. 1–4. https://doi.org/10.14288/workplace.v0i26.186161.

Stracqualursi, Veronica. "Kentucky Governor Says Teachers' Strike Left Children Vulnerable to Sexual Assault." *CNN*, 15 April 2018, https://tinyurl.com/4x8ew77d.

Strickland, Donna. *The Managerial Unconscious in the History of Composition Studies.* Southern Illinois UP, 2011.

Strober, Myra H., and David Tyack. "Why do Women Teach and Men Manage?: A Report on Research on Schools." *Signs: Journal of Women in Culture and Society*, vol. 5, no. 3, 1980, pp. 494–503.

Strunk, Katherine O. "School Closure Debates Put Teachers Unions Front and Center. *The Conversation.* 7 Jan. 2022, https://theconversation.com/school-closure-debates-put-teachers-unions-front-and-center-174517.

Tait, Vanessa. *Poor Workers' Unions: Rebuilding Labor from Below.* South End Press, 2005.

Tarlau, Rebecca. *Occupying Schools, Occupying Land: How the Landless Workers Movement Transformed Brazilian Education.* Oxford UP, 2019.

——. "From a Language to a Theory of Resistance: Critical Pedagogy, the Limits of 'Framing,' and Social Change." *Educational Theory*, vol. 64, no. 4, 2014, pp. 369–392. https://doi.org/10.1111/edth.12067.

Taylor, Clarence. *Reds at the Blackboard: Communism, Civil Rights, and the New York City Teachers Union.* Columbia UP, 2013.

Thandeka. *Learning to Be White: Money, Race, and God in America.* Bloomsbury Academic, 2005.

The Republic Staff. "What Are Arizona Teachers' 5 Demands?" *AZCentral*, 11 April 2018, https://tinyurl.com/w92dh7fw.

Thompson, Fred W., and Jon Bekken. *The Industrial Workers of the World: Its First One Hundred Years: 1905–2005.* Industrial Workers of the World, 2006.

Thompson, Todd. "Growing Opposition to Public Education Cuts in Oklahoma." *World Socialist Web Site*, 22 Feb. 2018, https://www.wsws.org/en/articles/2018/02/22/okla-f22.html.

Todd-Breland, Elizabeth. *A Political Education: Black Politics and Education Reform in Chicago Since the 1960s.* University of North Carolina Press, 2018.

Trotter, Matt. "Study Ranks Oklahoma as Fifth-Worst State for Women." *Public Radio Tulsa*, 9 Mar. 2020, https://tinyurl.com/4uj5mj87.

Uetricht, Micah. *Strike for America: Chicago Teachers Against Austerity.* Verso, 2014.

United Way OKC. "Disrupting Poverty: Research Brief." *Vital Signs*, Winter 2021/2022, https://tinyurl.com/54pwytmr.

Urban, Wayne J. *Gender, Race, and the National Education Association: Professionalism and Its Limitations.* Taylor & Francis, 2000.

U.S. Census. Quick Facts: Kentucky, https://www.census.gov/quickfacts/KY.

U.S. Census. Quick Facts: West Virginia, https://www.census.gov/quickfacts/WV.

Vance, James D. *Hillbilly Elegy.* HarperCollins, 2016.

Vergara-Camus, Leandro. *The MST, the Zapatistas and Peasant Alternatives to Neoliberalism.* Zed Books, 2014.

Villafranca, Omar. "Oklahoma Teachers Fight for Increased Funding: 'We're Doing This for our Kids.'" *CBS News*, 3 April 2018, https://www.cbsnews.com/news/oklahoma-teachers-fight-for-increased-funding-were-doing-this-for-our-kids/.

Voss, Kim, and Rachel Sherman. "Breaking the Iron Law of Oligarchy: Union Revitalization in the American Labor Movement." *American Journal of Sociology*, vol. 106, no. 2, 2000, pp. 303–349. https://doi.org/10.1086/316963.

Walker, Reagan. "Kentucky Schools Out for Funding Protests." *EdWeek*, 23 Mar. 1988, https://www.edweek.org/education/kentucky-schools-out-for-funding -protests/1988/03.

Walker, Vanessa Siddle. "African American Teaching in the South: 1940–1960." *American Educational Research Journal*, vol. 38, no. 4, 2001, pp. 751–779. https://doi.org/10.3102 /00028312038004751.

Washington, John. "4 Years After the Forced Disappearance of 43 Students, a Father Is Still Looking." *The Nation*, 12 Nov. 2018, https://www.thenation.com/article /archive/ayotzinapa-mexico-students-disappearance/.

Weiner, Lois. *The Future of Our Schools: Teachers Unions and Social Justice.* Haymarket Books, 2012.

——. "Heads Up! Chins Down!: Resisting the New Bipartisan Neoliberal Project in Education." *Network for Public Education.* 1 May 2021, https://tinyurl.com/39ad4k6x.

——. "Education Reforms and Capitalism's Changes to Work." *New Politics.* 23 Jan. 2022, https://tinyurl.com/426b2vz5.

Weiner, Lois, and Chloe Asselin. "Learning from Lacunae in Research: Making Sense of Teachers' Labor Activism." *REMIE: Multidisciplinary Journal of Educational Research*, vol. 10, no. 3, 2020, pp. 226–270. https://doi.org/10.17583/remie.2020.5090.

Weis, Lois, and Michelle Fine. "Critical Bifocality and Circuits of Privilege: Expanding Critical Ethnographic Theory and Design." *Harvard Educational Review*, vol. 82, no. 2, 2012, pp. 173–201. https://doi.org/10.17763/haer.82.2.v1jx34n441532242.

Wendler, Emily. "Penny Sales Tax for Education Seeks to Keep Teachers in State." *KGOU*, 20 Jan. 2016, https://tinyurl.com/ycyac44u.

Wendler, Emily and Ryan LaCroix. "'There is Wisdom in Shifting Focus': Oklahoma Teachers Union Calls Off Walkout." *KOSU*, 13 April 2018, https://tinyurl.com /y7jumtff.

West Virginia Industrial Workers of the World. "We Are Not Certain As of Now if Senate Will Meet to Discuss Pay Raise Tomorrow." *Facebook*, 28 Feb. 2018, https://www .facebook.com/WestVirginiaIWW.

Williams, David, and Bijan Hosseini. "An Oklahoma Lawmaker Criticized Teachers on a Facebook Video: Now One is Aiming for his Job." *CNN*, 4 April 2018, https://tinyurl .com/25n2e7yh.

Williams, Hampton S., and Leonard, Rex L. "A Study of Mississippi Teachers' Attitudes Toward the Use of Militant, Collective Actions." Paper presented at the annual meeting of the Mid-South Educational Research Association in Little Rock, Arkansas, 8–10 Nov. 1989.

Wilner, F. N. *Understanding the Railway Labor Act.* Simmons-Boardman, 2009.

Wilson, Dave. "Oklahoma State Cowboys Reward Football Coach Mike Gundy with $1M Salary Bump to $7.5M Per Year." *ESPN*, 25 Mar. 2022, https://tinyurl.com/yck73bjs.

Wilson, Ralph, and Isaac Kamola. *Free Speech and Koch Money: Manufacturing a Campus Culture War.* Pluto Press, 2021.

Wolcott, David B. *Cops and Kids: Policing Juvenile Delinquency in Urban America, 1890–1940.* Ohio State UP, 2005.

Wong, Alia. "Why the Los Angeles Teachers' Strike Is Different." *The Atlantic*, 14 Jan. 2019, https://tinyurl.com/5n95vh4f.

Young, Charles. "Frontier Communications Employees in West Virginia On Strike After Contract Expiration." *WV News*, 5 Mar. 2019, https://tinyurl.com/ym5zsann.

P&C

About the Authors

Erin Dyke is Associate Professor of Curriculum Studies at Oklahoma State University. Her primary line of research examines the pedagogies, organizing, and impacts of contemporary educator movements on educational practice and policy. Dyke and Muckian-Bates have published work in this area in the *Berkeley Review of Education* and *New Politics*. Dyke contributed to the edited volume *Walkout: Teacher Militancy, Activism, and School Reform*, and with Lauren Ware Stark and Rhiannon Maton, co-edited a four-part special issue series for *Critical Education* highlighting empirical studies of and organizer interviews with educator movements from across North America. With support from the Spencer Foundation, Dyke undertook a two-year community-based oral history study of the 2018 Oklahoma Education Walkouts (which informs this book) with a team of teacher-researchers, with whom she co-authored an article in *Critical Education* to address underrepresented narratives and perspectives in public accounting of the event. This research team curated a public collection of educators' oral history narratives of their strike experiences, published with the Oklahoma Oral History Research Program at OSU. Dyke has published ethnographic studies of liberatory curriculum and pedagogy in *Educational Studies, International Journal of Multicultural Education*, and *Journal of Education Human Resources*.

Brendan Muckian-Bates is a former West Virginia public educator turned non-profit worker. His specialization is gender studies, critical pedagogy, and social studies education. His work has appeared in *Jacobin, Berkeley Review of Education*, and *New Politics*.

P&C